photo by Jean-Luce Huré

Clyde H. Farnsworth has been a foreign correspondent of the *New York Times* since 1963. He is a winner of awards from the Overseas Press Club and Sigma Delta Chi, the national journalistic fraternity, for foreign reporting. A newsman since 1954, he has worked for the *New York Herald Tribune* and United Press International as well as the *Times*. He was born May 6, 1931, and educated in public schools in Mount Vernon, New York, and at Yale. After graduation he served in the 179th Infantry Regiment in Korea and was awarded a Bronze Star. He is married, the father of two children, and the author of one previous book, *No Money Down,* an exposé of the American credit industry.

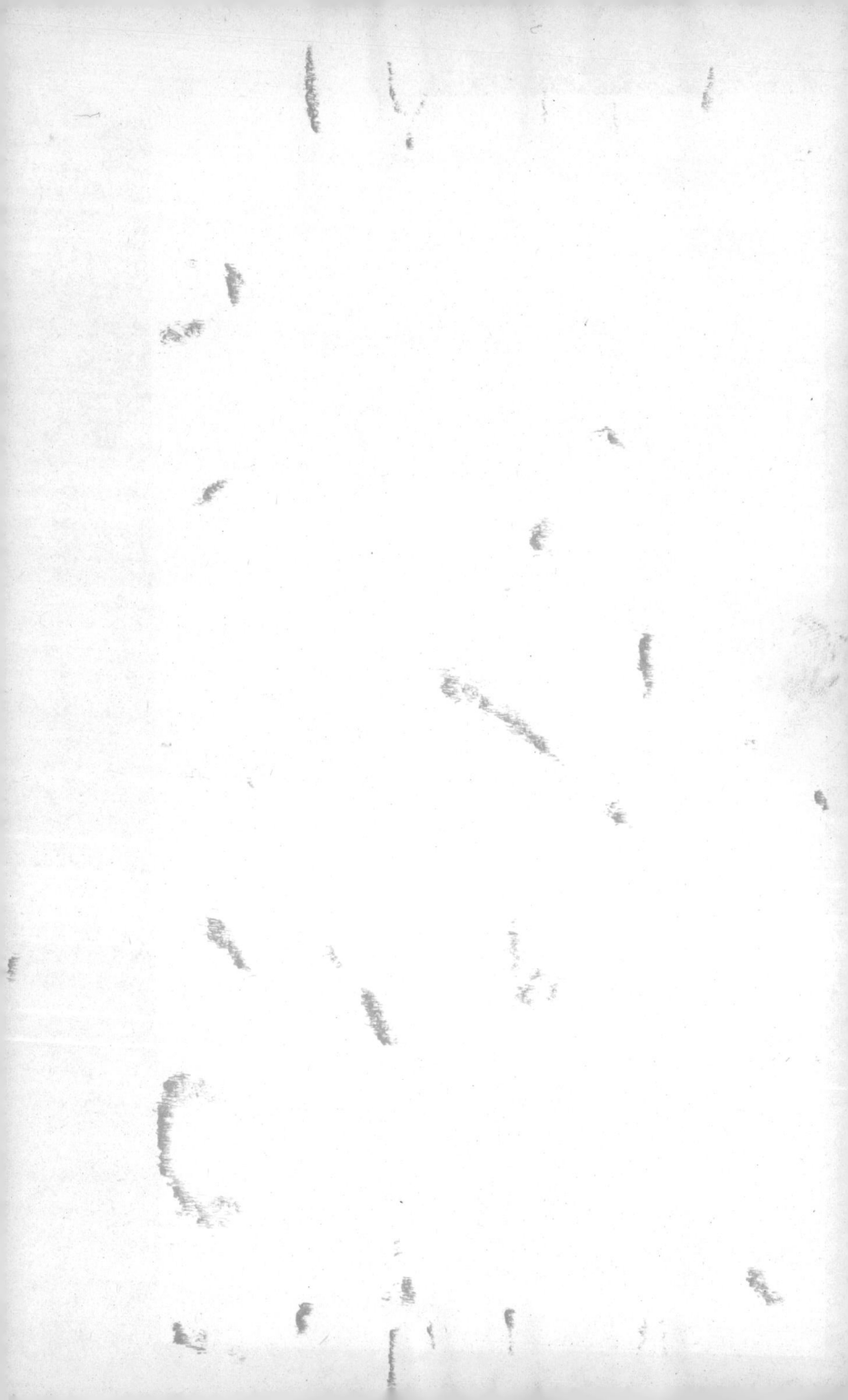

ARMAGEDDON IN THE MIDDLE EAST
by Dana Adams Schmidt

THE BLACK DILEMMA
by John Herbers

CONFLICT AND COMPROMISE:
THE DYNAMICS OF AMERICAN FOREIGN POLICY
by Richard Halloran

EASTERN EUROPE IN THE SOVIET SHADOW
by Harry Schwartz

MADMAN IN A LIFEBOAT:
ISSUES OF THE ENVIRONMENTAL CRISIS
by Gladwin Hill

OUT OF THIS NETTLE:
A HISTORY OF POSTWAR EUROPE
by Clyde H. Farnsworth

THE USSR TODAY
by Harry A. Rositzke

𝕿𝖍𝖊 𝕹𝖊𝖜 𝖄𝖔𝖗𝖐 𝕿𝖎𝖒𝖊𝖘

SURVEY SERIES

THEODORE M. BERNSTEIN
GENERAL EDITOR

THE NEW YORK TIMES Survey Series comprises books that deal comprehensively yet comprehensibly with subjects of wide interest, presenting the facts impartially and drawing conclusions honestly.

The series draws on the great information resources of *The New York Times* and on the talents, backgrounds and insights of specially qualified authors, mostly members of the *Times* staff.

The subjects range from the relatively particular problems of civilized life to the broadest conceivable problems concerning whether civilized life, or any kind of life, will continue to be possible on this planet.

The hope is that the books will be essentially informative, perhaps argumentative, but beyond that stimulative to useful, constructive thinking by the citizens who ultimately must share in civilization's decisions.

OUT OF THIS NETTLE:

A History of Postwar Europe

CLYDE H. FARNSWORTH

The John Day Company

AN Intext PUBLISHER / NEW YORK

Library of Congress Cataloging in Publication Data

Farnsworth, Clyde H
  Out of this nettle.

  (The New York times survey series)
  1. Europe—Economic conditions—1945–
2. European federation. 3. Europe—History—1945–
I. Title
HC240.F37   940.55   73-7409
ISBN 0–381–98248–3
ISBN 0–381–90010–X (pbk.)

Published in hardcover by
The John Day Company, 257 Park Avenue South, New York, N.Y. 10010.

Published in softcover by Intext Press, 257 Park Avenue South, New York, N.Y. 10010.
Published on the same day in Canada by Longman Canada Limited.

Printed in the United States of America

Contents

Prologue: A Definition   I

1 The Aftermath of the Storm   5
2 The Virtues of Necessity   19
3 The German Renaissance   36
4 A Kind of United States   52
5 Toward a Broader, Deeper Community   65
6 The Naysayers: British and French   82
7 Knock Three Times: End of an Era   103
8 From Sovereignty to Supranationality?   131
9 *Ostpolitik:* The Hazards and Hopes   157
10 The Quality of Continental Life   177
   Index   201

This book
is dedicated to
Clyde A. Farnsworth
and Barbara Farnsworth.
Their help was enormous.

Hotspur: 'Tis dangerous to take a cold, to sleep, to drink. But I tell you, my lord fool, out of this nettle danger, we pluck this flower safety.

Henry IV, Part I, Act 2

OUT
OF THIS
NETTLE:
A History of
Postwar Europe

Prologue:
A Definition

A European is someone who lives on the western peninsula of Asia. He inhabits one of those principal divisions of the land surface of the earth known as continents. Of those divisions, only Australia is smaller.

A European is

. . . a shopkeeper sipping a pint of Guinness at the burnished oak bar of the Coachman pub in Galway. He is talking about a bombing in Belfast that took twelve lives. "Terrible, terrible," he says.

. . . a wiry Swiss banker with his corpulent wife ensconced in the Zurich Opernhaus for a performance of *Fidelio*. A smile of self-satisfaction comes to his face as Rocco sings: "*Hat man nicht auch gold bei neben, kann man nicht glücklich sein.*" ("One cannot be happy without a little gold.")

. . . a farmer at St. Quentin in northern France, his eyes on the soil turned up by his one-horse plow as the Brussels-Paris express train flashes past at eighty miles an hour.

. . . a woman in Naples dressed in shapeless black studying the price of frozen calamari before dropping the package into the UPIM supermarket cart.

. . . the German, Italian, and Luxembourg technocrats in Brussels editing in French the text of a regulation on maximum axle weight for trucks of the Common Market.

. . . the Communist party secretary at Kiev, the space scientist at Dubna, and the construction worker at Riga—simultaneously annoyed by a shortage of ballpoint pens.

. . . and 325 million other people.

Europe is what lies between the Atlantic and the Urals.

In the western part of the peninsula one out of two families owns a car; three out of four have a television set. Slightly more than half of all Europeans are manual workers, and about 25 percent of all wives go out to work. Frenchmen work longer hours than Germans, Italians, Belgians, Dutchmen, and Luxembourgers, but they take longer vacations. In Luxembourg almost all families have a washing machine; in Portugal hardly any.

The French and Swiss tend to live in apartments; the British live in houses. The British, Germans, Swedes, and Norwegians pay their taxes; the Italians and the French, if they can help it, do not. It is almost impossible to get a good meal in Germany. It is almost impossible to get a bad meal in France.

The French and British go hunting on weekends. Czechoslovaks pick mushrooms in the woods. In the northern Bohemian town of Hradec Králové there is certainly one of the oddest stores in the world: it sells only mushrooms.

Europe is bureaucracy . . . the *carte d'identité* required of the foreign resident to import his furniture and formally establish the residence that is the condition for getting his *carte d'identité* . . . and the work permit that cannot be had until the worker has a steady job, which cannot be had until he has his work permit.

Europe is the bracing clean air high in the French Alps at Courchevel and the diesel stench of autobahns. It is Hitler and Beethoven.

"Everything has come to Europe and everything, or nearly everything, has come from it," said the French writer Paul Valéry.

Europe is 55 million Britons, 50 million Frenchmen, 80 million Germans (east and west), and, among others, 22,000 Liechtensteiners—all inhabiting an area a little smaller than the United States. In Western Europe alone ten major languages are spoken, not counting hundreds of dialects and the regional languages such as Gaelic, Basque, Schwizerdütsch, and Luxembourger.

It is a continent of contrasts rising from its multiple roots: Greek, Roman, Judaeo-Christian, Germanic, Mongol, Celtic, Arabic, Ottoman, Slav.

Out of the welter of tribes that settled on the peninsula, from those energetic mongrels who made war—and love—for centuries, has come a desire for unity. An association of states, the size of Charlemagne's and Napoleon's European empires, has been put together, not by conquest but by voluntary agreement. Its purpose is both to prevent future European wars and to strengthen the influence of a continent that once ruled the world.

1

The Aftermath of the Storm

Western Europe was fat, prosperous, and not a little smug in the early 1970s. London, Rotterdam, Liège, Cologne, Hamburg, and the other great and gutted cities of the war had been rebuilt. There were new and frequently unsightly concrete and glass shoeboxes jutting into the skylines, and in the caverns below the cobblestoned streets dancing couples swayed and bounced and drank scotch at $4 a shot. The discothèques were full of people, and the stores were full of goods. New supermarkets—with names like Carrefour, Inno, GB, UPIM, Super Bazaar, and Tesco—were changing shoppers' habits. Parking meters were sprouting like weeds in the cities, even in Paris, where it had long been considered an unalienable right to sling a car wherever one chose. In London a meter maid named Rita served as inspiration for the Beatles.

The old leaders had died—Churchill, de Gaulle, Adenauer, de Gasperi—men who at the apex of their careers seemed to symbolize their nations. They were replaced by a new breed of more pragmatic leaders, men with names like Edward Heath, Georges Pompidou, Willy Brandt, less smitten by a vision and more intent on resolving some of the practical problems of a coalescing continent. Perhaps nowhere, in the third decade after the war, was the change in leadership so dramatic as in Austria, the land of Hitler's birth, which had been integrated into his Third Reich, and where in 1970 Bruno Kreisky, a Socialist and a Jew, was elected chancellor. From Germany came an automobile, designed under Hitler

5

and named the People's Car, which was reproduced more times than Henry Ford's Model T. The jaunty Volkswagen was the new invader, beetling along French, Dutch, Belgian, and British highways, not to mention those of the United States.

The United States inspired the supermarkets, though all retained national traits (in France they were plentifully stocked with wine and cheese and in Italy with miles of pasta), and the United States inspired magazines that looked like *Time,* housing that looked like Levittown, clothes that owed more to Levi than Dior. Spurred on by the European attraction for American ideas and the cornucopia of dollars, American corporations bought huge slices of European industry. Europeans reacted ambivalently to the prospect of becoming an American industrial outpost. They wanted the technology and employment offered by American enterprises. Circumscribed by national frontiers, they felt both frustrated and challenged by the success of the American managers turning Western Europe into a single market. They resented the transfer of control of their industries from Europe to executive offices in New York. Later in the postwar period Americans themselves became anxious about the trend, especially about the jobs their investments brought to Europe at the expense of the United States.

These, then, were some of the elements of the New Europe. The contrasts with 1945 were stark. Those who lived through Europe's second civil war of the twentieth century remembered a ruptured continent. Its institutions had been discredited, its cities ravaged, its survivors disillusioned and displaced. From 1914 to 1945 five empires had either disappeared or were about to disappear: the British, French, German, Austro-Hungarian, and Ottoman. Hitler's "One Thousand Year Reich" had lasted twelve years. A sixth empire, that of Czarist Russia, had collapsed only to be rebuilt by Russian imperialists of another faith. East of the Elbe in 1945 the Soviet Union was primed for expansion. There was to be a *"cordon Stalinaire,"* the buffer zone of Stalin. Germany was a ruin. Britain and France were bankrupt. The United States had its legions in Western Europe backed by megatons from the new atomic weapon that had already been used to wipe out two Japanese cities.

As Washington and Moscow quarreled, it looked as if the old, suffering, hungry continent was being drawn into a new war. "A civilization is just as fragile as a life," Paul Valéry had written. In the carnage at Verdun, in the outrages of the Nazi epoch, in the breakdown of the wartime alliance and the confrontation of the superpowers, it seemed as if civilization itself might disappear.

The Second World War was by far the costliest in history. The United States spent more than $350 billion for the mobilization of more than 12 million men and the supply of war material to the Allies. Britain ran up huge debts to the Commonwealth and the United States and never quite got her balance sheet in order in the postwar period. France came through relatively lightly scathed until the Allies landed in Normandy and began squeezing the German armies toward the Rhine. The French calculated their losses in six war years at three times the prewar annual income. Italy figured a third of its national wealth had been wiped out. As for Germany, it was practically impossible to make a tally, so rampant was the destruction. The German public debt had risen nine-fold in the war years. Ashes of German cities were all there was to show.

No previous war had taken such a toll in human life. Where 8.5 million men died in the First World War, more than three times that number perished in the Second. It was total war this time that spared neither soldier nor civilian. The battlefield death figures alone were appalling: Soviet Union, 7.5 million; Germany, 2,850,-000; China, 2.2 million; Japan, 1,506,000; Britain and the Commonwealth, 544,600; Italy, 300,000; United States, 292,100; France, 210,700; total for smaller nations of Europe, 500,000. Civilian casualties were incalculable. At least 6 million persons died in the concentration and extermination camps. Hundreds of thousands more were killed in air raids.

And then there were the displaced persons. Again it was impossible to calculate the number of civilians who were uprooted from their homes. Estimates have run as high as 60 million. The Germans deported more than 4 million men to forced labor camps. At war's end three times that number of ethnic Germans fled or were expelled from German communities in Eastern Europe. A lawyer from southern Estonia was more fortunate than most. A nationalist political leader, he spent much of the war hiding in the forests alternately from the Russians and the Germans. He escaped from Estonia and joined the American army. At war's end he managed miraculously to link up with his family in a displaced persons camp in Germany. After some months, he got the necessary permission to take his wife, young son, and daughter to the United States, and in the early 1970s he was running a dairy farm in Vermont. For most of the displaced persons, the immediate postwar months—and years—were spent in the hovels of camps, treasuring a few symbolic possessions, waiting painfully for resettlement home, or somewhere.

The devastation of vast areas of farmland and the destruction of 40 percent of Europe's livestock led to severe food shortages. The Germans had opened the northern dikes of the Zuyder Zee, flooding hundreds of thousands of acres of Dutch farmland.* The pastures and Calvados-producing orchards of Normandy were sown with mines, as were the farmlands south of the Apennines and in the Po valley.

In the 1970s skyscrapers had risen over the ruins of the cities. Fresh layers of macadam covered former mine fields. Fiats, Peugeots, Volkswagens, and Triumphs raced along the undulating ribbons of superhighway and jammed and polluted the rebuilt cities. Well-dressed, nannied toddlers romped in the parks. The war, well beyond the memory of even those children's parents, was ancient history. There was no question of saving civilization. Only the very old quoted Valéry.

Europeans concentrated on their social and economic problems. While the tugs of rival nationalistic forces were still strong into the 1970s, what distinguished the Europe of the new decade from the ill-fated 1930s was that competition was economic, not military. There were crises over the valuation of national currencies, not over the build-up of national armies. Countries defended themselves not across Maginot Lines, but across barriers of exchange

*The owner of one of the flooded polders was a Dutch resistance leader named Sicco Mansholt, who later became chief farm specialist and then president of the Executive Commission of the European Economic Community.

controls. The invasions were mounted by the salesmen of Italian refrigerators, German trucks, French Cricket lighters, Dutch tape recorders, and Belgian hothouse grapes. The years since the war had seen the rise of the economist, the monetary specialist, the marketing man, the technologist and administrator—men who borrowed ideas from the United States, who perhaps even studied at the Harvard Business School or its European equivalents. They were convinced that they could take what the United States had to offer and then improve on it.

Although economic integration proceeded at a tediously slow pace, and political integration remained little more than a visionary's dream, what marked Europe a generation after the war was that the diverse peoples of the continent had drawn more closely together than at any time in their history. As the French weekly *L'Express* put it in the summer of 1970, "Would Spain go to war over Gibraltar, Austria over the Alto Adige, Bulgaria over Macedonia, Rumania over Bessarabia? No one really thinks so." In 1972 there were really no disputed frontiers.

Many Europeans believed that in social planning they could learn from the mistakes of the United States and so avoid the convulsions of the New World. They were perhaps a shade optimistic. Europe was developing just a little behind the United States as an urban, industrial, polyglot society. Prejudice was already showing up in the treatment of foreign workers, who were coming from the Mediterranean littoral and increasingly from black Africa. There were increasing tensions between labor and management. There were pressures for social reforms.

As production expanded after the war and demand for services increased, the main industrial countries of Western Europe found they simply did not have enough workers to man the machines, dig the ditches, pick up the garbage, sweep out the office buildings at night. So they turned to the less-developed, labor-surplus countries —Spain and Portugal, Algeria and Morocco, Turkey, Yugoslavia, Pakistan, the West Indies, and the countries of black Africa. Italy, often considered a separate, underdeveloped country, was also tapped as a labor source. The foreign workers lived apart from the social stream, in primitive shanty towns on the outskirts of Paris,

Munich, Düsseldorf, Milan, and other large cities. Their pay was low, and they didn't really compete for jobs, since the jobs they filled were those nobody else wanted. Yet frictions were quick to develop between the outsiders and the locals.*

The foreigners felt the frustrations of living in a consumer society without being able to participate. On the elegant Avenue Victor Hugo in Paris one day in 1972, three black street sweepers were taking a break. Leaning on their twig brooms in front of one shop displaying expensive sound equipment, they were overheard discussing the relative merits of Gründig versus Sony tape recorders. Since they earned no more than 75 cents an hour all the products in the window were well out of reach. They were penniless urchins in front of a candy shop.

All European workers were demanding a more egalitarian shareout of national wealth. Wages were still much higher in the United States in the early 1970s even after taking into account the higher European fringe benefits. And the cost of living in many European cities was at least as high. In 1972 the Fiat auto worker was earning about $2.50 an hour, while his counterpart in Detroit was making about $4.50. But not everyone in Europe fared as well as auto workers. In 1970 Paris department store employees went on strike to try to lift their minimum monthly wage from $144 to $180. And they were living in the city the American Department of Labor recorded in 1971 as the second most expensive in the world.† Yet, the wage gap between Western Europe and the United States was narrowing. Average pay increases in Europe in the early 1970s were running double the rate in the United States. American wages had been twice those of Sweden in the early 1960s. They were 50 percent higher in the early 1970s.

*Chapter 10 contains a fuller description of the foreign worker phenomenon in Europe.

†The labor department measured the cities in terms of what it cost for an American businessman to live the "American way of life" (for instance, shredded wheat for breakfast, which in France is costly, if you can find it, instead of simple bread and jam). No Frenchman would particularly want to live on an American diet. Even so, Paris costs were 50 percent higher than Washington, according to the index. Bangui, in the Central African Republic, had the stiffest prices.

Two out of five Europeans in 1970 were too young to have any memory of the war or its immediate aftermath of economic privation. Lacking this experience, European youth looked on society in ways different from the war-shaped generation. Growing up within a period of increasing prosperity, the new generation was less interested in obtaining economic advantages and more impressed by the need for social reforms. Youth also felt less fenced in by national frontiers, less distrustful of European neighbors.

The youth explosion in Europe, as in the United States, had an important influence on national events. In some cases student demonstrations led to the fall of governments. The Belgian administration resigned in 1967 after riots at Louvain University. Student unrest in Italy contributed to a series of government crises. In France, after students and workers took to the streets in May, 1968, Charles de Gaulle, while managing to contain the revolutionary forces, sensed that the tide of opinion was running against him and after a referendum stepped down as president of France less than a year later.

One of the main complaints of the new generation concerned the elitist system of education, in which university-level training was theoretically open to all but in fact was open to only a very small percentage of the elegible population. Students denounced anachronistic teaching methods, the lack of personal contact with professors, the failure of university authorities to take the student point of view into account.

Students thought that too much emphasis was being placed on the development of capitalist enterprise in Europe, at the expense of other values. At a European youth colloquium in Brussels in 1970, one discussion group concluded: "Neither trade unions nor political parties are effectively organized on the European level, and thus the social forces have no way of counterbalancing the economic power of private companies on the international level." Radical student groups sought to form alliances with trade unions, but workers reacted with little enthusiasm. There was an incompatibility between worker and student goals. Workers wanted more pay, better housing, a washing machine or dishwasher for their wives, more opportunities for their children, and rejected the students' sweeping generalizations about the worthlessness of society. The radical students naïvely saw workers as allies in the revolution. While students sometimes marched with workers in labor demonstrations, there was little students could do to aid workers in the collective-bargaining process.

Youths were more European in outlook than their parents. Frontiers were breached constantly in the summer as students, weighted with knapsacks and bedrolls (many traveling as mixed couples), hitchhiked all over the continent and mingled in the many cheap youth hostels where a bed cost $2.00 a night. Lacking memories of the war, they harbored few of the national prejudices of their parents. A German boy, born in Cologne, studied in Paris for a year "to get to know the French people." A French girl worked as an "au pair" in Pimlico. An English girl married a Spaniard, reared a son in France, and studied sociology at the Sorbonne. A Parisian hitchhiker, majoring in Germanic languages at the University of Munich, told an American who had stopped for him on the autobahn, "I like the German people."

While youths of 1970 took it more or less for granted, material wellbeing was something that had to be fought for in the grim, chaotic period immediately after the war. Economies were limping along then without even the basic necessities of food and fuel. "I recall Germany in 1945 as a study in disarray—a blasted surrealist landscape reminiscent in its macabre confusion of Faust's Walpurgisnacht on the Blocksberg," George Ball, the American lawyer-diplomat, wrote in *The Discipline of Power* (1968)." "Railroad marshalling yards," he continued, "looked like children's playrooms the day after Christmas. The industrial barons of the Ruhr presided over a twisted mass of bricks and mortar; for the moment they were junk merchants."

By April, 1945, Berlin had been devastated by 1,000 bomber raids of the American and British air forces, which dropped 76,000 tons of bombs, and by the artillery batteries of the approaching Soviet army, which fired 40,000 tons of shells on the city before occupying it on May 1. Hitler's bunkered chancery, where he and his mistress, Eva Braun, evidently killed themselves, eventually furnished the red marble for the memorial to the Red Army in East Berlin's Treptow Park.

Out of the rubble that was Berlin, Frankfurt, Hamburg, and the cities of the Ruhr came social chaos and a disastrous inflation. As after World War I, inflation was accompanied by a military occupation. In 1945 the Russians captured the Reichsmark plates and printed German money as fast as the presses would permit. Russian soldiers had been given a war's worth of back pay in Reichsmarks and used thousands of these marks to buy a Mickey Mouse watch or a can of beer. There was no real economic activity because money was of too little value. The black market flourished with cigarettes taking the place of money because they were convenient accounting units. But other things were bartered also, mainly to get food. Lawrence Fellows, a *New York Times* correspondent who had served in postwar Germany as a United States foreign service officer, recalled what it was like at the Potsdamerplatz, one of the great barter markets of Berlin. "The farmers stood on one side of the square and the others met them there with all they could scrounge from their own homes or steal from the bombed-out ones: paintings, silverware, typewriters, bits of decorative railings, chandeliers."* Children, he recollected, jumped onto moving trains to steal coal, which was hawked throughout the countryside for food.

To live in a society where money was practically useless made a deep impression on the Germans and accounted for their abiding fear of inflation in the late 1960s and early 1970s. The inflation after World War I had turned the social structure upside down. Hitler then found room to plant the seeds of national socialism.†

To try to prevent a recurrence of this tragedy, the Western Allies, led by the United States, acted with responsible German authorities this time to create a strong German mark. But until the *Wirtschaftswunder* or economic miracle, began, life was exceed-

---

New York Times, May 9, 1971, p. 28.

†When French and Belgian troops occupied the Ruhr, Germany's industrial heartland, in January, 1923, to force payment of reparations, the mark was valued at 18,000 to the dollar. By August of that year the figure rose to 4.6 million, and in November to 4.3 billion. It was in November that Hitler, following the rapid growth of the Nazi party in Bavaria, tried to seize power in Munich. After the abortive putsch, Hitler was sentenced to five years in prison. He served nine months, using the time to write *Mein Kampf.*

ingly difficult. An actress in Berlin recalled that she had been paid every day during that period at noon. Then she and her colleagues, to try to beat the next price increases, raced from the theater to the nearest bakery, their fists full of bills, which were enough to buy only a single roll. She borrowed from her father and bartered to make ends meet. Her rent was paid in margarine, two pounds a month. Her father, a textile merchant, had been wiped out by the runaway inflation, as were university professors, judges, and others with bonds or insurance policies or savings in the banks.

But the bad times brought out human resourcefulness. As the bitter 1945–46 winter approached, American blankets—fleecy white ones that were supposed to go on hospital beds—were appearing on the Kurfürstendamm modishly tailored as winter coats worn by the girls in nylons. Not all the girls were able to make the necessary friendships with GIs to get one of these blankets. One of the more unfortunate later told this story. The Red Cross had been distributing charitable bundles from American churches. Opening one of these, she found a gift Bible inscribed with the name and address of donors from St. Louis. She phrased a letter to the St. Louis couple, explaining the great need for blankets to keep warm that winter. Hoping for some stylish rose, creamy yellow, or mauve confection that could easily be turned into a coat, she eagerly awaited the response. At last a bulky package arrived. Opening it, she found an undeniably warm, but very unmodish patchwork quilt faintly smelling of mothballs.

While the German cities had been heavily bombed and shelled, the German industrial machine had been only partly damaged by the war. This helped pave the way for the *Wirtschaftswunder*. During the inflation of the 1920s, German industrialists had invested heavily in machine tools and other capital goods. These acquisitions, made protectively against erosion of the currency, gave Germany a massive industrial base and, together with the slave labor later drawn from all over occupied Europe (100,000 men in the factories of Alfred Krupp alone), kept the German companies operating at a relatively high state of efficiency during the war. Postwar surveys found that in 1943 the quantity of machine tools in Germany was three to four times as high as in either Britain or France. The round-the-clock bombing raids, ordered by

Winston Churchill and Franklin Roosevelt, were less effective in destroying the industrial base of Germany than in terrorizing and killing the civilian population.*

Economic disorder, privation, hunger, and suffering were not confined to Germany. By October, 1947, the cost of living index in Italy had risen to more than fifty times the prewar level. France, whose wheat fields had traditionally served as a granary for Europe, had to buy half a million tons of grain from Russia in 1947.† Frenchmen underwent even stricter rationing of bread than during the war.‡

The French recovery was complicated and delayed by the lack of adequate information on just what the nation's postwar resources were. Statistics had been faked during the war to deceive the Germans. When peace came, factory managers continued the practice of understating inventories and overstating wartime losses to obtain priorities in the allocation of scarce materials and to avoid having to make forced deliveries.

The British endured similar hardships. The recovery was more painful and slow in Britain than in any other Western European country. The large war debts weighed the economy down, reduced the scope for economic expansion. High tax rates to finance the "cradle to grave" social security system of the new Socialist government reduced incentives. The keynote of the immediate postwar period was austerity. Even much later the British economy was marked by alternating strokes of expansion and contraction, which came to be known in the jargon of the time as "stop-go."

As in France, Italy, and Germany, food and fuel shortages

*The bombings did have the effect of inducing the Nazis to move some industry eastward into Czechoslovakia, which gave that country a postwar industrial headstart.

†The pharmacist from Clermont-Ferrand in *The Sorrow and the Pity,* the documentary film about France during the war by Marcel Ophuls and André Harris, was asked what had been his greatest concern. Without hesitation he replied, "Eating."

‡France also ordered grain from the United States, thinking she would be getting wheat, but discovered after the contract had been signed that she had bought cornmeal instead. Parisians, as a result, were to complain for months about their strange-looking yellow bread.

plagued the British. The docks and the newly nationalized coal mines were hit by strikes because the labor unions, no longer restrained by the patriotism of the war years, sought to enforce demands for improved wages and working conditions. A headline in the *Daily Telegraph* of January 23, 1947, provided an idea of what life was like: "Bread ration may be cut. Peers hear review of food outlook. Less bacon and home meat. Beer supplies to be halved immediately." Britain, in fact, became the last of the Western European countries to abolish rationing—in 1951.

Some further insights into the war and immediate postwar conditions were provided in a pamphlet written by the Rev. E. M. Hadfield for his Roman Catholic parishioners in Pimlico, a London district on the Thames. In a history of the parish covering the years between 1939 and 1964, Father Hadfield had written: "On the night of July 13, 1944, one of our parishioners, on duty at the Horse Guards Parade, witnessed what appeared to be a flame streaking across the night sky—an eerie experience—no gunfire, just the sound of an aircraft engine, then, in the distance, the noise of an explosion, then silence. We were soon to know that these were pilotless aircraft, or flying bombs, soon to be nicknamed 'doodle bugs'* . . . four fell in Pimlico, one destroying the house on the site where the new church stands, killing 13 and wounding 150."

Father Hadfield wrote of the difficulties of constructing a new church. "At the end of the hostilities, labor, materials, etc., became scarcer and harder to obtain than at any time during the war. With the greatest of difficulties we managed to obtain a license to erect a temporary hut in the ruins of the old church in Claverton Street; having obtained this we had to fight every government department for every screw, nut and bolt, door handle, etc., to make the temporary hut into a church."

So severe was the postwar food shortage in Britain that the government actually took steps to try to change the eating habits of British families. Two million cans of an unknown food called snoek were imported from South Africa, a country in the sterling

---

*The Germans called them V-2s. They had been secretly readied at Peenemünde on the Baltic, where one of the chief engineers was Dr. Wernher von Braun.

area. This meant that Britain could pay with pounds and husband her sorely depleted dollar reserves. But the British didn't like snoek very much. The *Daily Express* polled twenty-five at random on their snoek-eating habits and found that only two had even bought a can. One said that snoek (a fish akin to barracuda) tasted terrible; the other said she fed it to her cat.

Europe was littered with the rubbish of war. Mines kept washing up on the beaches of Normandy for years after the Allied landing in June, 1944. Even into the 1970s unexploded bombs, like Neolithic relics, were being dug up all over the continent and gingerly disarmed by engineers.* Concrete blockhouses with the black eyes of machine gun apertures stared down on tourists driving in the French countryside two decades after the war. One German blockhouse, so solidly built that it was virtually impossible to destroy, remained into the early 1970s on a small Paris street not far from the Place de l'Étoile.

In England, wrote novelist Susan Cooper, there were "anti-aircraft posts in cornfields, banked with dribbling sandbags; concrete tank-traps lining the road, like idols left by some gloomy extinct race; mine fields and pillboxes lurking in the coastal dunes." She went on to observe that "at Taplow in Buckinghamshire, the national output of barbed wire rusted gently into an orange mountain."†

The war was over, but Europeans were not quite sure about the quality of peace that had descended. Soviet divisions were massed in the east, with very little to stop them from rolling across Western

---

*Here is what happened within the space of one week a quarter-century after the war. On September 7, 1971, construction workers came upon an unexploded World War II German bomb less than 3,000 feet from the main runway at Orly airport. A week later, a 1,100-pound German bomb was found in Nanterre, a suburb of Paris and had to be exploded because disarming operations were too risky. Meanwhile, West German bomb-disposal squads defused two 100-pound World War II bombs found during excavation work on the huge U.S. Rhein-Main airbase near Frankfurt. Police in Munich reported at the same time that a local bomb-disposal crew rendered safe a 500-pound World War II bomb found at Riem International airport.

†*Age of Austerity, 1945–1951*, edited by Michael Sissons and Philip French, Penguin Books, 1964, p. 39.

Europe except the presence of the United States. The Soviet Union consolidated its position by establishing Communist dictatorships in one country after the other in Eastern Europe. Misunderstandings and suspicions on both sides led to the outbreak of the Cold War, and the United States committed itself to the defense of Western Europe.

Local Communist parties were actively seeking to foment revolution in the western countries. At the war's end, Communist-led guerrilla forces took over the administration of many towns and villages in France, and for the next three or four months, until the central government in Paris was able to enforce authority, there were summary executions of suspected collaborators after trials by kangaroo courts. Communist parties all over Western Europe sought to capitalize on the economic chaos and political disorder, promising bread and Utopia for the working class. They were checked in attempting to gain power legitimately. As experience showed in Eastern Europe, they needed the presence of Soviet armies to acquire power illegitimately.

Nowhere was the political and social uncertainty greater than in Germany. One of the major postwar problems was to find a way to insure that Germany would never again be able to start another war. President Roosevelt's secretary of the treasury, Henry Morgenthau, conceived a plan for keeping the German war-making potential forever repressed by completely destroying the German industrial base and converting the country into a vast farmland. Born of the emotionalism of the later war years, when one of the favorite pastimes of American students was to devise ingenious ways of torturing Hitler, Goering, and Goebbels, the idea was quickly pigeonholed in the first rounds of the Cold War.

A strong Germany, Washington decided (with some misgivings expressed by France), was essential to bolster the defenses of the West. The harsh peace terms imposed on the Germans by the Versailles Treaty in 1919 had increased the appeal of Hitler's national socialism. This time Germany was to be rebuilt and democracy encouraged, but Germany was to be molded into a broad framework of European partnership and prosperity.

2

The Virtues
of Necessity

When the war drew to a close, the pealing of bells soon gave way to sober reflections on the ways to fit the broken pieces of Europe together again. Here was an unparalleled opportunity, in the flux of the moment, to reshape the continent and somehow create the institutions that would contain nationalistic forces and perhaps bring an end to European civil wars.

There was a heady, visionary spirit in the air. Over "working breakfasts" in Washington, in the smoking rooms of the clubs on Pall Mall, at Downing Street, and on Pennsylvania Avenue, men spoke seriously of international cooperation, one world, of European and world government.

"Those who cannot remember the past are condemned to repeat it," George Santayana, the American philosopher, once said. In Washington, the center of world power in 1945, the searing experiences of the Great Depression—the soup kitchens, jobless men selling apples ("Brother, can you spare a dime," the song of the period went)—and the struggles against Hitler in Europe and Hirohito in the Pacific were vividly recalled. To avoid repeating the past the policy-makers of the day set the world on a new course marked by three fundamental changes in the approach to postwar problems.

The first was the abandonment of peacetime isolationism by the United States. Cautiously at first, and then too vigorously in later years, the United States went into the business of global interventionism. The Senate's rejection of American participation in the League of Nations in 1919 had long been recognized as a reason for the instability of the interwar years. Signaling the turn in the new era was the bipartisan interest (it became almost an obsession) in Washington in establishing new international organizations, beginning with the United Nations as a successor body to the defunct League of Nations, to promote peace and stability. A charter for the United Nations was drafted in San Francisco in April, 1945, and temporary headquarters were later set up at Lake Success on Long Island. With a gift of land from John D. Rockefeller, Jr., and a loan from the United States government of $65 million, the permanent headquarters went up along the East River in Manhattan in 1951.

Another change was in the treatment of the vanquished. The reparations exacted after World War I (mainly out of the French desire for vengeance after France's 1870 humiliation by the Prussians at Sedan) had both crippled Germany economically and given the Nazi party grist for its propaganda mills. In the general elections in Germany in 1932, a year of deep economic depression, Hitler's National Socialist party polled only 15 percent less than the combined vote for the German democratic parties. That fact could not be ignored. To prevent the forces of darkness from rising again out of the nation's economic distress, the Atlantic Allies decided to rebuild Germany and hopefully construct democracy through prosperity. Never before in history had victors been so generous to a foe.

Finally, the policy-makers agreed that, after the convulsions of competing protectionism in the interwar period, new economic and trade structures had to be built to stimulate the free flow of goods and money and keep nations outward-looking and open politically. International organizations with alphabet-soup initials—IMF, IRBD, CEEC, OEEC, GATT—were created as forums where nations could talk over their economic problems. The idea was to generate a collective responsibility for keeping the world on a liberal tack. Mechanics were worked out for nations to help each other economically, so that there would be no need to resort to "measures destructive of national or international prosperity," as it was put in the Articles of Agreement of the International Monetary Fund (IMF), one of the most important of the new organizations. One specialist, Frank Paish, an economics professor at the University of London, commenting on the situation later in the postwar period, made this revealing observation: "If the International Monetary Fund and the central banks had existed in 1929, and if the rest of the world had done for Germany in 1930 one-quarter of what the rest of the world had done for this country [Britain] between 1964 and 1968, there would never have been the rise of the Nazi party. It was sheer lack of knowledge which caused the Great Depression."

Even while the Allied armies were blasting their way across Norman hedgerows in July, 1944, the economic specialists of forty-four countries—known as the Wartime United Nations—were meeting at Bretton Woods, New Hampshire, to try to agree on a new world money and payments system that would promote the twin objectives of multilateral trade expansion and full employment. The breakdown of the old system had led to the Great Depression. Essentially, there hadn't been enough internationally acceptable money around to finance world trade; so trade dried up. Compounding the troubles was the restrictive environment produced as countries tried to gain maximum advantage over their partners by building ever higher barriers around domestic markets and enacting competitive devaluations. Everybody wanted to sell, but nobody could buy—a classic formula for economic ruin. The Bretton Woods experts' main job then was to do something about getting an adquate supply of acceptable money.

Gold was the traditionally acceptable asset, but there were many drawbacks to a gold standard, not the least of which was its subjection of the world economy to dependence on the health of the gold-mining industry. There was no rational reason why the prosperity of Chicago, Liverpool, or Hamburg had to be in any way related to the outtakings of metal from, say, the West Witwatersrand mine.

In the so-called Golden Age before World War I—*La Belle Epoque*—all of Europe's currencies were linked to gold. In other words, if one didn't like his paper money, he could turn it in for the equivalent in gold—and probably tear a hole in his pocket. In this way the currencies of Europe were also fixed in relation to each other. This made them practically universally acceptable.

The gold standard provided a stability that made life not unpleasant for the privileged classes. Apart from a few lagniappes, public spending to improve the lot of the working man was nonexistent. The masses were left in an *oubliette* of poverty. This comfortable, orderly way of life for the privileged few was overturned in the 1914–18 war and its aftermath. Arms had to be financed. The masses became more vocal and insistent in their demands for social justice. Since there were only limited supplies of gold, the printing presses of each nation rolled out cheap paper money. The result was inflation.

In reaction to the debasement of money and the destruction of savings, the hard money men came back into power, and by 1928 the gold standard had been widely reestablished. But that led to equal, if not greater, problems for Europe and the world. As mentioned earlier, each country wanted to give up as little gold as possible to its neighbors, and so built up barriers that curbed the quantities of goods its citizens could buy from abroad. But as the effects of these restrictions came to be felt in rising unemployment worldwide, there developed a new wave of defections from the gold standard. By 1937 hardly a single country was left on it. The gold standard seemed inappropriate for a world of rising expectations.

The monetary problems had to be shoved aside as the Second World War broke out in Europe, but even during the war a good deal of thinking was going on in Washington and London over the shape of a new system. Late in 1941 John Maynard Keynes, the most influential economist of the first half of the twentieth century, began working out a detailed plan for an international clearing union which would act more or less as a world bank for governments, issuing an international money known as Bancor, as well as credits to its members. Obligations would be imposed on countries that were chronic debtors (those that had more expenditures abroad than receipts) to take corrective action, either by acting on their exchange rates or adopting appropriate fiscal and monetary policies at home, to return to equilibrium. Similar obligations would be imposed on countries that were chronically in surplus (those that took in money from abroad) so that they, too, would be under pressure to return to equilibrium.

The United States produced a plan of its own. It didn't much like the idea of an international central bank issuing money to the world. It preferred to play this role itself by issuing dollars to the world. Americans pushed through what came to be known as the gold exchange and later simply the dollar standard. All currencies would be convertible into dollars, and only dollars would be convertible into gold. Since dollars were backed at that time not only by most of the gold in the world but also by the world's most powerful economy, nations could easily hold dollars as assets in their reserves knowing that those dollars were as "good as gold." Dollars would then become a convenient standard against which to measure the value of all other currencies. And from this it followed that dollars would be used in the exchange markets as a valve by nations wanting to maintain the stability of their exchange rates. For instance, if the French authorities saw the value of the franc falling they could conveniently buy francs in the market with the dollars in their reserves, and this, of course, would tend to prop up the rate for francs. Conversely, if the value of the franc was rising, they could conveniently sell francs to the market and acquire dollars. This, of course, would tend to curb any increase in the value of the franc.

The United States bought Keynes's ideas only insofar as it was prepared to see the creation of an international stabilization fund on which countries in temporary balance-of-payments difficulties could draw. This became the International Monetary Fund. The United States was not interested in a joint leadership position for Britain, which was implicit in the Keynes wartime proposals. As for Keynes's idea that obligations should be accepted by chronic-surplus as well as chronic-deficit countries to return to balance-of-payments equilibrium, the United States saw itself more or less in perpetual surplus and was therefore against any onerous obligations on the surplus countries. It wanted deficit countries to tighten their belts through fiscal and monetary austerity and to devalue only when they were in "fundamental disequilbrium," or in other words, only as a last resort if other measures failed to restore equilibrium. These principles were accepted at the time. Later, when the United States itself became a debtor country, it pressed for a more balanced system with obligations for surplus as well as deficit countries to adjust.

Keynes and the American under-secretary of the treasury for international monetary affairs, Harry Dexter White, had several meetings during the war years to try to come to an understanding. "To some extent it was a battle between the rasp and the rapier," Roy Jenkins, chancellor of the exchequer in the late 1960s, wrote in an essay on Keynes. "On the whole it was the rasp that won. Keynes's intellect was a match for most things, but not for the power of the United States in wartime."

What grew out of Bretton Woods then were: the gold exchange standard; fixed exchange rates with modest permissible fluctuations measured against the dollar as the key currency: and two new institutions, the International Monetary Fund and the International Bank for Reconstruction and Development (World Bank). As it worked out, the Bank became a fund and the Fund a bank.

On at least two counts Keynes had been ahead of his time. In the next quarter-century the IMF began issuing an internationally managed reserve asset. Instead of being called Bancor the new asset was known as Special Drawing Rights or SDRs. And with the United States pressing for changes, conventional wisdom in the 1970s finally came to accept that chronic-surplus countries shared obligations with deficit countries to return to equilibrium.

The initial purpose of the World Bank was to provide funds for the rebuilding of the war-devastated industries of Europe. Later, when Europe was on its feet, the Bank concentrated on financing projects in the developing countries of Asia, Latin America, and Africa. Opening shop in June, 1946, the institution made one-third of its loans to the nations of Europe during its first decade of operations. Later Europe had so prospered that by 1970 the only European states to receive any World Bank financing were Cyprus, Yugoslavia, Greece, and Spain. The Bank was long criticized for following too niggardly a lending policy by not opening up enough to the very poor countries. It was also accused of buttressing right-wing dictatorships by lending money to Greece and Spain. Somewhat more liberal policies were followed after Robert S. McNamara, secretary of defense under Presidents Kennedy and Johnson, took over as the bank chief in 1968. But since McNamara himself was closely identified with the intensification of the war in Vietnam, the bank came under fresh attack as being a symbol of American neo-colonialism. At a bankers' meeting in Copenhagen in 1970, as McNamara was being jeered by young Danish hecklers, he was heard telling an aide, "That's real hospitality for you—I feel right at home."

Both the World Bank and its sister organization, the IMF, represented a radically new effort to bring the world closer together by establishing a collective responsibility for helping nations in distress. Both drew their main financial support from the United States because it was about the only country that had any money in those days.

The IMF began functioning in March, 1947. While organized as a specialized agency of the United Nations, it operated autonomously from headquarters in Washington, shared with its Bretton Woods twin, the World Bank. Each body had a separate secretariat, financial structure, and membership. The Fund was a pool of gold and currencies requisitioned from members on the basis of their economic strength. From this pool, loans were made to countries that were spending more than they were earning. The loans were to serve as temporary aids to help countries pay their bills while their governments acted to restore balance to the external accounts. As members drew from the common pool, the IMF international secretariat had increasing authority to tell the borrower how to run its economic affairs. In the 1960s the British were subjected to this somewhat painful indignity as they went deeper and deeper into their credit lines with the Fund.

In 1971, membership of the IMF stood at 115, but included only one Communist country, Yugoslavia. The following year Rumania joined. Czechoslovakia and Poland were early members but resigned after Communist regimes were installed. Cuba walked out in 1964 after Fidel Castro came to power. The Soviet Union sent delegates to the Bretton Woods negotiations, but since all the major decisions were being made by the United States, the Russians pulled out. Moscow saw the Fund and Bank as part of a capitalist conspiracy, but it had more immediate and practical objections to joining the new institutions. Ever secretive about financial matters, Moscow could not accept the requirement that members submit economic data regularly to the Fund headquarters.

In spite of the Communist boycott the system set up at Bretton Woods had an enormously constructive influence in the first quarter-century after the war, generating robust growth of commercial exchanges and a rise in living standards throughout the Western world. Easy access to dollars, the facility to borrow money when in balance-of-payments trouble, and stability of exchange rates encouraged countries to break down the barriers they had built up around their markets and spurred businessmen into making new investments and hiring more workers.

During the years immediately following the war, the United States was willing to part with its surpluses and provide a base for expanding commercial exchanges on the theory that everybody would be lifted by a rising tide. The policy succeeded, but then much later things started going wrong. The pivotal position of the dollar had been justified in 1945 when the United States stood out as the economic giant of the world, but by the early 1970s Western Europe and Japan were no longer the scrawny-looking pygmies of the immediate postwar period. Partly because of that earlier American generosity, they were challenging American preeminence in trade and technology and accumulating the bulk of the world's monetary reserves (money that's held in national coffers, for instance, Fort Knox in the United States). Accompanying the change in economic power relationships was the hemorrhage of dollars overseas, far exceeding the intake by the United States of foreign money. Dollars were being spent on the junkets of American tourists, on the investments of American corporations, on wars in the Far East and troop garrisons in Europe, and on foreign aid to the poor countries. So long as the sales of American products abroad exceeded sales of foreign products in the United States the overall balance of payments was kept under control. The trade earnings were about the only plus next to all those minuses on the balance sheet. The only other significant plus was income from investments abroad. Then, in the late 1960s, trade turned sour, largely because of inflation in the United States, which lifted the price of American goods abroad and made cheaper foreign goods easier to sell in the United States. The inflation, in turn, was the result of the Vietnam War, which had been fought even though nobody wanted to pay for it. In 1971 the United States ran its first trade deficits of the twentieth century, and on August 15 of that year, with the banks of foreign governments holding five times more dollars than the United States had gold in Fort Knox, President Nixon officially suspended the dollar's convertibility into gold, signaling the end of the Bretton Woods system.

In the immediate postwar period, as in the early 1970s, nations sought monetary stability, while at the same time trying to dismantle trade barriers. Even before the Second World War the United States began shifting away from protectionism, and during the wartime collaboration it pressed the Allies into adopting similar positions. Easy lip service was paid to the idea with free trade clauses duly inserted in the Atlantic Charter of 1941, the Lend-Lease Agreements of 1943, the Bretton Woods Agreement of 1944, and the British-American Loan Agreement of 1945. Before the war ended the United States proposed to the Economic and Social Council of the new United Nations Organization that an international body be set up to enforce equality of trading opportunity.

But in view of gold and dollar shortages outside the United States most other nations in the immediate postwar years were still anxious to protect their weaker economies from American competition by maintaining high tariff walls or even more pervasive and effective nontariff barriers. These can be anything that keep foreign goods out of a country. Some examples: taxes on automobile imports into many European countries levied on the basis of engine size—making big American cars cost more; Buy-American provisions in some purchasing regulations of the United States government—keeping foreign contractors from getting the business; administrative controls in Japan that bar imports of computers. All of these and thousands more were being applied into the early

1970s. "Trying to do something about nontariff barriers," Franklin Roosevelt once observed, "is like trying to dynamite a fog."

In the summer of 1947, following an American invitation to twenty-three governments to meet in Geneva, pairs of governments negotiated mutual reductions of import duties, which were then generalized so that all the negotiating parties would benefit from the bilateral concessions. Also, at the Geneva meeting, the delegates drew up a code of conduct to encourage liberal, multilateral trading relationships and the abandonment of protectionism. The set of rules was known as the General Agreement on Tariffs and Trade (GATT). A small international secretariat worked with governments to try to enforce the code, operating from the serenity of the salmon pink Villa le Bocage (where Tolstoy once lived) above Lake Geneva. In subsequent years the GATT signatories, which included all the major Western trading nations, negotiated a series of supplementary tariff-cutting agreements, which, together with the new monetary machinery, led to the rapid growth of world trade through the early 1970s.

GATT was actually second best. When the covenant was signed, no one thought it would ever play any kind of significant role in the future because negotiations were about to get under way to establish a far more potent institution, the International Trade Organization, with a far more rigorous set of rules. After a lengthy meeting of fifty-six countries in Havana, from Novemeber, 1947, to March, 1948, the idea, which had been proposed by the United States, looked less and less attractive. Governments at that time, and Congress in the United States, simply were not willing to go too far in liberalizing trade because of the effects this might have in the short run in reducing domestic employment.

While some progress had been registered in creating new monetary and trade institutions, the clash between competing ideologies of East and West was assuming ominous proportions. Armies of the Soviet Union did not withdraw from Eastern Europe after the war. Their presence helped Moscow consolidate political authority in a band of satellite states from the Baltic to the Adriatic. In the West there were strong and active Communist parties seeking to overthrow the weak postwar governments and capitalize on general misery. Communists were already in the cabinets in France and Belgium, threatening a coup d'état in Italy, and waging civil war in Greece.

Gradually, the United States again got involved. It was the only country with the capacity to contain Soviet aggressiveness. Recalling the prewar failure to recognize the danger of Hitler until too late, Washington came to believe that its postwar mission was to contain Stalin. Perhaps it represented a Manichean view of the world, but Stalin in those days was seen in some of the same terms of darkness and evil as Hitler. As after every major war, there were strident calls for cuts in taxes and defense spending and for action to "bring the boys home." But the American people ended up supporting the policies of containment because they were frightened by the destruction of the wartime alliance and by the big black headlines of Communist takeovers in one state after the other.

The story of American postwar interventionism begins in Greece. In the postwar division of the world into sometimes vaguely, sometimes sharply, defined spheres of influence, Greece fell under Britain. Communist guerrillas, getting guns from Yugoslavia and Bulgaria across the border, had tried to seize power in Athens as early as December, 1944. While unsuccessful, they nevertheless controlled vast stretches of the countryside and waged an effective campaign of harassment. Their next attempt at a putsch followed the April, 1946, general elections, which were boycotted by the Communists and were easily won by King George II. With British help, the right-wing regime of the king managed to stay in power by repulsing the new Communist thrusts. But Clement Attlee, whose Labor government had replaced Winston Churchill's wartime coalition, had neither the bankroll nor the resolve to conduct more than a holding operation against the Greek Communists. On the grounds that an anti-Communist Greece was vital for safeguarding Middle East oil supplies, Britain poured $250 million into Greece between 1944 and 1947, but this wasn't enough. The Greek economy, in the crush of inflation, was at the point of collapse and needed far more help than Britain, increasingly preoccupied by domestic needs, thought she could afford, either in political or economic terms. In February, 1947, Foreign Secretary Ernest

Bevin served notice that his country was at the end of its tether. If Greece, and neighboring Turkey, which was under similar though less concentrated pressures, were to be kept out of the Communist orbit, Washington would have to do something.

The deterioration of the situation in Greece came against stunning reverses for the West in other areas of Europe. At Fulton, Missouri, a year earlier, Winston Churchill drew the picture in these somber terms:

> From Stettin in the Baltic to Trieste in the Adriatic, an iron curtain has descended across the continent. Behind that line lie all the capitals of the ancient states of central and eastern Europe. Warsaw, Berlin, Prague, Vienna, Budapest, Belgrade, Bucharest and Sofia, all these famous cities and populations lie in what I must call the Soviet sphere, and all are subject in one form or another, not only to Soviet influence but to a very high and, in many cases, increasing measure of control from Moscow.*

Truman's advisers convinced him that he had to act, and on March 12, 1947, he went to Congress to request a $400 million aid package for Greece and Turkey. Every nation had two alternatives, Truman told Congress, a way of life based on the will of the majority and distinguished by free institutions or a way of life "based upon the will of a minority forcibly imposed upon the majority." He went on to say, "It must be the policy of the United States to support free peoples who are resisting attempted subjugation."

To James Reston of *The New York Times,* the mood of Congress was "grim and resentful." There was a tendency, Reston wrote, to "blame the British and the Administration—the British for going broke and passing the baton to us, and the Administration for asking Congress so suddenly to assume such tremendous responsibilities."

The chairman of the Senate Foreign Relations Committee, Arthur H. Vandenberg, told Truman that if he wanted to get his

*This speech was given at Westminster College, Fulton, Missouri, on March 5, 1946. For full text see *New York Times,* March 6, 1946, p. 4, cols. 1 and 2.

money he would have to "scare the hell" out of the country. Dean Acheson, the elegant, Yale-educated diplomat who later became secretary of state, proceeded to do just that. Acheson spoke of an "unbridgeable chasm" between Russia and the United States and declared that no two powers had been so far apart on fundamental issues since Rome and Carthage. Within less than three months Turman had the aid bill on his desk for signature.

The threat of Communist takeovers was, as Truman later put it, "only half the walnut." The other major postwar problem was the staggering accumulation of wealth by the United States, which somehow had to be shared out with the Western partners to establish foundations for economic growth and political stability.

The self-interest of the United States was involved. Once on its feet, American planners thought, Western Europe would be a stronger ally in the Cold War, a major market for American products, and an ideal foreign base for American companies eager to expand abroad.

The immediate postwar task was to boost the industrial, food, and fuel production of Western Europe, which had been checked by the lack of investment in capital goods and the critical shortage of foreign exchange to buy raw materials. The new monetary and trading systems would help over the longer run. But other action was needed right away.

A former cotton merchant, Will Clayton, under-secretary of state for economic affairs, had an influence on the policy taking shape in Washington for the other half of Truman's walnut. Clayton was asked by Secretary of State George C. Marshall to take a trip to Europe. But it was not to be just another government-sponsored junket. As a businessman, Clayton was to report his personal impressions of what was wrong on the continent and what had to be done. In the report back to Marshall, those impressions echoed Benjamin Franklin's "for want of a nail, the shoe was lost. . . ." The troubles, said Clayton, lay with "the peasant who would not produce more than he and his family and his cattle could eat because with the money he might get from selling his surplus produce in the market he could not buy buttons and thread or cloth or farm tools." Additionally, "The manufacturer of buttons and thread and cloth and farm tools could not produce for want of materials and fuel and because workers, being unable to satisfy their wants with money, were refusing to work."

On June 5, 1947, at Harvard commencement exercises, Secretary of State Marshall read a speech that proclaimed to the world the American intention to help Europe, but only on terms whereby the Europeans would also help themselves. What had started as special assistance for beleaguered Greece and Turkey was extended in the Marshall Plan to a formal program, unprecedented in generosity, for American financial and moral support for a strong, united Europe that would no longer be the breeding ground for war.

Marshall restated the problem in his Harvard speech along lines already invoked by Clayton:

> The modern system of division of labor upon which the exchange of products is based is in danger of breaking down. . . The remedy lies in breaking the vicious circle and restoring the confidence of the European people in the economic future of their own countries and of Europe as a whole. The manufacturer and the farmer throughout wide areas must be able and willing to exchange their product for currencies the continuing value of which is not open to question.

Marshall said it was "logical" for the United States to assist in the return of normal economic health "without which there can be no political stability and no assured peace." American policy was to be directed not against any one country, or doctrine, he stressed, but against "hunger, poverty, desperation and chaos." Yet, Marshall emphasized, it could not be a completely American show.

> It would be neither fitting nor efficacious for this government to undertake to draw up unilaterally a program designed to place Europe on its feet economically. This is the business of the Europeans. The initiative, I think, must come from Europe. The role of this country should consist of friendly aid in the drafting of a European program and of later support of such a program as far as it may be practical for us to do so. The program should be a joint one, agreed to by a number, if not all, European nations.*

*For full text, see the *New York Times*, June 6, 1947, p. 2, col. 3.

So, in other words, Europeans finally had to stop squabbling among themselves and put their shoulders to the common task. The first priority was their own recovery, toward which they would have to work together if they were to get any help from the United States. Hopefully, in Marshall's view, the cooperation would deepen into the first tentative arrangements for economic integration, and as this, in turn, developed into something meaningful, a political confederation of some sorts would emerge.

Marshall started a process of history that would need decades to play itself out. These were old states with different regimes, languages, and traditions and a deep distrust of each other. It was too facile and simplistic to think that they could suddenly solidify into a United States of Europe, and those who thought in these terms were headed for grave disappointment. But, in the long run, a distinct coalescence did come about, in reaction primarily to external forces: first, the military threat from the Soviet Union and later, the economic challenge of the United States.

Marshall invited all European countries except Francisco Franco's Spain to set up an organization that would coordinate the reconstruction efforts. Sixteen countries—Austria, Belgium, Denmark, France, Greece, Iceland, Ireland, Italy, Luxembourg, the Netherlands, Norway, Portugal, Sweden, Switzerland, Turkey, and the United Kingdom—responded. Only five weeks after the Harvard address, the sixteen countries sent delegates to an elegant former Rothschild mansion, the Château de la Muette, across the Boulevard Périphérique from the Bois de Boulogne in Paris, to begin work on a four-year European recovery program. They set up the Committee of European Economic Cooperation,* which drew up a balance sheet of what Europe had and lacked, and then drafted a program to boost production in essential economic sectors. This all occurred within ten weeks, speed unheard of in the annals of bureaucracy.

Truman persuaded the predominantly Republican Congress to

*This, in a later incarnation, became the Organization for Economic Cooperation and Development, an institution representing the rich countries of the world. In 1972 there were twenty-three members—nineteen from Western Europe, plus the United States, Canada, Japan, and Australia.

appropriate funds both for emergency interim aid in 1947 and for the more broadly based European Recovery Program, which began in April, 1948. The ERP set up the administrative apparatus for the distribution of Marshall aid annually appropriated by Congress. Congressional sentiment was perhaps best summed up by Republican Senate Leader Vandenberg: "Within the purviews of this [Marshall] plan are 270 million people of the stock which has largely made America. . . .They are struggling against great and ominous odds to regain their feet. They must not be allowed to fail."

Between 1948 and 1952 Congress voted credits and grants to Western Europe of $13.6 billion. This was on top of the more than $9 billion the United States had already transferred since the war. The largest sums went to Britain and France, followed by Italy and Germany.

To British Foreign Secretary Ernest Bevin the American aid represented "the most unsordid act in history." Twenty-five years later, also at a Harvard commencement address, West German Chancellor Willy Brandt said thank you by announcing formation of the German Marshall Plan Fund to promote better Atlantic relations.

Although there was an open invitation to participate, the Soviet Union and, inevitably, all the countries of Eastern Europe rejected the Marshall Plan as they had declined to participate in the Bretton Woods institutions. Again Moscow's opposition was rooted in the deep suspicion of any foreign interference in internal Soviet economic affairs. Additionally, Moscow feared that the Eastern European satellites would somehow be drawn into the Western orbit. One Eastern country, Czechoslovakia, accepted the invitation to attend the Paris meeting at which the reconstruction program was drawn up. But after Premier Klement Gottwald and Foreign Minister Jan Masaryk were summoned to Moscow the invitation was promptly turned down. Still another element was Kremlin distrust of American intentions over Germany. Because of the interlocking manufacturing and raw material relationships between Germany and the other countries of Europe, Washington knew that Europe's productivity could not be restored without a mighty German contribution. But Stalin could not understand why a victorious power could show magnanimity to the losers of the war.

Each country wanted to boost exports to increase foreign exchange earnings, but no country was prepared to buy the others' products. That was the situation Europeans found themselves in before Marshall money started arriving. Only with those fresh dollars, that bought the machinery that created the jobs that boosted the purchasing power that led to prosperity, did the Europeans become less protective. They began removing quantitative restrictions on trade and granted limited bilateral credits to each other to help finance increased exchanges.

By July, 1950, they had established their own multilateral clearance system, the European Payments Union, for settling their accounts at regular intervals, like bridge players who pay their debts at the end of the evening instead of at the end of each rubber. While the British Socialist government under Clement Attlee joined in the European Payments Union, Britain refused to participate in other European integration moves. There had even been talk of a customs union in the early Marshall Plan days, but British delegates gave it all very short shrift, and in the process offended their continental partners.

These were the opening rounds in the long postwar debate over Britain's role in Europe and the world. At that moment British insularity had both the Socialist and Tory seal of approval. Churchill said, after he had reentered 10 Downing Street in 1951, that if it came to a choice between Britain being moored to the continent or staying out in the open sea, he knew his countrymen would opt for the open sea. To most Britons the continent could only be regarded with distance and suspicion. "Frogs are slightly better than huns or wops, but abroad is utterably bloody and all foreigners are fiends," said Nancy Mitford's Uncle Matthew in *The Pursuit of Love,** and most Britons could certainly not disagree.

On the other hand, France much favored European integration because it seemed to be the best way to redirect Germany's energies away from aggressive nationalism. Later in the postwar period, when France had the atomic bomb, she lost interest in this idea, but for the moment she wanted European institutions that would help keep the force across the Rhine across the Rhine.

* *The Nancy Mitford Omnibus,* Hamish Hamilton, London, 1956, p. 91.

3

The German Renaissance

In the second two weeks of July, 1945, Harry Truman, Joseph Stalin, and the British wartime coalition leaders Winston Churchill and Clement Attlee, but no French leader, met at Potsdam, a town fifteen miles southwest of Berlin (where Frederick the Great had once entertained Voltaire), to decide what to do with a beaten Germany. A month earlier, the wartime Allies, including France this time, had carved the country west of the Oder and Neisse rivers into four occupation zones and had set up the Allied Control Council, consisting of the four military commanders and their political advisers, as the administrative agency. Although it was in the Soviet zone, Berlin came under the special authority of all four powers and was governed by an interallied commission. At Potsdam the Allies agreed not to partition Germany but to treat the defeated country as an economic unit with central administrative departments. At the same time the Potsdam signatories made Germany a much smaller country. They lopped off in the east, in the former German kingdom of Prussia where those stiff-backed generals came from, an amount of land equal to a quarter of the size of Germany immediately after World War I. The Soviet Union was given the northern half of East Prussia. The territories east of the Oder and Neisse rivers, "pending the final delineation of Poland's frontiers," were left under Polish administration, separated from the Russian zone.

The hope to treat the four occupation zones as a single economic unit did not materialize. For one thing, France didn't like it. France had been offended by what she considered as the slighting treatment of her allies, and this made her a prickly partner. On substantitve grounds her interest was in keeping Germany as weak as possible to reduce any future military threat from across the Rhine. While the French attitude created tensions in the Western camp, there was the widening rift between Washington and Moscow over nearly all aspects of Germany policy, which ruled out any economic merger.

The Soviet Union took massive reparations to strip the vanquished foe and bolster its own postwar recovery. Not only did it hungrily swallow the production of German factories, but also it dismantled some of the factories themselves and carted them off to Russia.

The French, meanwhile, achieved one of their postwar goals by detaching the Saar industrial belt, near Luxembourg, and making it into an autonomous territory economically attached to France. An international authority was created to control the coal and steel industries of the Ruhr basin.

With all this wrenching dislocation, a prostrate Germany was once again experiencing, in Bismark's phrase, "the nightmare of foreign coalitions."

Initially, the Allies' top priority was to root out and destroy, once and for all, the foundations of German militarism. The Western powers soon found themsevles, however, faced with a much different problem, the economic weakness and demoralization of the defeated nation. There was a desperate housing shortage. There was not enough food and practically no work. More than ten square miles of Berlin's built-up districts had been demolished in the wartime bombing and shelling, far greater destruction than London had suffered. More people died at Dresden than at Hiroshima. Into the rubble of the German cities poured hundreds of thousands of refugees, Germans from the seized Eastern territories now under Polish administration, Sudeten Germans expelled from Czechoslovakia, and others.

Washington responded to the critical situation by pumping in dollars and supplies. Then as a step toward more effective economic management the Americans went to the British and proposed a merger of their two zones. If merger with the Russians was ruled out, nevertheless a start could be made in the unification process. Against the objections of both the Soviet Union and France, the British-American Bizone came into being on January 1, 1947.

To build a democratic base, parliaments (*Landtage*) were established in the German states (*Länder*), which then elected delegates to a German Economic Council in the Bizone. The Council, which later got authority in the French zone as well, assumed responsibility, under Allied supervision, for reconstruction of the country. It became the nucleus of the future West German government.

In the elections to the state parliaments the two largest parties to emerge in all three zones were the Christlich Demokratische Union, Christian Democratic Union (CDU), and the Sozialdemokratische Partei Deutschlands, Social Democratic party of Germany (SPD). These remained the principal parties for more than two decades after West Germany became a republic. The CDU, which ran German affairs uninterruptedly until the late 1960s, leaned to the right. The SPD, with its roots in the prewar trade union movement, leaned to the left.

One of the major tasks of the Economic Council was to draw up a plan for currency reform. In the first three years after the war, Germany suffered from what in economic jargon is called "suppressed hyperinflation." Money had little meaning. Some workers, for example, were being paid in the aluminum pots they were making. To eat, they had to scour the countryside to find someone with extra potatoes to trade for their pots. A cigarette was the closest thing to money.

The man who finally provided the formula for stability was Professor Ludwig Erhard, a rotund, cigar-chomping economics professor who believed that if free market forces were encouraged, Germany could move into an era of growth and price stability. As the director of the Bizone's Council, Erhard got the opportunity to put his ideas into practice. Working closely with Americans, he abolished controls that were impeding production and in a cur-

rency reform started a process that would give German money a
real value. One new deutsche mark was issued for every ten of the
near worthless old reichsmarks.

The idea was to let the economy respond freely to competitive
forces. As production rose to meet pent-up consumer demands, the
new currency would have real buying power. Statistics showed it
was the tonic the country needed. The reforms were enacted on
June 20, 1948, and in the last six months of that year output was
equal to 75 percent of the 1936 level, compared with 45 percent in
the previous six months. Steel production doubled in 1948 over the
previous year.

The reform was criticized by the SPD opposition on the Bizone
Economic Council and by the trade unions on grounds that it gave
capitalists far more than the workers. It was also assailed by Moscow.

Communist parties in the West, counting on popular discontent
to build up their strength, were trying to create as much social and
economic disorder as possible. Communist-led strikes spread
throughout Western Europe in 1947 and 1948, provoked in the case
of France by the firing of Communist ministers from the government of Paul Ramadier. Other governments found they could not
work with Communists. In Belgium, Communist ministers resigned during a coal industry dispute in March, 1947, and were
excluded from a new government formed by Social Democratic
leader Paul-Henri Spaak. In Italy, Christian Democratic leader
Alcide de Gasperi defied Communists and Socialists by forming a
government without them in May, 1947.

The great test of Communist strength in the West came during
the campaigning for seats in the Italian National Assembly in the
general elections of April, 1948. The Communists campaigned
hard, but no harder than the non-Communists, who had the active
support of the Roman Catholic priests in the villages and most
Italian-descended Americans in the United States. So concerned
was the Truman administration that Italy would swing Communist
that the administration threatened, rather heavy-handedly, to cut
off Marshall Aid to that country if the Communists won and called
on Italian Americans, as their patriotic duty, to write to family and

friends to impress on them the importance of a non-Communist vote.

As it was, the Communist coup in Czechoslovakia and the tragic death by defenestration of the Prague foreign minister, Jan Masaryk, which hit the headlines during the Italian election battles, were probably far more decisive in the election results than anything the United States or the Vatican said. De Gasperi's Christian Democrats won nearly half the vote, and a center coalition of Christian Democrats, Liberals, Republicans, and Social Democrats was quickly put together. De Gasperi and his centrists gave Italy stable government for more than a decade and helped provide conditions for rapid economic growth, even though living standards remained unacceptably low in the Mezzogiorno (Italy's south).

Developments took a different turn east of the Elbe.

Linguistically, three-quarters of the population of the Soviet Union are Slavs. But the Soviet Academy of Sciences has counted 169 ethnic groups in ten major divisons—Indo-European, Caucasian, Semitic, Finno-Ugrian, Nenets, Turkish, Mongol, Tungus-Manchurian, Palaeo-Asiatic, and what are simply called "tribes from the Far East with an ancient culture." In language and tradition, most of Eastern Europe is Slavic, except for Albania, Hungary, and Rumania. But here too there are strong national differences. Czechoslovakia, Hungary, and Poland are mainly Roman Catholic; Bulgaria and Rumania are Orthodox. Albania is 70 percent Moslem. Yugoslavia is a mixture of all three. Czechoslovakia was one of the most advanced industrialized states of Europe before the war, Bohemia having been industrialized about the same time as the English Midlands, whereas the other Eastern countries were mainly agrarian. Several had been monarchies—Bulgaria, Hungary, Rumania, Albania, and Yugoslavia—at the outset of the war. Bulgaria, Hungary, and Rumania joined Hitler; the others joined at the side of the Allies.

What they had in common now was the presence of Soviet troops. Local Communist chieftains therefore had a high trump in the power game. Used in combination with election rigging and systematic elimination of the opposition by violence or other means, the presence of the troops gave the Communists control in one state after the other—Yugoslavia, Poland, Bulgaria, Hungary, Rumania, Albania, and finally Czechoslovakia.

Marshall Tito's Communist partisans, backed by the Soviet divisions that rolled into Serbia in October, 1944, formed a people's front that took control in Yugoslavia in March, 1945, and wiped out opposition leaders one by one. During the resistance against the Germans, Tito's partisans and the right-wing Chetniks under Serbian General Draja Mihailovich, who commanded the allegiance of most of the Yugoslav exiles, were fighting their own private civil war. In 1946 Mihailovich was tried for treason and shot. The Roman Catholic Archbishop of Zagreb, Aloysius Stepinac, accused of cooperating with Croatian fascists during the war, drew a sixteen-year sentence.

With his enemies dealt with, Tito established a federal republic with a constitution modeled after the Soviet Constitution of 1936. Decentralization in language and culture of the six constituent republics—Croatia (the richest), Serbia, Slovenia, Bosnia-Herzegovina, Macedonia, and Montenegro (the poorest)—was accompanied by extreme centralization of the state bureaucracy and the Communist party that controlled it.

While Tito pursued a foreign policy that was subservient to Moscow in the immediate postwar period, his appointments and promotions in the army, police, and civil bureaucracy assured a staff whose first loyalty was to him.

Tito's became a nationalistic form of Communism, producing what Stalin himself called "something between de Gaulle's France and the Soviet Union." Regimes in the other Communist states, at the moment, dutifully followed the Moscow tune.

Tito's deviation created tensions and finally a rupture between Moscow and Belgrade. So angry did Stalin get that he exclaimed at one Kremlin meeting, according to an oft-told tale in Belgrade, "I will shake my finger and there will be no more Tito." Tito, of course, endured, one reason being the loyalty of his cadre.

In June, 1948, the Yugoslav leader was formally excommunicated from the newly established Cominform, or Communist Information Bureau, which, as a measure of Stalin's earlier confidence and esteem, had been installed in Belgrade. The base of the organization, which Moscow used to propagate the faith after inauguration of the Marshall Plan, was subsequently moved to Bucharest.

While intensifying the dissemination of Communist propaganda, Moscow tightened the network of trade and economic agreements with the satellite countries after Tito's expulsion from the Cominform. As the black sheep, Tito got no aid from Moscow and was forced to turn to the West for sustenance. Seeing a chink in the Communist armor, the West promptly accommodated him. The contributions and influences of the West and the ever greater need for Yugoslav self-reliance within a hostile Communist camp eventually produced substantial changes in the country's economic system. The changes had as their major objective the improvement of efficiency so that Yugoslavia could compete more effectively in world markets. Gradually, decision-making was decentralized so that production could be regulated not so much to meet targets set by bureaucrats as to respond to demands of the market. Worker councils were established as the local base, but these councils, ostensibly demonstrating that workers owned the means of production, hired professional managers to run things. Profits were encouraged and bonuses handed out as the incentives to make the economy work better.

These deviations from the principle of monolithic economic control, which was central to the Communist dogma of the time, led to a larger amount of personal freedom in Yugoslavia than in other Communist countries. Yet, it was still a police state. Making money was tolerated but opposition to the Communist party was not. The influence on other Communist countries was enormous. In 1968, when Hungary adopted measures similar to those of Yugoslavia, it was impossible to resist calling this highly significant movement in the affairs of the Eastern states "Goulash Communism."

One of Tito's heresies was his belief in a "strong monolithic entity" for the Balkan peoples. Stalin, who had suppressed nationalistic forces whenever they emerged, refused to accept any regional power centers in his empire. So ruthless was the quelling of "bourgeois nationalism" in the Ukraine in 1939 that many Ukranians welcomed Hitler's armies as liberators in 1942, but the "liberators" proved even more brutal than Stalin. Soviet leaders always feared the weakening or breakup of their Union of Soviet Socialist Republics if its diverse nationalities were permitted real freedom to express themselves. A sensational book published in the West in the late 1960s by the Soviet writer Andrei Amalrik, who was later imprisoned, predicted the dissolution of the Soviet Union in the 1980s.

Of all the states on the western frontier of the Soviet Union in 1945, only Finland managed to remain independent. Just before the outbreak of World War II, the Finns fought the Winter War of 1938-39 against the Soviet Union, a war that was started by Stalin because of his growing insecurity over the rise of Hitler. Finland's southeastern frontier, drawn when the kings of Sweden controlled northern Europe, was uncomfortably close to Leningrad. If Finland fell to a potential aggressor of the Soviet Union, that aggressor's armies would be within easy striking distance of the Soviet hinterland. Stalin attacked Finland to roll the frontier back. The Finns fought courageously to keep their land but were no match for Goliath, and when the final settlement was made they had to give up one-tenth of their territory, including most of the province of Karelia, to the Russians.

Hitler attacked the Soviet Union in November, 1942, and, as Stalin had anticipated, used Finland as the jumping-off point for assault in the north. The Finns welcomed the Germans because they wanted to get their territory back from the Russians. When the tide of the war turned, Soviet armies again pushed into southeastern Finland. Every able-bodied Finn, and some not quite so able-bodied, was sent to the front to slow the Russian juggernaut. Thus, within five years Finland and Russia had fought two wars. A 1945 settlement gave Stalin back the territory he had taken after the Winter War, $300 million of reparations, and the naval base at Porkkala, only eighteen miles from Helsinki. In 1955, agreement was reached to return the base. It was one of the rare instances in the postwar period when the Soviet Union gave anything back.

The Finns' costly struggle to keep the Soviet armies at bay

doubtless was the major factor in preserving independence. The Finns also were lucky. Soviet forces were thinly spread in 1945, and while they could easily have crushed Finland had they been concentrated in the north, this would have meant withdrawing divisions pursuing the Germans into Eastern Europe farther south, and for Stalin the dividends were greater in this latter region.

Not wanting to press their luck, the Finns, in free elections in 1946, turned to a Communist prime minister, Mauro Pekkala, who remained in power until 1948. But there were no Russian armies in Finland, and this made all the difference. Communists never got control of the police, the army, or other institutions to consolidate their grip over the country.

In April, 1948, still under the Pekkala government, Finland and the Soviet Union signed a treaty of mutual assistance binding Finland to fight in defense of the Soviet Union if the latter was ever attacked through Finland. Finland still retained democratic processes, however, and three months later a Social Democratic government came to power. While Moscow was preoccupied with developments in Prague, the new Finnish government was careful not to do anything that might antagonize Stalin. Urho Kekkonen, the Agrarian party leader, became prime minister in a new coalition in 1950, and he also managed to placate Stalin. One of his first acts was to sign a five-year trade treaty with Moscow. Under Kekkonen Finland swung deftly out of the Soviet orbit to become a neutral state with a prosperous, Western-oriented economy.

Czechoslovakia was a different story. As the disputes intensified over occupation policies in Germany, Moscow recognized the prime strategic importance of Czechoslovakia, sandwiched between Germany on the west and Russia on the east. Events in early 1948 were leading to the establishment of a divided Germany. Stalin, therefore, was determined to fix his hold on Prague.

Again, there was the advantage of having the Red Army in the Czechoslovak capital. During the war, General Eisenhower's American forces, positioned to reach Prague before the Russians did, did not do so. On May 4, 1945, Eisenhower's spearhead was only fifty-six miles from the capital when mainly non-Communist resistance fighters started a series of demonstrations against the

Nazis. The Prague guerrillas appealed to Eisenhower to take the city quickly to forestall almost certain Nazi retaliation. For reasons that are still puzzling the American forces stayed put. It was not until much later before some of the mystery was cleared up. A lieutenant of Alexander Dubcek, Prague party leader in 1968, reported that Communists who were in the leadership of the wartime resistance movement had been in contact with the Americans and had rejected all offers of assistance. The Soviet army didn't get to Prague until May 11, giving the Gestapo ample time to round up and massacre the non-Communist resistance leadership.

Something similar had happened to Warsaw the year before. The Soviet authorities, having discredited the legal Polish government in London, smuggled faithful Communists into what had been an anti-Communist nation to supplant the leaders of the indigenous resistance to the Nazi occupation. When the Red Army reached the Vistula River, near Warsaw, in July, 1944, Moscow called for a general rising in the capital to support the troops. The commander of the "home army," acting on Moscow's request, relayed by the London exile regime, dutifully responded with an open struggle, while the RedArmy stood for sixty-three days motionless on the river line. The non-Communist resistance was decimated, and when the Red Army moved again toward Warsaw it disarmed and deported members of the home army. Poland was thus locked tightly into the postwar Soviet sphere. The conquest of Czechoslovakia took longer.

President Eduard Benes, the prewar Czechoslovak leader who had set up a government in exile in London, returned to Prague on May 16, 1945, to establish a provisional government, including seven Communists and a left-wing socialist as premier. After a quarter of a million alleged wartime collaborators were struck off the voting lists, the country went to the polls in May, 1946. Communists got the largest vote—38 percent—and Communist leader Klement Gottwald became premier in a coalition government.

Gottwald embarked on a recovery program in which economic production rose and increasing trade contacts were made with the West. A drought hit Czechoslovak agriculture particularly severely in 1947, which prompted Gottwald to respond to the

American offer of Marshall Plan aid. Gottwald had his knuckles rapped by Stalin for that. After being summoned to Moscow, the Czechoslovak leader began plotting a Communist putsch, timing it to occur just before elections that were due in March, 1948. Stalin's veto of Marshall aid caused deep resentment in the country, and the Communists were unsure of maintaining anything like the percentage of votes they had received in May, 1946.

The incident that led to the coup was the abrupt dismissal by Communist Interior Minister Vaclav Nosek of non-Communist commissioners in the police force and their replacement by Communists. When the eleven anti-Communist ministers resigned in protest on February 20, the Communists brought police reserves from outside Prague and staged demonstrations. Opposition newspapers were suppressed, student counterdemonstrations were crushed, and hundreds of persons were arrested. Five days later, President Benes gave in and accepted a new Gottwald cabinet, which was overwhelmingly Communist.

On March 10, the body of Jan Masaryk, the non-Communist foreign minister whose father Thomas had founded the Czechoslovak republic, was discovered on the pavement under a window of his office at the foreign ministry in Prague. He may have jumped or he may have been pushed out the window by Communist thugs: it was never clear. Perhaps it made little difference. Even if he took his own life, his death represented an act of murder. Masaryk was a symbol of Czechoslovak independence, which had died. In the ensuing elections there was no choice except to vote for the Communist-led national front or to spoil the ballots. Some 6.4 million votes were cast for the Communist Front, some 1.5 million ballots were spoiled. Benes, who had been the protégé of Thomas Masaryk, resigned on June 7, and died three months later.

The Prague coup electrified the West. People could identify with Masaryk, Benes, and the student protesters, just as they did with Alexander Dubcek and a new generation of students twenty years later. The immediate result was something that perhaps Stalin hadn't counted on: a stiffening of non-Communist resistance in Western Europe. Less than two months after the Prague coup, the Communists suffered their heavy setback in Italian general elections. Within a week of Masaryk's death, Britain, France, Belgium, the Netherlands, and Luxembourg signed a multilateral defense pact in Brussels, the first of the postwar era directed at the Soviet threat. Thirteen months later, the North Atlantic Treaty Organization was formed to bolster the defenses of the West.

The Prague coup came against badly deteriorating relations between Moscow and Washington over Germany. As the United States and Britain, in their newly merged Bizone, went ahead with plans to set up a democratically based German government in the West, with a new currency and a more solidly based economy, the Soviet military administration reacted by squeezing Berlin. The city, itself divided into sectors governed by the wartime Allies, was an enclave in the eastern zone of Germany, 110 miles by autobahn from the western zone. Late in 1947, the Soviets began requiring permits for interzonal traffic with the city. By March 20, 1948, when the Russians withdrew their representative from the Allied Control Council, the body set up in 1945 to run Germany, they were already prohibiting the transfer of property between the Western zones and Berlin and were sharply reducing truck traffic. The squeeze continued, with permits suddenly required for Western troop movements into Berlin, the announcement of a two-day suspension of civilian access to the city, the interruption of rail traffic, and the closing of canal and highway traffic. Moscow's objective: to drive out the Allied garrisons and secure East German control of the entire city.

Washington's analysis was that Stalin, while playing dangerously, did not want a war. Instead of sending in armed convoys of trucks, which might have sparked a conflagration by miscalculation, the United States organized the supply of Berlin by air and refused to be diverted from its course, which was to get a West German government on its feet. Around the clock, the C-47s and C-54s droned through the Western corridor into East Germany, ferrying supplies into the beleagured Western sectors of Berlin. The blockade was finally lifted on September 30, 1949, by which time 2.3 million tons of food, fuel, and raw materials had been flown into Tempelhof airport.

Unable to squeeze the Western garrisons out of the city, Moscow divided the city administratively. The Western allies responded by giving increased authority to Mayor Ernst Reuter, who was later succeeded by fellow Socialist, Willy Brandt. As West Germany prospered under the new reforms of Ludwig Erhard, so did West Berlin. The airlift demonstrated that, short of a war the Russians would have to start themselves, West Berlin would long remain a democratic, capitalist-oriented enclave, deep inside East Germany.

Work was meanwhile going forward to draw up a constitution for the embryonic Federal Republic of Germany. This was done by a council of sixty-five members from the state parliaments of the three Western zones of Germany,* under the chairmanship of Konrad Adenauer. A Rhinelander, born in Cologne in 1876, Adenauer had solid anti-Nazi credentials, made even more impressive by his arrest in 1944 after the plot to kill Hitler. Charles de Gaulle was later to call him "that good German."

The parliamentary council concluded its deliberations on the draft constitution in May, 1949, and submitted it for ratification to the eleven provincial assemblies and to the Allied military governors. All of the assemblies approved the constitution except Bavaria's, which preferred a looser federation, but was willing to go along with the majority. The three Allied governors endorsed the constitution after expressing certain reservations, the most important of which dealt with article 23, declaring West Berlin as the twelfth state of the republic. The constitution, inclusive of article 23, was ratified anyway, but up to the 1970s there remained a certain ambiguity over Berlin's legal status, which generated frictions between East and West from time to time. West Berlin sent twenty-two members to the Bundestag, the German parliament, but they were "delegated," not elected, and did not have voting rights. West Berlin's status as a state was marked mainly in ceremonial ways. But even this caused strong reactions in the East and further squeezes on the city.

The constitution, which, despite the objections of Bavarians, reserved more powers for the state administrations than the prewar Weimar Republic, provided for a president and two legislative

*The French zone was merged with the Bizone in April, 1949.

chambers—the Bundestag, whose members chose the federal chancellor, and the Bundesrat, representing the eleven incontrovertible state governments. Elections to the Bundestag, to determine the political composition of a West German government, took place in August, 1949. The two parties that favored a rapid return to a free economy, the Adenauer Christian Democrats and the smaller Free Democrats (Freie Demokratische Partei, or FDP), got a majority and formed a right-wing coalition under Adenauer, but there was a strong, vocal, Socialist minority that believed in state ownership of heavy industry and a controlled economy.

With Berlin a divided city, the seat of the new government was established at the sleepy Rhenish town of Bonn, the birthplace of Beethoven, just upriver from Adenauer's birthplace at Cologne. Under Adenauer, who had twice been mayor of Cologne, and who followed a policy of close cooperation with both France and the United States, the Federal Republic formed a distinctive personality and eased its way into the Western councils. The new nation's problems were immense: it faced the open hostility of the Soviet Union and the distrust of France; it feared a new war, not of its own making this time but one in which it again would be a battlefield. It began life with a crippled economy, and, although a recovery program offered prospects for a more promising future, many years would be needed before unemployment was reduced, and the refugees from the Eastern territories fully absorbed.

Two months after the Bundestag elections, the "people's council" of East Germany transformed itself into a provisional "people's chamber," or Volkskammer for the German Democratic Republic. Three days later a chamber of states, the Länderkammer, was appointed, and the two houses elected a president, Wilhelm Pieck. The hold of the Soviets in the Eastern zone was not relaxed. One of the first acts of the new East German government was its announcement of the acceptance of the loss of the Eastern territories to Poland. On July 6, 1950, an agreement recognizing the Oder-Neisse line as the permanent frontier was signed by the two governments.

Power politics and competing ideologies were responsible for the division of Germany. As the wartime alliance sputtered and then broke down, Washington and Moscow began tugging at Europe. The United States wanted to check Soviet influence by anchoring a democratic West Germany to the new Western alliance it began to construct after the coup in Prague. There were several theories about Moscow's aims. Some thought that Stalin seriously considered trying to take over all of Europe. "The Russians need only a good pair of shoes to reach Brest," the American military commander in Germany, General Lyman T. Lemnitzer, said in the emotionally explosive post-Prague 1948 period. Others maintained that the Kremlin was acting defensively to neutralize what it considered as the threat that the emerging West Germany would represent to Soviet security. What Stalin finally got was a Communist-dominated buffer zone between the Soviet Union and a Western Europe in which American economic and political influence was growing.

The fear of Soviet expansionism was certainly the dominant consideration in the West in 1948, when the Brussels Defense Treaty was signed and secret talks began over the construction of the wider North Atlantic Treaty Organization (NATO). In the icy Cold War climate, President Truman had already urged Congress to restore selective service, and in response to the growing anti-Soviet mood in the country, Senator Arthur H. Vandenberg, chairman of the Senate Foreign Relations Committee, got a resolution adopted in the Senate in favor of "such regional and other collective arrangements as are based on continuous and effective self-help and mutual aid." It was the sign that Congress would buy a regional defense treaty.

On April 4, 1949, representatives of twelve countries signed the North Atlantic Treaty in Washington. The signatory nations were Belgium, Canada, Denmark, France, Iceland, Italy, Luxembourg, the Netherlands, Norway, Portugal, the United Kingdom, and the United States. Greece and Turkey signed during the Korean War. West Germany signed the alliance in 1954.

The parties agreed that

> an armed attack against one or more of them . . . shall be considered an attack against them all; [and consequently they agreed

that] if such an armed attack occurs, each of them, in exercise of the right of individual or collective self-defense . . . will assist the party or parties so attacked by taking forthwith, individually and in concert with the other parties, such action as it deems necessary, including the use of armed force, to restore and maintain the security of the Atlantic area.

Under the Marshall Plan, the Americans were pumping billions of dollars into the recovery of Western Europe. Now Washington was committed militarily and politically to Europe's defense. For the United States, the alliance represented a complete break with its peacetime tradition of neutrality and isolationism. Soon after the NATO agreement was signed, the Berlin blockade ended. In the following year, the United States got into an armed conflict—not in Europe, but in Asia—when North Korean troops marched south across the 38th parallel. In Europe things took a different turn.

4

A Kind of
United States

Around the year 200 B.C., a group of Greek coastal towns banded together to form the Achaean League, under the leadership of a general named Philopoemen. They wanted to protect themselves against pirates and against the armies of more powerful Greek city-states such as Sparta. While preserving internal freedom of action, the Achaean towns formed a central administration, which set up uniform standards of measures and coinage, imposed taxes, ran an army, negotiated treaties, and made war or peace. This federal structure survived for several hundred years until it was finally broken up by the Romans.

The Western European states after World War II also faced an external threat, from the aggressive military policies of the Soviet Union and later from the aggressive economic policies of the United States. The idea of linking independent states in a federal structure, as Philopoemen had done, also had appeal for Europeans as a means to end those European civil wars. Churchill in 1946 had called for "a kind of United States of Europe," in which the peoples of the continent could "dwell in peace, safety and freedom."

The idea of uniting all disparate peoples of the continent had been floated for centuries, but the only practical results were achieved in the age of warrior conquerors—the Romans, Charlemagne, Napoleon, Hitler. After World War II, for the first time, it seemed that the peoples of the continent could be brought together by a common will and purpose.

This was implicit in the way the Marshall Plan was framed: Europeans had to help themselves if they were to get help from the United States. After being drawn into two wars on the European continent in a generation, Americans felt it was in their enlightened self-interest to help the unification process along as much as possible. "Why can't those Europeans just get together?" many Americans asked.

The key to stability in Western Europe was a good relationship between France and Germany. Leaders of both countries were thinking of an institutional association that would be open to other countries. France wanted a body that would act as a restraint on German expansionism. Germany wanted a body that would offer it equal status after the defeat of 1945.

Well before Hitler came to power, Konrad Adenauer had written that "a lasting peace between France and Germany can only be attained through the establishment of a community of economic interests between the two countries." In March, 1950, the new German chancellor signaled that his country was ready for a French initiative by suggesting that France and Germany should work toward a political-economic union that would be open to other European powers.

On May 9, 1950, two months after Adenauer's statement, newsmen were summoned to a press conference along the left bank of the Seine at the Quai d'Orsay, the French foreign ministry, to hear Robert Schuman, the foreign minister, call for a pooling of the French and German coal and steel industries in an organization that other countries of Europe might join. "It is no longer the moment for vain words, but for a bold, constructive act," said Mr. Schuman, a Luxembourg-born Alsatian who had fought in the German army in World War I. The European Coal and Steel Community, and after a somewhat longer gestation, the European Economic Community, were the offspring of that May day in Paris.

The Schuman declaration was the culmination of several earlier initiatives.

Even before the end of World War II, Belgium, the Netherlands, and Luxembourg signed the Benelux Convention of September 5, 1944, under which they agreed to abolish customs duties in internal

Benelux trade while establishing common duties in trade with the outside world. This accord had served as the model for American-promoted efforts within the Committee of European Economic Cooperation, the Marshall Aid distributing agency in Paris, to create a European-wide customs union. The British showed no interest, and the idea was buried.

Similarly the British were uninspired by a French plan to give the secretary-general of the CEEC and his executive board powers to make major policy decisions if support could be mustered from a majority of the member states. This time the Benelux countries were also unenthusiastic, fearful that they would be overruled by the larger countries.

None of the pre-1950 endeavors stirred up quite so much excitement as the Council of Europe or created so much disappointment afterward. Founded in May, 1949, in a spirit of unabashedly ebullient optimism, the Council was to be the vehicle for that "United States of Europe" that Churchill talked about. "I came to Strasbourg [Council headquarters] convinced of the need for a United States of Europe," said Paul-Henri Spaak, the Belgian foreign minister and first president of the Council. "I leave with the certainty that union is possible."

The hopes that the Council, which was run by a consultative assembly of parliamentarians and government ministers, would become the nucleus for a European government were quickly dashed. In the crunch, member countries were unwilling to cede any real sovereign power. The Council got impressive quarters, across the street from a large park in residential Strasbourg, but authority to do little more than act as a sounding board for ideas. Although it never achieved its political goals (de Gaulle was later to call it an "empty carcass"), the Council salvaged what it could by doing useful work in the social, cultural, and legal fields and was still active into the 1970s. One of its most notable achievements was the European Convention on Human Rights of November 4, 1950, which established a European Court of Human Rights in which individuals could lodge complaints against governments. In 1971 the Council of Europe got agreement to standardize the pitch of orchestras around a treble A tone of 440 vibrations a second, an important accomplishment for the musical world.

Jean Monnet, Schuman's chief aide in the French foreign ministry, was probably the man most responsible for maintaining the momentum of integration as the disillusionment set in over the failures of the Council of Europe to unite the continent politically. He occupied a singular place in the history of Europe over the next fifteen years as the "instigator" (as the French called him) of the European Communities.

Monnet was born in 1888 in the village of Cognac in southwestern France, where his family operated a business producing and selling, not surprisingly, cognac. A diminutive, spritely, warm, entertaining, fiercely ambitious man, Monnet joined the family company as a salesman, prospered, traveled, played the money markets, prospered some more, and as an international financier suddenly found himself advising governments. At thirty-one his meteoric rise, incidentally without any university training, had put him in line to become deputy secretary-general of the League of Nations. After a distinguished interwar career and his exile from France during the occupation, he headed the planning commission that mapped France's postwar economic rehabilitation and was then tapped to be the aide of Robert Schuman.

Monnet was an idea man who loved to tinker in the affairs of government. He was also one of the world's most successful promoters. No one could claim more credit than he for the entry, after so many false starts, of Britain into the European Communities.

In his thinking about Europe Monnet accepted the reality of its diversity. Grandiose conceptions such as the Council of Europe were impractical because they did not recognize this reality. In conversation with American friends Monnet would contrast viniculture in California and France. In the wine-growing regions of California, he would observe, only about a dozen different types of grapes could be identified, against more than one hundred types within an area of less than four hundred square miles in the region of France where he was born. So what was needed to pull together a continent in which there was such variety in a single region, he reasoned, was not the fuzzy and misleading notion of European togetherness but a collective action at "one limited but decisive point."

Monnet drew up a memo for Schuman suggesting that coal and

steel were "decisive points." It turned out to be the right move and the right time because Europeans wanted to do something concrete and constructive together.

Events outside were also pushing Europe in this direction. In September, 1949, President Truman announced that the Soviet Union had exploded a nuclear bomb. In June, 1950, North Korean armies invaded South Korea. In Washington and the capitals of Europe the message was clear: to influence events outside the continent Europe had to unite and get stronger.

On March 19, 1951, less than a year after the Schuman press conference, the governments of France, Italy, West Germany, and the Benelux countries initialed a draft treaty in Paris covering the establishment of a European Coal and Steel Community. After the six parliaments ratified it, the treaty, valid for fifty years, came into effect in June, 1952.

The long-term objective of the European Coal and Steel Community was to introduce, in Schuman's words, "the germ of a broader and deeper community between countries long opposed to one another by bloody conflicts," but the immediate aim was nuts and bolts: to bring about a "fusion of markets" by removing tariffs and other barriers to trade in coal and steel inside the Community. More exchanges would hopefully lead to greater economic expansion and higher standards of living for everybody, encouraging, in turn, more efforts toward political union. Institutions were set up to guide this transformation: a High Authority to act as the executive body, Monnet becoming its first president; a Court of Justice to rule in legal disputes; a Common Assembly appointed by national parliaments, and a Council of Ministers where representatives of the member states would meet with representatives of the High Authority to make the decisions for the Community.

Some of the objectives were certainly met. Freer trade in steel did help to stimulate economic activity. The Coal and Steel Community did become the germ of the "broader and deeper" European Economic Community that came into existence later in the decade.

But free competition never came about and probably never will. Each national administration faced the social problems of a labor-intensive coal-mining industry in a general state of decline because of the competition of oil. Where the dimensions of the problem were greatest, in France and Belgium, the administrations followed national policy objectives, which meant continued protectionism of one form or another. The steel industries of the member states, at the same time, were becoming concentrated in fewer and bigger enterprises, a trend the Community sought to encourage in the belief that size is related to efficiency. In Germany, the steel companies organized themselves into four main selling groups, smacking a little of the prewar cartels. A chummy European steel club was formed, which would probably never have run the gauntlet of American antitrust enforcement.

Three broad principles of policy kept the British Labor government from participating in the continental experiment in coal and steel: refusal to cede any sovereignty whatsoever to a supranational body such as the High Authority; the desire to keep lines open to the Commonwealth; the attempt to construct a more egalitarian society in Britain, which the British Socialist politicians feared would be undermined by any union with the non-Socialist governments of the continent. The resulting aloofness perpetuated the impression that somehow the British, like the rich of F. Scott Fitzgerald, were very different from you and me.

Before the Schuman plan was announced, Monnet sought Britain's advance support. In the negotiations to form the Community, he tried to get a British commitment to join. The British never quite said no, but the conditions they set for membership were equivalent to a rejection. With superb disdain the British figured the continentals would never go ahead on their own.

The whole story might have been different if, ten years earlier, Monnet had been successful with another idea. It was June, 1940, just before the fall of France. Monnet, who was in London, proposed a union between France and Britain, under which there would have been a joint war cabinet, dual citizenship, a customs union, a single currency, the pooling of all resources and the sharing of war reparations. Recognizing the impracticability of the proposition, Churchill nevertheless was interested because, in France's exhausted condition, Britain would have dominated the union. The French administration, under Paul Reynaud, had no interest at all. Anti-British feelings after the withdrawal of British forces at Dunkirk (leaving the French in disarray before the Germans) set French public opinion against the idea. It was officially spiked when Reynaud, who had set up a temporary seat of government at Bordeaux during the German advance in June, decided to quit France. He was offered a plane flying the British flag and refused it. Later de Gaulle ridiculed Monnet's idea. It was as foolish as trying to integrate King George and President Lebrun, or the Horse Guards and the Garde Républicaine, he said. A union of Britain and France may have been unworkable, but the idea did have an important influence on the sweep of European history because it served as inspiration for the 1944 Benelux customs union, which in turn was the precursor of the Coal and Steel Community.

Six weeks after the Schuman declaration divisions from North Korea, spearheaded by tank columns, crossed the 38th parallel and invaded South Korea. The North Koreans presumably expected no military response from Washington, which appeared to have put Korea outside the non-Communist defense perimeter. The United States, having written off the government of Chiang Kai-shek as an investment, had done relatively little to prevent Mao Tse-tung's Communist forces from taking over China the year before, but President Truman reacted swiftly and angrily to the action of the North Korean Communist leader Kim Il Sung by ordering units of the Cavalry Division and the 24th Division, softened by years of garrison duty in Japan, to Korea to help South Korean troops try to check the invader. Heavy losses were taken by the defenders, who were rolled back to a perimeter around the southern port city of Pusan. Then, as more American units, swollen by draftees, and forces from fifteen other members of the United Nations, began reinforcing the defenders, the tide changed, and the war was carried north to the Yalu River on the border with China. Peking then provided a massive army to reinforce the armies of the north.

The Korean War, the first of the ferocious postwar "limited wars," raged up and down that ravaged peninsula for three years, and, although it took place halfway around the globe, it came to have a strong influence on European events. Washington was convinced that the invasion had been stage-managed by the Soviet Union, the big arms supplier of North Korea, and that the Korean hostilities were the prelude to further Soviet pressures in Europe. With the American commitment in Korea, it was therefore imperative to the Washington planners that Western Europe, and particularly West Germany, be in a better position to defend itself. The Allies had little to put in the way of two hundred Soviet divisions in Eastern Europe.

Less than three months after Kim Il Sung's army struck south across the 38th parallel, the American secretary of state, Dean Acheson, who had just replaced Marshall, dramatically stepped up the pressure on the Europeans by declaring in a speech that NATO forces should include German divisions. This was still a frightening prospect for the Europeans, and particularly the French, but the Americans kept up the pressure, hinting that their resolve to defend Europe would weaken considerably if West Germany was not rearmed.

Again it was up to the French to come up with some ideas, and they did, with the European Defense Community. The French government put the EDC plan before the National Assembly, which approved it overwhelmingly—343 votes to 225—on October 24, 1950.

The EDC, which Monnet also had a hand in preparing, solved the defense problem by putting German and other national forces into a "European" army under "European" federal control. As it finally took shape, the idea was to create a European army of forty divisions to replace the national armies. Mixed manning—Frenchmen and Germans, for instance, in the same platoon or company —was a problem that was finally resolved by the decision to organize units on a national basis up to division level and then to integrate them into the mixed command structure. So, there would be German and French divisions in the European army. All the troops would wear the same uniform.

The same states that formed the European Coal and Steel Community were also in on the Defense Community negotiations— France, West Germany, Italy, Belgium, the Netherlands, and Luxembourg. Once again Britain wanted no part of the continental

venture but did express willingness to sign a treaty of mutual
assistance with the Europeans if the EDC ever got off the ground.
Later the British said they would assign one armored division to
the European army but would not participate in either military or
political integration.

Federalists, arguing that there could be no European army unless Europe existed as a political unit, introduced an article into the
draft defense treaty demanding the creation of a political organization "of a federal or a confederal nature." Without even waiting for
the defense treaty to be ratified, ministers of the six would-be
members of the new community requested that a special ad hoc
assembly be created to draw up a treaty for political union. This
was a sign of the way the external forces were pulling the Europeans together. On March 9, 1953, two and one half years after the
French National Assembly approved the idea of the Defense Community, Paul-Henri Spaak, chairman of the ad hoc assembly, formally presented the proposed treaty to the Six.

The draft provided for a European executive council, a council
of national ministers, a court of justice, a parliament consisting of
a senate whose members were to be chosen by national parliaments
and a "people's chamber" directly elected by citizens of the member states. Member governments would coordinate foreign policies
and prepare to create a customs union.

In the coming months, hundreds of government experts met at
one conference after the other to examine the ad hoc assembly's
draft. The proliferation of meetings and of the committees appointed to work out fresh proposals was now the sign that enthusiasm for the whole project was waning. With the death of Stalin on
March 5, 1953, and the end of the Korean War just four months
later, the world was moving into a less intense phase of the Cold
War. As tensions eased, there was naturally more questioning of
the need for a beefed-up defense establishment and for the political
union that went with it. The argument was heard increasingly that
NATO defense was enough. "Some men of great integrity are
naturally anxious about the dissolution of their homelands," said
French Foreign Minister Georges Bidault, raising sovereignty as
an issue. Communist parties in France and Italy played on the fears

of German rearmament even within an integrated defense organization. Britain's refusal to join gave another weapon to opponents. Without Britain, they said, there wouldn't be enough counterweight within the organization to the emerging power of West Germany.

The long story of the Defense Community finally ended in the French National Assembly in August, 1954, when the deputies refused to ratify the treaty. France's new premier, Pierre Mendès-France, then a radical socialist (liberal) who was perhaps best known for his efforts to get Frenchmen to drink milk instead of wine (France had the highest alcoholism rate in the world), became head of a Fourth Republic coalition in June, four weeks after the fall of the French garrison at Dienbienphu to the Vietminh Communists under Ho Chi Minh.

Mendès-France was primarily interested in getting France out of Indochina, and some commentators, such as Sorbonne Professor Raymond Aron, suggested that there was a link between this objective and French rejection of the treaty. The new French premier had threatened to resign if a ceasefire, being negotiated at Geneva, was not arranged before July 20. The suspicion of Aron and some others was that Soviet Foreign Minister Molotov and Mendès-France reached a secret agreement under which Moscow would support a ceasefire in return for French assurances that there would be no Defense Community. The Geneva accords were signed on July 21, providing for a ceasefire and the temporary partition of Vietnam into northern and southern zones until reunification by elections that were supposed to be held (but never were) in 1956.

In the National Assembly voting on the Defense Community, Mendès-France, who during the debate refused to endorse the project, abstained along with forty-two other deputies. The lack of government support doomed the treaty: the vote was 319 against and 264 in favor.

What the whole thing boiled down to was that Europe simply wasn't ready for a unified military establishment. As Professor Richard N. Cooper of Yale has observed, three factors signify nationhood in today's world: a foreign policy, a national military establishment, and a national currency. Two decades after the National Assembly beat down the idea of a European army, the Europeans still had not revived it, although they were proceeding cautiously both in the fields of money and foreign policy.

Washington policy-makers were highly critical of the Vietnam accords, mainly because the partition provision would place millions under Communism in the north. The National Security Council had been so opposed to the Geneva negotiations, a Pentagon analyst related, according to accounts published by *The New York Times,* that "the President was urged to inform Paris that French acquiescence in a Communist takeover of Indochina would bear on its status as one of the 'Big Three' and that "United States aid to France would automatically cease."*

While it pledged not to disturb the Geneva accords, the United States refused to sign them and persisted with its demands to rearm Germany. The pressure this time resulted in such a watered-down version of the Defense Community that even Britain could join. This was the Western European Union, set up by the six coal and steel partners and Britain in December, 1954, as a loose military alliance without any supranational trappings. Under the treaty West Germany was permitted to have an army of twelve divisions but was barred from making atomic, biological, or chemical weapons.† Following ratification of the WEU treaty, the Bonn government was admitted to NATO. One of the paradoxes of the situation was that those who opposed German rearmament under what would have been the tight control of the Defense Community accepted it under the much looser control of the WEU. One explanation is that people were getting bored with the issue. Another reason was that in view of the intense American pressure German rearmament seemed inevitable.

***The Pentagon Papers,* Bantam Books, New York, 1971, p. 5.

†Britain pledged that she would not withdraw her four NATO divisions from the continent without approval of a majority of the WEU members. In another move edging her closer to Europe, Britain signed an association agreement with the Coal and Steel Community in September, 1954, providing for the exchange of technical information and the establishment of a permanent delegation of the High Authority in London.

The rejection of the EDC by the French Assembly only temporarily halted discussion of political union by the six continental powers. At a foreign ministers' conference at Messina in Sicily in June, 1955, France, West Germany, Italy, Belgium, the Netherlands, and Luxembourg decided to have another go. Symbolically, it was an ideal spot. Founded by pirates, Messina fell into the hands of the Persians, Athenians, Carthaginians, Romans, an assortment of medieval European dynasties, the Bourbons, and finally Cavour, who unified Italy and constructed the republic around the time of the American Civil War. The town is just across the straits from the mainland (waters where Homer placed the monster Scylla and the whirlpool Charybdis) and may one day be connected to the mainland by a bridge that would run twice the length of the Verazzano-Narrows span over New York harbor.

The foreign ministers met in Messina on June 1 and 2, 1955, to consider two main ideas: the creation of an atomic energy community, which would function like the coal and steel organization at one of Monnet's "limited but decisive points"; and a full-scale customs union in which the Six would eliminate tariffs and other barriers in trade with each other and levy a common tariff in dealings with the outside. Germany and the Netherlands, with fast-developing competitive industries, plumped for the customs union. France, with her weak industry and protectionist policies, was more interested in the nuclear energy pool.

After the two-day conference, the six ministers published the following resolution, which was to serve as a cornerstone of the construction of Europe over the next decade:

> . . . the time has come to make a fresh advance toward the building of Europe. They [the governments] are of the opinion that this must be achieved, first of all, in the economic field. They consider that it is necessary to work for the establishment of a united Europe by the development of common institutions, the progressive fusion of national economies, the creation of a common market, and the progressive harmonization of their social policies. Such a policy seems to them indispensable if Europe is to maintain her position in the world, regain her influence and prestige, and

achieve a continuing increase in the standard of living of her population.

The foreign ministers at Messina set up a committee, again under that chunky Belgian workhouse Paul-Henri Spaak, to put the ideas into the practical form of treaties the Six could sign. The Spaak committee developed the proposals for the European Atomic Energy Community (Euratom) and the European Economic Community (known as the Common Market because its objective was the establishment of a single European market for industrial and farm goods) and incorporated them into treaties that were signed in Rome on March 25, 1957.

With campaigning by Monnet, who had resigned as president of the Coal and Steel High Authority and set up his Action Committee for a United States of Europe* to lobby governments, the treaties were ratified by overwhelming majorities in the six member countries by mid-December that year and went into force on January 1, 1958.

But once again it was questionable whether the new exercise would have come to much were it not for another set of international political crises, this time in the Middle East, that pointed up the weaknesses of a politically and economically fractured Western Europe.

*A pressure group of non-Communist parliamentarians for European integration and British membership in the Communities.

5

Toward a Broader, Deeper Community

On July 20, 1956, President Gamal Abdel Nasser of Egypt nationalized the British- and French-owned Suez Canal to advance the cause of Arab nationalism and his own position as a leader in the Arab world. It was a dramatic gesture of defiance of the West and pointed up one of the weaknesses of Western Europe: its dependence on the Middle East for energy supplies. Nasser's action came as the Soviet Union was enlarging its influence in Cairo, which further increased the tensions in the Western capitals. Nasser was skillfully playing the West off against Moscow. The American secretary of state, John Foster Dulles, rebuffed by Egypt's refusal to participate in a Middle East defense system, showed his displeasure by vetoing promised World Bank financing for the Aswan high dam, which Egypt was building in the upper Nile as a major source of hydroelectric power. Nasser promptly turned to the Soviets, who came up with the needed financing and technical assistance.

Nationalization of the canal, constructed by the French engineer Ferdinand de Lesseps, in the 1860s, was a shock, strategically, financially, and psychologically, to Britain and France, and leaders of both countries conspired to take the canal back by force without informing the United States. One of France's motives was to crush the principal backer of the rebels she was then fighting in Algeria. Israel, struggling to maintain herself in a hostile Arab world (Arab lands had been appropriated to establish the Jewish state), was

65

brought into the plans as an only too willing ally. Israel had developed a potent aggressive army to enforce its survival rights and believed with Clausewitz that attack was the best defense.

On October 29, 1956, Israeli armor rumbled across the Sinai desert, and within five days Israeli forces, having occupied most of the craggy peninsula, stood on the east bank of the Suez Canal. When British and French units intervened as part of the prearranged strike plan, the anger and outrage registered in Moscow, the United Nations, and Washington were so great that the two European powers ignominiously had to call a halt to the operation. The wounds on both sides left by this colonialist misadventure took a long time to heal. Even in the mid-1960s, Americans living in London were told by British friends, "You let us down at Suez."

The effects on the European integration drive were profound. Here was the continent that had once controlled the world unable now to conduct an independent foreign policy. The object had been to "teach Nasser a lesson," but it was the Europeans who were taught the lesson—that only in union could they apply influence in the world. Another point came through. For its industrial society to survive, Europe had to import energy. Arab nationalism now represented a threat to traditional sources of petroleum supply. It was therefore essential to develop new energy sources, such as the atom.

The governments of the Six appointed a commission of "three wise men"—Francesco Giordani, an Italian atomic scientist; Louis Armand, the engineer who rebuilt France's railroad system after the war; and Franz Etzel, a German engineer from the Coal and Steel High Authority—to report on Europe's future energy needs. Their conclusion: Europe faced a long-term energy shortage and in nuclear development for peaceful purposes was far behind the United States, Britain, and the Soviet Union. Thus, on two scores, energy and independence, the parliaments of the Six and public opinion were prepared in the months following Suez to move toward the "broader and deeper community" that Robert Schuman had spoken of in 1950.

While the Middle Eastern adventure showed divisions in the Atlantic world, a revolution in Hungary and riots in Polish cities

showed the cracks in the empire of the Soviet Union. In the intensification of the Cold War that followed the repression of the
popular risings in the East, Western Europe was again seen as
vulnerable, another important element in the background of the
1957 treaties.

Following the death of Stalin in 1953, Eastern Europe had moved
into an exciting but all too brief phase of liberalization.

Imre Nagy, the only leader in Hungary with any popular following, succeeded the Stalinist Matyas Rakosi as premier and
launched policies for somewhat greater economic and political
freedom. By the spring of 1955 Rakosi again got the upper hand.
But the seeds of liberalization had already germinated. Hungarian
intellectuals organized a series of mass public debates, demanding,
among other things, freedom of the press. Rakosi was unable to
control events and resigned. He was replaced by another Stalinist,
Ernö Gerö. Disturbances continued until, by September, 1956,
Hungarian writers and university students were in open revolt
against the party. On October 23, six days before the Israelis
crossed into the Sinai peninsula, the Hungarian students began to
demonstrate in the streets, following a denunciation of the "revolution" by Gerö. Shots were exchanged outside the state radio building. A colossal statue of Stalin was pulled off its pedestal and
smashed. Passions raged. Nagy was called back to power, but even
he couldn't control events.

Insurgents, joined by a majority of the Hungarian army, occupied public buildings and industrial plants. Workers and peasants took to arms. Religious leader Joseph Cardinal Mindszenty,
who had been sentenced to life imprisonment for "espionage" in
1949, was liberated. On November 1, Nagy repudiated the Warsaw
Communist defense treaty, which had been signed the previous
year by the East bloc countries and Russia (in reaction to the
formation of NATO), and asked for international recognition of
Hungary's status of neutrality.

The rebels were egged on by broadcasts beamed to Hungary
from American-controlled radio stations in the West, suggesting
that the rebellion would be supported by the Western powers. In
the end the West did nothing.

On November 4, three days after Nagy's repudiation of the Warsaw pact, hundreds of Soviet tanks rumbled into Budapest, and after savagely restoring order the Soviet command placed a young Communist party functionary, Janos Kadar, who had been imprisoned under Rakosi, in charge. Cardinal Mindszenty found asylum in the American Embassy on Szabadsaj (Freedom) Street, where he stayed until 1971. Nagy was executed. Although Moscow would probably have acted in Hungary anyway in 1956, the Suez invasion helped the Soviet Union divert world attention from what its tanks and troops were doing in Budapest.

Poland, meanwhile, was having its troubles on a smaller scale. On June 28, 1956, workers in the industrial city of Poznan took to the streets, protesting low wages and high prices. By October, the unrest had developed into a full-scale uprising against the Soviet Union's political, military, and economic hold.

The Poznan riots began at a locomotive and railway car works named after Stalin. Instead of going to their machines, the workers rallied in the factory yard, then set out toward the Communist-named Freedom Square in the center of the city. According to Henry Kamm, a *New York Times* correspondent,

> . . . soon the cry of "bread and freedom" rose from what had begun as a demonstration over economic grievance. The crowd, now joined by women and children, chanted for all they did not have and wanted. They shouted for the release of Stefan Cardinal Wyszynski, the primate of Poland, whom the Stalinist rulers had banished to inactivity in enforced residence in an out-of-the-way religious institution. They demanded the right to revive such prewar institutions as the Boy Scouts. They confronted the authorities with protests over the privileges that made officials' lives easier than the others.*

In the end, at least fifty-four were dead and two hundred wounded.

Unrest spread to other Polish cities. Poland seemed on the brink of revolution. Wladyslaw Gomulka, who had been under house arrest, was brought back to the Polish leadership as the only man

New York Times December 17, 1970, p. 12, col. 3.

with sufficient standing both in Warsaw and Moscow to maintain the authority of the party, restore order, and bargain for Kremlin concessions.

The events in both Hungary and Poland followed Nikita S. Khrushchev's denunciation earlier in 1956 of the Stalin terror. The new Moscow party chief promised better times but knew that to hold his job he would have to keep the empire intact. A slackening of discipline was incompatible with this objective, as Nagy had signaled with his proclamation of Hungarian neutrality. The restoration of discipline, through the use of brute force in Hungary, left Western Europe again with a sense of helplessness and ineffectiveness.

Against the background of Suez, Warsaw, and Budapest, it took only nine months to draft the treaties for the European Atomic Energy Community (Euratom) and the European Economic Community (EEC) and six months, after the formal signing on March 25, 1957, on Rome's Capitoline Hill, to get them ratified. What specifically did they seek to accomplish?

The main purpose of Euratom was to advance and coordinate research and development in atomic energy for peacetime purposes. Cheap electricity, nuclear-generated steam heat for homes, atomic ships, planes, cars, and trains were among the things envisaged in what was seen as the dawn of a new era for Europe.

So long as cheap atomic energy was simply a gleam in the eye of a scientist or a cluster of figures on his scratch pad, all of this sounded eminently reasonable. But once nuclear energy became commercial, as was about to happen, other forces would begin working. Industrial companies had little interest in sharing their knowhow with competitors. Governments were therefore less interested in underwriting joint research efforts and decided to put up money only where they were certain of an immediate financial return. Few thought in terms of an integrated European community effort from which everyone might benefit later.

Then there were the politics of the atom. The French government under General de Gaulle, who came to power the year after the treaty was signed, wanted Euratom, regardless of the cost, to develop in a direction that would free it from dependence on

American supplies of fissionable material. The Germans and other Euratom members were chiefly interested in getting low-cost energy. Under de Gaulle, France accelerated her atomic weapons program and later more or less turned her back on Euratom.

So by the late 1960s, Euratom had become simply another intergovernmental agency scrambling for money to stay in business. Its most useful work had been in the subsidiary field of controls, to insure that enriched uranium brought from the United States was not being diverted into bombs and missiles. Euratom hobbled along into the 1970s with a much depleted corps of scientists and technicians at its research centers at Ispra in Italy, Karlsruhe in West Germany, Geel in Belgium, and Petten in Holland. Its future was linked to the prospects for general European technological cooperation, which in the first flush of Common Market enlargement in 1973 looked better than at any time since 1957.

The excitement caused by peacetime atomic development in 1957* drew most attention to the Euratom treaty. But it was the other treaty, launching the European Economic Community, that provided the drive for integration in the succeeding decades. Here was that Benelux customs union of 1944 finally put into a wider setting. Rejected by the British in the bigger European grouping of the Paris Marshall aid distribution committee, the customs union was being adopted now by the continental powers themselves. French gloves, Italian shoes, German machine tools, Belgian chocolates, Dutch paints, and Luxembourg ceramics would eventually circulate duty-free within the bloc. A common tariff around the bloc would be levied against anything coming from the outside, such as American machine tools or British cars. If a French manufacturer in Lille needed textile machinery and had narrowed his choice to suppliers in Britain and Germany, the elimination of the tariffs between France and Germany gave the German equipment a big advantage over the British. But the way it developed here was really a lot more business for everybody, including those outside

---

*Some of that excitement was registered in the symbol chosen to represent the era at the 1958 Brussels World Fair, the giant Atomium (model of an atom) that continued to stand, into the 1970s, at the Brussels Park of Laeken.

who sold to the EEC states, because of the stimulus that tariff cutting gave to European consumption. Those inside the bloc ended up with a bigger share of the bigger pie.

The model for this, of course, was the United States, which was already a large customs union. Clocks made in Thomaston, Connecticut, were sold duty-free in New York City, while a tariff was levied on a similar clock coming from Switzerland to New York. In addition, the United States had a single currency, freely permitted workers in Indiana to move to Ohio, get a job and still come under Social Security, allowed a doctor to transfer his practice from New Mexico to California, gave the North Carolina textile manager the chance to buy the South Carolina mill he had his eye on without having to pay prohibitive taxes to either state, and made it easy for the widow with savings in a Maine bank or bonds in Minnesota to transfer them to Florida. Similar things were envisaged for the Common Market. And once the things fell into place, then Europe would be set for political union.

It was going to prove exceedingly difficult, much more so than those men in the heady days of 1957 ever imagined. Again the American experience was apposite. It took decades to establish, for instance, even an imperfect monetary union in the United States —and Americans all spoke the same language.

The community founders set up in their Rome Treaty elaborate machinery to effect some of the changes. There was a schedule, for instance, for tariff cuts to insure that the momentum toward abolition of trade barriers would be maintained. In the end the states cut tariffs even faster than the treaty prescribed. The states contributed money to a Community pool to facilitate the retraining and resettlement of workers whose jobs disappeared because of integration and competition. A European Investment Bank was formed to "contribute to the balanced and even development of the Common Market," and ended up making most of its loans for projects in depressed regions such as Italy's south. Free movement of labor was laid down in the treaty for achievement in stages, and, like tariff abolition, the program was completed ahead of schedule. Under the program, employers could no longer discriminate against a Community national by giving priority of employment or placement to their own citizens. Community workers also enjoyed a priority over nationals from outside the bloc.* And former colonies of the member states were singled out for special assistance in the treaty through a Development Aid Fund and through preferences they received in selling in the Community market.

The first fifteen years of the EEC's existence consisted mainly of the dismantling of internal barriers. It was not until the Community started on its monetary union project in the early 1970s that the more positive character of progress could be discerned. At the summit meeting of the enlarged community in Paris in October, 1972, there were fresh advances toward European confederation.

Organizationally, the Treaty of Rome set up the Common Market along lines similar to the Coal and Steel Community. The major institutions were: an Executive Commission of bureaucrats, or "Eurocrats," as they quickly came to be known; a Council of Ministers from the member states which met several times a month; a European Parliament with largely consultative powers made up of members of national parliaments; a Court of Justice to which disputes under the treaty could be referred; an Economic and Social Committee, and other specialized bodies that were consulted in the policymaking process.

The Commission, headed by a president (appointed for a renewable two-year term) and, in 1973, thirteen other commissioners† (appointed for renewable four-year terms), and which in the same year employed some five thousand Eurocrats, was responsible for initiating new policies for consideration by the Council of Ministers, the highest decision-making authority. The Commission pro-

*In 1971 and 1972 Italy, the Community's major labor surplus country, formally accused West Germany and Belgium of violating the priority principle by giving work to Turkish, Yugoslav, Algerian, and other non-Community nationals before Italians. The Italian Labor Minister said the employers in the north preferred the outsiders because they were more docile and less demanding than Italians.

†Nine commissioners, two each from France, West Germany, and Italy, and one each from the Benelux countries in the period before enlargement. After enlargement on January 1, 1973, Britain also got to name two commissioners, while Ireland and Denmark, the other two new members, named one each, raising the total number to thirteen.

posed; the Council disposed. If the Council could not agree, the Commission tried to formulate compromises, thus acting as "honest broker" among the states. In preparing its proposals, the Commission sounded out experts from the national administrations and from specialist groups. Its proposals, then, already represented a compromise of sorts before they reached the Council.

The Commission was also responsible for implementation of Community policy. Its written orders to enforce Council decisions had the force of law in all member countries. If a member state or enterprise within the bloc failed to accept a Council decision or a provision of the Treaty of Rome, it was in violation of the law. The Commission then filed charges in the Court of Justice. Most of the Commission's watchdog actions were in the antitrust field. It issued "cease and desist" orders against companies it found acting in restraint of competition and levied fines against those that disobeyed. Appeals went to the Court of Justice.

Thus, the Commission, which organized itself into about two dozen divisions,* had a triple function: initiator of Community action, mediator in disputes, and watchdog of the Treaty and Council decisions.

The body was organized by the Rome Treaty fathers to be the executive branch of a European federal government, but national governments, and particularly the France of de Gaulle, were reluctant to let any real power fall from their hands. Even with the restrictions the Commission had a good deal more influence than the secretariat of any other international organization.

One area where Commission influence expanded over the years was in commercial relations with non-Community countries. The treaty prescribed that the Commission was to become the Community's sole negotiating agent, and it did so become, consulting always with the technical experts of the member states.

The Commission Eurocrats worked in about two dozen divisions from a cluster of Kafkaesque modern buildings near the triumphal

---

*Dealing with: legal affairs, economic and financial policy, external relations, industrial affairs, research and technology, agriculture, development aid, antitrust policy, atomic energy, social affairs, transport, and regional policy.

arch where King Leopold I was welcomed after Belgium broke away from Holland in 1830. One of the streets alongside a Commission building is still known as the Avenue de la Joyeuse Entrée. Some of the Community civil servants also worked in Luxembourg, in the City of Luxembourg's only skyscraper, a twenty-three-story tower overlooking the cowfields on the town's periphery. Luxembourg, because it was an important steel center, had been the home of the Coal and Steel Community, and there was a competition between the Grand Duchy and Brussels over which would serve as the headquarters of the New Europe. Finally Brussels was selected as the chief capital with Luxembourg in a supporting role. Convenience and Belgium's position as one of the smaller countries that would not be able to dominate the institutions were behind the choice. Brussels was only two or three hours by car or train from four of the other five capitals of the member states. Following the 1967 merger of the administrations of the three communities, Luxembourg retained the Court of Justice and became an alternate meeting place for the European Parliament based in Strasbourg. For three months a year Luxembourg's twenty-three-story European center became the meeting place of the Council of Ministers.

The Council of Ministers brought together ministers of foreign affairs, agriculture, finance, transport, and other national departments for meetings in Brussels or Luxembourg several times a month to take decisions based on the Commission's proposals. Discussions centered on such things as farm prices (perhaps the most controversial of all issues), relations with the United States, enlargement of the Community, establishment of a common policy for transportation or energy. The Council decided on everything the Community did. For the major decisions of overall policy the foreign ministers usually met. When momentous questions involving, say, new membership or monetary union had to be decided, there were jumbo councils of foreign, finance, and often farm ministers, accompanied by platoons of advisers, and these often became marathons, lasting days—and nights—on end. All-night sittings became more and more frequent as the councils touched on bigger and more complex issues in the late 1960s and early 1970s.

At one of these in 1970 the then Dutch foreign minister, Joseph Luns, a charming nonconformist, startled his colleagues by announcing in somber terms, almost as if he was going to veto a proposal, that his feet were tired. He duly took off his shoes and walked around the council chamber the whole night proudly displaying his fire-engine-red socks.

Politically it was easier to sell a decision taken at 5 A.M. after wrangling all night if the decision didn't go exactly the way one member state wanted. The minister could argue back home that he had done as much as possible for his constituents. Normally, the major agreements were designed as a package of accords, giving every minister something to take home. The trade-off most frequently involved France and West Germany. When the two most powerful states of the bloc were in accord, progress was generally smooth. If one member was unwilling to concede on a vital point and bow to the will of the others—France's long opposition to British membership was the most glaring example—it was never overruled. The others simply waited until the vetoing state became more cooperative and willing to compromise. Finally, when Britain joined, the Big Powers became a triumvirate.

The union was too fragile in its first fifteen years to manage its decisions by anything other than unanimous voting. The Treaty of Rome had prescribed majority voting after January 1, 1966, but after one of the deepest crises in the Community's brief existence, the provision was never applied to issues of overriding national importance. On issues of lesser importance a weighted majority system did go into effect. Germany, France, and Italy each cast four votes; Holland and Belgium had two each; Luxembourg had one. Twelve out of seventeen votes were needed to carry a measure. This weighted system was devised so that big countries could not gang up against the little ones.

In the end the Council struck a compromise on a proposal from the Commission or referred it back to the Committee of Permanent Representatives, a body of less senior state representatives who headed the permanent delegations of their governments in Brussels. This institution, springing from the committee of national delegations (the Spaak Committee) that drafted the Rome Treaty, acquired powers never foreseen in the treaty as the second most important decision-making group. The ambassadors met twice a week with the representatives of the Commission and prepared the ground for Council meetings by thrashing out controversial ideas and sketching tentative outlines for compromise. Their quiet, unsung work was essential to getting things done at the Council meetings. While these men were faithful to their governments' interests, they were perhaps more dedicated to the ideals of a united Europe than their colleagues in the national capitals. The reason was only a little below the surface. As Norman Macrae, a writer for *The Economist* put it, in a survey of the prospects for European unity called "The Phoenix Is Short-Sighted":

> Intelligent men who live permanently in the atmosphere of Brussels—with enthusiasm for unity in the air and with able and idealistic "Eurocrats" as their most frequent guests and hosts at dinner parties—tend to get caught in that enthusiasm.*

The Court of Justice, as the Community's Supreme Court, interpreted Community law. Initially, the court had seven judges, and upon enlargement of the Community on January 1, 1973, it had nine, like the American Supreme Court. The judges dealt with civil cases arising from the EEC, Euratom, and Coal and Steel treaties as well as controversies stemming from Council decisions. Like the American Supreme Court it settled disputes between the member states themselves, over issues related to the Community. Gradually, as the Community life embraced more and more of the life of the member states, the Court of Justice became increasingly important. Its rulings were especially watched by international businessmen whose activities were ever under the regulatory eye of the EEC Commission, that hybrid body that acted as the overall administrative authority for the EEC as well as an enforcement agency. The Court was not always in favor of what the Commission was trying to do. For instance, in a landmark antitrust case in 1973 it refused to permit the Commission to break up the merger of the Continen-

*The Economist, May 16, 1970, p. 52.

tal Can Company with a Dutch company, Thomassen and Drijver-Verblifa. The Commission's tough antitrust chief Willy Schlieder, a former German union lawyer, had ordered the merger unraveled because of his contention that it gave the American company a monopoly in the metal container business. "We have to prevent future monopolies from being born," Mr. Schlieder told this reporter once in an interview. But the Court of Justice said, in effect, "That's all very well, but you simply don't have the proper legal tools." Article 86 of the Treaty of Rome, the EEC Constitution, prohibits companies from taking "improper advantage" of a dominant market position. Mr. Schlieder had tried to use this as the antimerger club, but the Court said it was not so intended by the Treaty of Rome. Throughout much of its history the American Supreme Court tended to interpret the Constitution and the laws of the United States liberally to enlarge the scope of federal authority. The Continental case showed that the EEC Court, probably because it was still dealing with a loose union of sovereign states, preferred to interpret the treaties and laws of the Community in narrow fashion. Somewhat incongruously the Court of Justice, sitting in a burnished steel building in Luxembourg, operated across the road from a Holiday Inn motel.

The Community was also to be subject, under the Treaty of Rome, to a degree of democratic control through the so-called European Parliament in Strasbourg, that ancient town of Vauban fortresses and foie gras on the French side of the Rhine. At least until the early 1970s the European Parliament was among the least effective institutions of the Common Market and was regarded essentially as a debating society. There were several good reasons for this. First of all, the Parliament had no real power. Its main functions were to scrutinize the budgets of Community institutions (without having any say itself in those budgets) and to confront Commissioners with occasionally awkward questions. By a two-thirds majority it could dismiss the Commissioners, but it had no say in appointing new ones, which made this power meaningless. A second reason for its lack of effectiveness was that its 183 members, including the 41 new Danish, Irish, and British delegates who arrived on January 1, 1973, were not elected to the Parliament but appointed from their national legislatures. This led to a situation in which it was generally the poorer quality delegates who came to Strasbourg, because those who felt that they had a promising career in their national assemblies could not afford to take the time off. It was in part a vicious circle. So long as there was no real power the more gifted and ambitious politicians would keep out of Strasbourg.

When the British finally joined the Common Market they tried to hasten the process of a more equal power share-out between the European Parliament and the Council of Ministers. Peter Kirk, the chief of the British Conservative delegation to Strasbourg in 1973, proposed that a special committee of members should be set up to investigate how the Parliament could use its existing powers more effectively. "The more we have examined the situation, the more astonished we are at the latent power which this Parliament could have if only it would use it," Kirk declared.

As a result of a decision taken at the end of 1969, the European Parliament was given a small voice in determining the Community budget after 1975. By a vote of three-fifths of its members, the Parliament would be able to override the Council of Ministers' budget decisions and increase spending in these sectors: administration, Euratom, the European Social Fund, and the Community Food Aid Program for developing countries. The gradual assumption of the authority to raise money led to the transfer of power from the British kings to Parliament at Westminster between the seventeenth and nineteenth centuries. The 1969 decision might have started a similar process in the European Community. And the British could certainly be counted on to help the process along.

In addition to its lack of power, there were some other differences between the European Parliament and the Parliament at Westminster that made the former a far more somnolent body. One was in the shape of the two chambers. The small House of Commons, looking a little like a cock-fighting pit, where Government and Opposition face each other and rail at each other, provides a stimulating cut and thrust that is absent at Strasbourg, where delegates are ranged more formally across a vast semicircle in blocks according to their political affiliations. Everything in Stras-

bourg is organized through a stiff bureaucracy known as the Parliament Bureau, which is controlled by the Parliamentary groups.
Everything that a delegate proposes has to be cleared first by the
Parliament Bureau. Often it takes weeks. "One consequence of this
inflexibility," observed Richard Evens, Parliamentary Correspondent of the *Financial Times* with typical British understatement, "is
that debates totally lack fire."

With its untested institutions and highly complex decision-making procedures, the Community began to move forward in 1958
under the leadership of the first Commission president, German
law professor Walter Hallstein. Number-two man in the German
foreign ministry before his appointment, Hallstein had represented
his country both in the Schuman Plan negotiations and at Messina.
A proud, energetic, solemn man who didn't laugh easily, Hallstein
saw himself in somewhat exalted terms as the President of Europe
(newspapers called him "Mr. Europe") and saw the Commission
he headed as the new supergovernment. In protocol he demanded
to be received as a head of state. "We are not in business," he often
said, "but in politics." His conceptions went for the most part
unchallenged in those days and gave him the drive to push ahead
with the immediate job, as he saw it, of "fusing markets and
economies into one"—that is, cutting away at the jungle of barriers
inside the bloc.

Hallstein and his associates in those halcyon days, when it was
thought that "Europe" could be built by 1970, progressed spectacu-
larly in getting the process of economic integration under way.
They persuaded national governments to cut their tariffs faster
than originally planned, to remove quantitative restrictions, and at
least consider knocking down elusive nontariff barriers such as
discriminatory safety regulations. They began to work out a common agricultural policy. They set a timetable for removing the
restrictions on the movement of labor and took cautious first steps
to free the movement of capital. The first studies were undertaken
to harmonize the tax structures of the members through introduc-
tion of the value-added tax (a kind of sales tax) with its neutral
economic impact. Integration had not yet reached the stage where
it would begin to hurt in some sectors. Nor had the process yet

really begun to challenge the authority of the national governments.

Europe was in an expansionary economic cycle. The lowering of tariffs inside the bloc was an added stimulus to business. Companies prospered and jobs were plentiful—workers had to be imported. Even France, protectionist at least since the days of Colbert, and frightened by the prospect of cheap German, Dutch, and Italian goods flooding her markets, gave almost as good as she got in the industrial sector, while her peasants got the benefits of a wider market and higher prices for their abundant farm products.

As the internal tariffs dropped, Italy began producing new, well-designed small refrigerators and exported them all over the continent, along with elegant shoes, colorful knitwear, and Fiat cars. Who had ever heard of a Daffodil automobile before the Common Market? But as the tariffs fell, the Dutch produced their Dafs (DAF actually stands for van Doorn's Automobil Fabrieken) in record numbers. The port cities of the Community—Antwerp, Rotterdam, Hamburg—were booming. Flemish millionaires popped up in Antwerp and built huge homes for their families in outlying suburbs such as Brasschaat, where French nannies almost outnumbered the children.

Companies began thinking of merging across frontiers, and although this was to be a slow process, a Belgian and a German enterprise started the ball rolling when they combined into Agfa-Gevaert to try to combat Eastman Kodak. And the American companies, many of which were convinced that Europe would someday be a single market bigger than the United States, were starting to move in, setting up headquarters in places like Brussels, London, and Geneva.

In trade, in investments, in the spillover of technology and managerial skills, a dynamic force was at work in the Common Market that gave it a very special character, in which Britain took no part. Excluding herself to begin with, and later being excluded by the Six, Britain ended up with growth and productivity less than half that of the Community. Although the Six had started out with different economic structures, their rates of growth were approaching each other as a result of the forces unleashed by the Common

Market. By 1970, the Six were trading half their exports with each other inside their common tariff wall. In each of the six countries, imports from the other five were by far the fastest-growing element of total consumption.

How did Britain and the new Community deal with each other?

6

The Naysayers: British and French

Cherishing an unqualified belief in their own superiority, the British felt little attachment for things European. One old newspaper headline had become something of a national joke: "Fog Over the Channel, Continent Isolated." Though the British didn't realize it, the isolation was theirs.

As Arnold Toynbee, among others, has pointed out, Britain's attitude toward continental Western Europe was governed by the failure of medieval England to carve out an empire in France. After the interminable wars between the Valois of France and the Plantagenets of England, the English were handed a humiliating defeat in 1429 by that dazzling, legendary figure Joan of Arc. Joan not only exposed the English colonial designs but assured her triumph in history by getting the English to make her a martyr in the Old Market Square of Rouen in 1431. Thereafter Britain confined her military intervention on the continent to preventing any continental country from uniting Europe by military conquest. Over the centuries, Britain fought against the Bourbons, the Hapsburgs, Napoleon, the Hohenzollerns, and Hitler to maintain a balance of power on the continent.

Even though the Common Market was the first continental organization of countries established voluntarily and not by force, the British found it difficult to consider the EEC as much more than another one of those coalitions that, over the centuries, they had tried to dissolve. To Macmillan, who replaced Anthony Eden (later

Lord Avon) as prime minister, the Common Market was purely and simply a "continental blockade," as he once told de Gaulle, adding, "We shall have to declare at least a tariff war against it."

At first the British didn't consider the integration moves very significant, because they doubted that the continental powers, rivals for so long, could ever do anything voluntarily. Then, when it seemed as if the continentals were really serious in their determination to go ahead again after the Messina conference, the British played a more active role in the deliberations in order to try to shape the new structure so that it would be compatible with British interests.

A fundamental conflict had developed over the way the British and the continentals viewed things. The continentals wanted a deeper, tighter, stronger, more rigid organization than the British were prepared to accept. The continentals wanted a customs union that would evolve into an economic and political union. The British wanted a far looser free trade area.

There were two main points that the continentals developed in making their arguments. The first dealt with Germany. Only if Germany were integrated within a deep union of European nations could the threat be contained of both revived German nationalism and another one of those secret German-Russian arrangements that had spelled so much trouble in the past. The second point was that only a deep union could enable Europe to build the mass market that would open the way to economies of scale, wider commercial exchanges, more technological cooperation, and other advantages that would increase Europe's competitiveness and the standards of living of its people.

The British argued that the same objectives could be achieved without the rigid organization contemplated by the continentals. But essentially the chief British interest was in a grouping that Britain could join while still maintaining Commonwealth ties and the "special relationship" with the United States.

When Britain realized she could not stop the continentals from going ahead with their customs union, she ingeniously proposed that this new customs union be part of a larger European free trade area. In other words, France, West Germany, Italy, Belgium, the

Netherlands, and Luxembourg could go ahead and set up internal free trade and a common external tariff. Twelve other countries and the EEC bloc of the Six would then reciprocally cut their tariffs down to zero in trade with each other. Unlike the Six, the Twelve would not have a common external tariff, but instead would levy individual tariffs in exchanges outside Europe.

That old Marshall aid distribution agency, which had been transformed into an eighteen-nation Western European cooperative body known now as the Organization for European Economic Cooperation,* became the forum in which the British proposals were discussed.

The plan represented British diplomacy at its sharpest because Britain would be able to meet her main objectives in one fell swoop: defend her continental markets, retain complete independence, and remain at the center of the Commonwealth preference system. British companies were afraid that they would be hurt if the Six went ahead on their own. Italian Fiats would enjoy a competitive advantage over British Morris Minors or Swedish Volvos in the French market because the Fiats would not have to pay tariffs inside the customs union, while the Volvos and Morris Minors coming from outside the customs union would. Similarly, German machine tools competing in Belgium and Holland would have advantages over British, Swedish, or Austrian machine tools.

The British saw their Commonwealth and world role threatened by too close a liaison with the continentals. Both roles were, in fact, declining. Hugh Thomas, in his essay on the Suez crisis in 1956, quipped that Britain was "now too feeble to be even perfidious."

The Commonwealth preference system was based on mutual trade concessions in the vast—but hardly homogeneous—bloc consisting of Britain's former colonial possessions. In the clubs of Pall Mall and the pubs of Yorkshire, the Commonwealth, as the symbol of Britain's past glory, was not something to be given up lightly, especially when the preference system meant cheap food for British

---

*Later the OEEC would change its name again to the Organization for Economic Cooperation and Development and take in industrialized countries from other continents. The United States, Canada, Japan, and Australia had joined by 1972.

housewives. Under agreements made at the Imperial Economic Conference in Ottawa in 1932, which continued in effect after the postwar decolonization, food and raw materials, the principal products of the Commonwealth, came into Britain under especially favorable terms. The Commonwealth territories, in turn, offered special terms for British industrial goods. But the rules of a European customs union, if Britain were a member, would force her to trade less with the worldwide Commonwealth and more with the continent of Europe. Because of those common protective walls around the EEC, butter from New Zealand, tea from Ceylon, oranges from South Africa, wheat from Canada, sugar from Trinidad and Tobago would no longer enjoy the same privileged access. So, in the end, the British housewife would have to pay more.

France was insisting on this common protection for agriculture as well as industry in hopes of selling more of her own farm products and keeping her large peasant population happy. For France, it was a trade-off of agricultural advantages in other countries' markets for greater access by other countries to French consumer and industrial markets. She feared, excessively as it later turned out, that her industry would be swamped by Dutch and Italian and Belgian and mainly German competition once tariffs disappeared inside the customs union. French industry had been coddled by high tariffs since the days of Jean-Baptiste Colbert and Louis XIV and was uncertain what would happen in the cold shower of the Common Market.

So while the British wanted to keep on buying their cheap food from the Commonwealth, the French were pressing for a protectionist (high-cost food) policy in the Common Market. It was a point of obvious conflict. Had Britain joined the customs union, the battles between the two ancient rivals might have been so great as to threaten the new Community's very existence. As it was, the British simply weren't ready yet to make a move. British-Commonwealth trade was still too important to jeopardize. Trade with the continent, while growing, was as yet only marginal. Not until the middle of the next deacade were the developing regional trading patterns to make an influence in political decisions.

Yet the British in 1958 were still hoping, even after the first

Common Market tariff cuts were made, that the wider industrial free trade zone of the eighteen Western European nations would come into being. Negotiations to this end were being conducted at the Paris OEEC headquarters at the Château de la Muette and, not unexpectedly, ran into great difficulties. There were problems about nontariff barriers and about trade diversion (the handling of imports into a low-tariff country that were then free to move into a high-tariff country). The Six asked themselves, wouldn't the achievement of a Western European free trade area weaken their resolve to form their deeper economic and political union? Obviously, Britain wouldn't mind if it did. And then there was the problem of agriculture. France and Italy, the two high-tariff countries in the Common Market and the ones with the biggest farm populations, would be opening up their consumer markets to practically all the West European states. Since the British proposals did not include agriculture, France and Italy would gain no wider outlets for their farm products beyond those that would be established inside the Common Market. So for France and Italy it did not look like a very good deal.

There were complications also with the United States, which was strongly opposed to the British proposals. Eighteen countries of Europe, all of which had benefited to some extent from American postwar aid, were now considering what amounted to massive discrimination against American exports when, having found a new prosperity, they might have been expected to liberalize their trade with the rest of the world. The United States supported the Common Market and wanted Britain to join it,* even though this smaller bloc also meant discrimination against American products. The difference was that the Market had a clear political goal— "even closer union among the European peoples," as the preamble to this Treaty of Rome put it—and set up the institutions to achieve this. Furthermore, the Market sought to root Germany in a bloc of democratic countries, restraining the nationalism that had

---

*American pressure created ill feelings, particularly among British left-wing Socialists who saw the Market as a product of the Cold War and as a means for perpetuating it.

caused so much of Europe's troubles. The free trade area had a commercial purpose only.

"You have become entangled in something so complex you'll never extricate yourselves from it," Reginald Maudling, the British minister who drew up the free trade proposals, told the Spaak Committee in 1956. Maudling's words applied just as appropriately to the endless debates in the OEEC over the free trade area. It took a major event to bring the curtain down, and this finally occurred when General de Gaulle took power in France on June 1, 1958. Less than six months later, on November 14, 1958, the new French minister of information, Jacques Soustelle, said that it was "impossible to create the free trade area as wished for by the British." De Gaulle had rung down the curtain, and that was that.

Macmillan didn't go so far as to declare the tariff war he had been considering against the continent, but he did form a peripheral alliance a year later under the Treaty of Stockholm that set up the European Free Trade Association (EFTA). This was a disparate grouping of seven countries on the fringes of the Common Market. They had little in common except a desire to protect their commercial interests as integration proceeded within the Common Market.

There was backward, autocratic, pristine Portugal. There were the industrialized neutrals, Sweden, Austria, and Switzerland. There were three NATO members, Norway, Denmark, and Great Britain. Later Finland, another neutral, and Iceland, another NATO country, joined the club, Finland as an associate member. The EFTA countries agreed to reduce, eventually to zero, the tariffs they levied against each others' industrial goods but made no effort to establish deeper economic and social policies of cooperation.

The peripheral states were acting to defend their interests, but unfortunately, in that process, Western Europe was being divided into rival trading blocs. It was not the way to unify the continent. The hopeful element was that EFTA's goals were limited and its functions recognized as temporary. Its objective was its own dissolution (certainly an unusual goal for any organization) when the conditions were ripe for wider union.

Between 1960 and 1970 the trade exchanges of EFTA members with each other, spurred by successive tariff cuts, were impressive. The internal trade volume expanded two and one half times. Among the Scandinavian countries volume more than tripled, keeping pace with EEC growth and encouraging economic integration in the north.

The Nordic countries had tried for many years to form a deeper association. Political differences frustrated efforts to create a Nordic customs union, but during the EFTA years they saw themselves more and more closely linked economically and socially. They developed a common labor market (a Finn, for example, could take a job in Sweden and immediately qualify for benefits under the lush Swedish social security program); they eliminated passport control for inter-Nordic travel; Norway, Denmark, and Sweden (though not Finland) merged their airlines; they concerted on a number of other joint projects and developed interparliamentary links through regular meetings of the Nordic Council.

During the Kennedy Round of tariff-cutting negotiations in the mid-1960s (in which the major trading nations slashed their tariffs by about one-third) the Scandinavian countries took a common position because their trading interests were so similar. But in later negotiations to join the Common Market, where political as well as economic interests were involved, they found their national preoccupations so varied that they had to negotiate from weaker individual positions.

Denmark felt the need for Common Market membership so strongly (because of its dependence on Germany as a market for meat and dairy products) that it was prepared to break Nordic ranks and join even if the other Scandinavian countries did not. While Danish farmers felt they could easily compete inside the Common Market, the less efficient Norwegian farmers, on much poorer land, were worried about losing the valuable national subsidies that kept their incomes up. Norwegian fishermen were afraid that their rich coastal preserves, perhaps the richest fishing ground in the world, would be raided by trawlers from other Common Market countries. Sweden and Finland were both concerned with finding the formulas of accommodation that would satisfy economic needs without compromising political neutrality.

Sweden, which had not fought in a war since 1815, had profited handsomely from its neutral status during World War II, when iron ore from the biggest European mine at Kiruna, near the Arctic Circle, was sold to the Ruhr steel mills and transformed into guns and tanks for Hitler. Finland (see chapter 3) accepted a contractual neutrality with the Soviet Union as the price for maintaining its independence. Norway and Denmark, on the other hand, saw their security in terms of a close alliance with the United States. Norway, with its sparsely settled northern lands bordering the Soviet Union, felt especially vulnerable to any expansionary moves by the Soviets and was thus among the strongest early backers of the NATO alliance.

"I don't know what to do with de Gaulle," Roosevelt once wrote to Churchill after the war. "Perhaps you would like to make him governor of Madagascar."* As leader of the Free French, General Charles André Joseph Marie de Gaulle, tall, proud, astringent, a soldier of unusual intellect,† a patriot and visionary, had come into frequent conflict with Roosevelt and Churchill. Roosevelt in particular took exception to de Gaulle's messianic (more Joan of Arc than Jesus Christ) complex‡ and much preferred to deal with more

---

*Declassified documents released by the State Department, February 15, 1971.

†De Gaulle fought at Verdun in 1916, where he was wounded and captured by the Germans. After the war he served on the French general staff, in the army occupying the Rhineland and in Lebanon. In the 1930s he wrote three books—*Le Fil de l'Épée* (1931), *Vers L'Armée de Métier* (1934), and *La France et Son Armée* (1938)—which revealed considerable literary skills and a vision of strategy at variance with the orthodox views of the times. De Gaulle argued for a highly mechanized and mobile professional army while accepted opinion favored reliance on the draft and the entrenchments of the Maginot Line. So widespread was the view of the impregnability of the Maginot Line that in 1940, just before France fell, collections were taken to plant rose bushes around the Maginot Line trenches to make life more pleasant for the troops.

‡As British historian A.J.P. Taylor puts it: "Instead of starting as a hero and becoming a legend General De Gaulle started as a legend and became a hero on the way." (*Europe: Grandeur and Decline,* London, Penguin Books, 1967, p. 299.)

amenable types like Monnet, the anglophile, who spent most of the war on the British Supply Council in Washington.

De Gaulle himself relates that the United States and Britain simply did not understand France and seemed intent on excluding France—or at least himself (and as far as he was concerned the two were inseparable)—from planning the shape of postwar Europe. France had beeen excluded, in fact, from the Yalta Conference of February, 1945, at which Roosevelt, Churchill, and Stalin more or less divided the world into spheres of influence, and again from the Potsdam conference in July (see chapter 3) where the future of Germany was on the table. Exclusion from the postwar directorate was, to him, an Anglo-Saxon affront that was not easy to suffer.

Some differences between France and the United States remained long after the war, particularly over foreign policy priorities. The United States primarily wanted to prevent expansion of Soviet influence in Europe, and then to anchor Germany to the Western alliance. France was absorbed, on the other hand, in reestablishing herself, in strengthening her position vis-à-vis the reviving German giant and in holding on to, then getting rid of, her dependencies, first in southeast Asia and then in North Africa.

In May, 1958, the "colons" (French settlers in Algeria) and army paratroop units under General Jacques Massu began massive demonstrations in Algiers against the Paris authority. They suspected that the Fourth Republic intended to make peace with the Algerian guerrillas of the National Liberation Front and grant independence to what was, administratively, a part of metropolitan France. They turned to sixty-seven-year-old de Gaulle, who, after his brief postwar rule, had been waiting for twelve years for the indecisive, corrupt, and at times almost farcical Fourth Republic (counted since the overthrow of Louis XVI) to crumble. The choice before President René Coty was either power to de Gaulle or army mutiny and probable civil war. By June 1, de Gaulle was voted into office by the National Assembly.

Although it was the colons who returned him to the Élysée Palace from his hermitage at Colombey-les-deux-Églises ("*Je vous ai compris*—I have understood you," he told throngs of French settlers in Algiers), de Gaulle decided early on that the struggle to

keep hold of the colony was not worth the cost in lives and resources. By 1962 he had done what he had been called on to
prevent. He negotiated Algeria's independence. The settlers some
of whom represented third and fourth generations of Frenchmen
in Algiers and who were known as Pieds Noirs, or Black Feet
(when debarking in Algeria in the first half of the nineteenth century, they had struck the Arabs, who wore babouches, or light,
pointed slippers, by their black leather footwear), had to return to
France. Many of these never forgave de Gaulle's "double cross."
Some formed a "secret army" whose aim was to assassinate de
Gaulle, take over the administration in Paris, and get Algeria back.
In the early 1960s plastic bombings and machine-gunnings in the
streets of Paris were almost a daily occurrence. Once the scars had
healed, France became stronger economically and politically and
played a dominant role in European affairs.

De Gaulle believed that the nation-state was the only political
reality. His credo: absolute independence must at all costs be maintained. Europe, in his view, could never have a single government.
He envisaged, instead, an association of states that were in general
agreement on political, economic, military, social, and cultural
matters. France was the natural center for such an association, and
the association itself would become the center of a global organization concerned with production, trade, and security. In other
words, to de Gaulle, France would become the center of the world.

It was not difficult to see how such ideas would be in basic
conflict with the concept of federalism embedded in the Common
Market. Nor was it hard to see confrontation with Washington and
NATO. De Gaulle was convinced that nothing that had been
accomplished since the war without his personal participation was
either useful or valid.

Some observers thought that de Gaulle might proceed right
away to pull France out of the Common Market. But while he was
proud, de Gaulle was not reckless. His immediate calculations
were that so long as the Common Market remained purely and
simply a trading bloc, there might be advantages in it for France.
There was time to reshape it or replace it later, after he had
consolidated his power.

De Gaulle's position led to a remarkable state of affairs, the irony of which was pointed out by Professor Raymond Aron of the University of Paris: "The men of the Fifth Republic [the constitutional government under de Gaulle] loved the EEC not at all but gave it life; the men of the Fourth Republic loved the EEC but would they have given it life?" Aron's point was: Probably not, because they could not have acted strongly enough.

Seven months after coming to office, on December 27, 1958, de Gaulle authorized the devaluation of the franc by 17.5 percent. This single act made it possible for France to participate in the Common Market's first tariff reductions, scheduled to take effect the following month. Without it, French industry was in danger of being overwhelmed, which of course would have called into question France's continued membership. By sharply reducing the value of the franc in terms of other currencies, French goods automatically became cheaper in foreign markets. Similarly, foreign goods became more costly inside France. The devaluation, in other words, gave the French a competitive edge.

It was not until May, 1960, before de Gaulle began to attack the Common Market institutions in a move aimed at reshaping the Community to a Gaullist design. The first assault came with this seemingly innocuous declaration: "The path to be followed must be that of organized cooperation between states while waiting to achieve, perhaps, an imposing confederation." Shortly afterward, the General proposed that a committee be formed to draft a political treaty for the Common Market countries. The treaty would create several new joint political institutions: a council of heads of government, permanent secretariat based in Paris, four specialized councils for politics, economics, defense, and culture, and an assembly of delegates from the national parliaments. The intent now became clear: to create an organizational rival to the Common Market without the supranational trappings, something that would remain firmly in the control of each individual government.

France's partners went along with the idea that a political treaty snould be drafted. But they stubbornly resisted any attempts to unaercut the institutions of the Common Market. Christian Fouchet, one of de Gaulle's most faithful followers, who was to serve as both education minister and interior minister in later Gaullist governments, became the French representative and the chairman of the committee and, for the next two years, the Six became embroiled in controversy over how to shape a political community.

Ever since the failure of the European Defense Community the Six had felt that their ties would not be complete without deeper political cooperation. So de Gaulle's initiative was not entirely unwelcome. But France's five partners wanted a complement to, not a replacement for, the institutions of the Economic Community.

De Gaulle persisted and through his deputy, Fouchet, submitted specific proposals that brought the clash out into the open and created the division (France against the Five) that was to mark the debates of the Community throughout the 1960s.

The first Fouchet Plan provided for meetings three times a year of a council of government leaders, at which decisions would be taken unanimously; a political commission composed of foreign ministry officials who would prepare the council meetings, and a parliament of national delegates who could pose questions and make recommendations but who would have no power. The Five were highly critical. They didn't like the absence of an independent executive or a strong parliament. They wanted majority rather than unanimous voting in the council. But they reserved most of their diplomatic energy to attack another provision of Fouchet Plan I: the idea that the embryonic political community would dominate the economic community. The French wanted the economic community merged into the political community; the Five wanted it the other way round. For the layman, the issues became terribly esoteric.

France came up with another plan, Fouchet II, but this made matters even worse, since the French had hardened their stand. Economic affairs, instead of being absorbed into the political community at a later date, were to fall directly under the control of the political community. The Five submitted counterproposals so far out on the limb of supranationalism as to be totally unacceptable to France.

The political talks were finally suspended but not until they

showed an unbridgeable gap between the federalism championed
mainly by the Benelux countries and the nationalism of General de
Gaulle. Each side was suspicious of the other's motives and finally
retreated to entrenched positions separated by the no-man's-land
that was to remain part of the European scene for a decade or
more.

While de Gaulle sought to impose his political ideas on the
Common Market, he launched a parallel offensive against NATO,
which, as he commented in his memoirs, was "outmoded, un-
balanced, and preponderant in Anglo-Saxon influence." His first
major act on this field of battle was the memorandum he sent on
September 14, 1958, to President Eisenhower and Prime Minister
Macmillan, proposing a tripartite directorate of the three powers
in running NATO. Washington didn't take the proposal seriously,
and de Gaulle himself indicated that he didn't really expect the
United States to take it seriously. His real intention was to use the
rejection as the rationale for French withdrawal from the military
alliance. Within months of the memorandum, de Gaulle announced that France would not permit atomic missiles on her soil,
except under her own control. Starting with the French Mediterranean fleet, he gradually pulled out French units from the integrated NATO command. France had started to develop an atomic
bomb under the Fourth Republic, and de Gaulle immediately ordered the program stepped up. French defense contractors began
building the planes, rockets, and submarines to deliver the weapon.
Continental powers, de Gaulle declared, had the "right and duty"
to have their own defense systems. It was "intolerable," he said, for
a great state to leave its destiny up to the decisions and actions of
another state.

During the 1950s, NATO strategy had been based on massive
retaliation, the terrifying doctrine of John Foster Dulles under
which atomic weapons would have been used immediately against
cities in the Soviet Union if the Red Army crossed into Western
Europe. In August, 1961, some eight months after President
Kennedy took office, an event occurred in Germany that was to call
into question the validity of this concept. Just after midnight on

August 13, East German troops and border police occupied cross-ing points on the East Berlin side of the dividing line between the Russian and Western sectors of the city and installed roadblocks and barbed-wire barricades. It was the beginning of the Berlin Wall, constructed to stop the flood of East German refugees to the West. It was an offensive action by the Soviet Union—a challenge to the shared control of the city—for a defensive purpose. It was intended, as the Bavarian political leader and former Bonn defense minister Franz-Josef Strauss put it, "to enable the German Demo-cratic Republic, which was slowly being robbed of its biological substance through the flight of its people, to consolidate."

President Kennedy let four days elapse before a formal protest from the West was delivered to Moscow, a sign of his extreme caution in responding. The then West Berlin Mayor Willy Brandt wrote to Kennedy to protest the feeble Western reaction. Accord-ing to Arthur Schlesinger, Jr., in his book *A Thousand Days,* Kennedy replied that the "brutal" border closing represented a Soviet decision that only war could reverse and that no one sup-posed that "we would go to war on this point." Even so, Kennedy sent Vice-President Lyndon Johnson to the city to "show the flag" —in other words, to tell the Russians that the United States would not be pushed out of Berlin. If there were to be hostilities, it would be the other side that started them. At the same time the tiny American garrison in West Berlin was bolstered by 1,308 American troops dispatched along the autobahn from West Germany.

The wall was built and the city divided, but Kennedy, later visiting Berlin himself and emotionally telling a mass gathering at the Rathausplatz, *"Ich bin ein Berliner,"* again even more dramati-cally underscored the American commitment to the Western sec-tor.

The Berlin episode meant the end of the Dulles massive retalia-tion strategy. It was an incident that drove home to American planners the necessity of being able to respond flexibly to Soviet challenges. With the inevitable "hotpoints" of confrontation be-tween East and West, the use of atomic weapons was now seen as the ultimate threat in a gradually intensified series of responses, each designed to meet the seriousness of the challenge. It now seemed possible to contain troubles and defend the interests of the West without destroying the world.

De Gaulle was suspicious of the flexible response doctrine. Probably with good reason, he had no confidence in the American will to go to war with Russia to defend Western Europe. It was in recognition of the realities of distance, American domestic preoccupations, and American economic and political interests that would sometimes conflict with Western Europe's that de Gaulle continued to press ahead with the French nuclear deterrent. The bomb, in his view, put France automatically in the Big Power league because, theoretically at least, she would have the power to trigger a major war simply by dropping the weapon on an aggressor.

There was another important reason for de Gaulle's *force de frappe:* Germany.

The bomb was an insurance policy for security along the Rhine. In the minds of many Frenchmen, justifiably or not, Germany still represented the potential enemy. Russia was too far away. France and Russia were traditional allies; not so France and Germany. A French television commentator, perhaps unwittingly, demonstrated these feelings when he described French military equipment being shown in a parade on the Champs-Élysées on Bastille Day, 1971. As the camera focused on a huge military truck, the news analyst explained that the truck was designed to provide floating lengths of interlocking track that could be used by military vehicles in crossing rivers. Which rivers? It was not the Volga nor the Elbe nor the Thames that he cited, but the Rhine.

In 1968, the French strategist, General Charles Ailleret, published an article that attracted wide attention. General Ailleret said the French nuclear arsenal had the capability of striking out not just toward the Soviet Union but in all directions, or, as he put it, *"tous azimuts."* Paris military specialists said he was deliberately reminding the Germans that France intended to remain Germany's military superior, even though Germany was stronger economically. As already noted, Germany had been barred under the Western European Union Treaty of 1954 from making atomic weapons. By 1968 the French-German alliance forged by de Gaulle and Adenauer was coming under strain because of a monetary quarrel between the two countries. France was beginning to worry about Germany's overwhelming economic superiority and, in fact, under Pompidou in the 1970s made the catching up with Germany economically her number-one priority. At a press conference on September 23, 1971, Pompidou told Frenchmen that while they may have been lagging behind the Germans, they nevertheless retained certain "trump cards" in the competition with Germany. "We have our geography. We have, why not say it, a certain political, even moral, prestige. . . ."

The United States was totally unenthusiastic about France's nuclear pretensions. It turned down French requests to purchase essential elements for the French deterrent, such as equipment for processing uranium ore, blueprints for nuclear submarines, guidance systems and fuel for missiles. Later the United States blocked the sale of large computers to France. France was finally offered Polaris missiles, but only under condition that control of the warheads be kept by Washington. De Gaulle refused this offer and moved ahead with his own plans, doggedly and independently.

In the early 1960s, the *force de frappe* was characterized scornfully in American circles as a "pop gun," but later Washington developed a certain respect for it. In July, 1965, the United States was rather embarrassed by the disclosure that its photo-reconnaissance planes were eyeing the Pierrelatte uranium plant in the Rhone Valley, an indication that Washington was keeping very close tabs on French weapons development.

Again, French-American differences arose over priorities. Washington, fearing an accidentally-triggered Armageddon, directed its energies toward nuclear disarmament. A treaty banning the spread of nuclear weapons was finally agreed to in the late 1960s, but France (together with China) refused to sign it. De Gaulle found it intolerable that decisions vitally affecting France would be taken in Washington. The bomb was the passkey to independence.

Gaullist feelings, especially over the excessive weight of Washington in the alliance, were shared by other Europeans and led to a number of American gestures toward European sensitivity in the early 1960s. Kennedy brought into some of the top policy-making jobs a group of men who were convinced that Europe, so long as its peoples were drawing closer together, should play a bigger role in the alliance. Perhaps the most influential was George Ball, that associate of Monnet, who became under-secretary of state for economic affairs, and later the under-secretary, the number-two man in the State Department. Ball and the others were responsible for what came to be known as the "two pillar" policy, under which the United States and a united Europe would share equally the responsibilities of the world.

There were two concrete expressions of Kennedy's policy of trying to deal on a more equal basis with Europe. One was the Kennedy Round of tariff cuts; the other was nuclear sharing. The first succeeded, but just barely. The other failed. The failure of nuclear sharing showed that so long as Europe was in its long, uneven transition phase toward unity, and so long as the United States held an overwhelming nuclear superiority, an equal partnership simply could not exist. The difficult and complex Kennedy Round tariff discussions showed that even where Europe was able to speak with a single voice—in the area of trade—the dialogue between equals would be difficult, because Europe's economic interests were already beginning to conflict substantially with those of the United States. And in the 1970s, as the process of European integration accelerated, and as the United States faced increasingly tough social, economic, and monetary problems, there were some reservations in Washington about American support for European unity.

The abortive nuclear sharing idea involved a plan to establish a multilateral nuclear force, composed of the NATO countries. The United States was to share its nuclear technology to give the force its atomic punch. But Washington would maintain a veto—and a free initiative—on the actual use of the weapon.

It was hoped that the project would prevent the proliferation of nuclear weapons and give a sense of participation to the NATO allies, especially to the Germans, who were uncomfortable (some observers said claustrophobic) about having their ancient rivals, France and Russia, in possession of nuclear weapons while Bonn had permanently renounced them. France, as could be expected, took a dim view of the multilateral force, lost no time in ridiculing the idea (General Pierre Gallois, one of the chief French strategic thinkers, called it "the multilateral farce"), and hinted that if the United States went ahead without France, France would pull out of NATO.

Unwilling to provoke an open clash, the United States eased the pressure, and the project was quietly shelved after the British sought to save everyone's face by proposing a careful study of alternatives.

The Kennedy Round confrontations dramatically revealed how the trade interests conflicted. President Kennedy had pushed a Trade Expansion Act through Congress in 1962 empowering the administration to negotiate deep tariff cuts with the other trading nations. The act was drafted with the idea that Britain would join the Common Market and that the enlarged European trading bloc might pose a threat to world trade growth unless tariff barriers were substantially reduced at the same time. The fear was that Europeans would tend to trade more with each other and less with the United States and other countries, a process that might distort world trade patterns and lead to a resurgence of protectionism and nationalism unless it was accompanied by massive liberalization.

After remaining aloof in the 1950s, the British had finally applied for membership in the Common Market in 1961 (see chapter 7). Then, in January, 1963, de Gaulle vetoed the application. Despite the veto the negotiating parties in the Kennedy Round decided to continue their talks. Any results would not be as promising as those originally envisaged, but they still could be important.

From the outset, the talks proved difficult, with arguments— chiefly between the United States and the Common Market— proliferating over the most minuscule points. Broadly speaking, the United States wanted to sell more farm products to Europe, and the Europeans wanted to sell more of their industrial products in the United States. There were, therefore, the possibilities for a deal. But the matter was complicated by the Common Market's increasingly protectionist farm policy, which was designed to pre- serve markets for European (mainly French) farmers, who had already become a social problem for their governments. Success hung in the balance until virtually the last moments of the Congressional deadline.

Considering the complex political and economic issues that faced the Atlantic world in May, 1967, when the negotiations were wound up, the Kennedy Round was an amazing achievement. It represented the most ambitious attempt ever made to achieve a liberalization of world trade. Fifty-three countries, accounting for 80 percent of world trade, finally agreed to an average 33 percent cut in their tariffs, some liberalization of trade in agriculture, and a program of food aid for underdeveloped nations. Trade in the products on which concessions were agreed to amounted to $40 billion per year. This was about eight times more than was achieved in the previous round of world tariff-cutting negotiations, the Dillon Round in 1960–1961. The battles over farm trade liberalization, however, pointed to troubles ahead for American-EEC relations in the 1970s.

The Supreme Headquarters Allied Powers Europe (SHAPE) was based in Rocquencourt, a hamlet outside of Paris, for the first decade and a half of NATO's existence. A succession of American generals, named by the President of the United States, ran the outfit. These generals controlled the units earmarked to the NATO command by the member countries.

General de Gaulle had already served notice that he didn't like the setup very much, and, as noted earlier in this chapter, had been gradually pulling French units out of the integrated command structure. In September, 1965, de Gaulle began to launch his frontal attack against the alliance. "The subordination known as integration . . . which hands over our fate to foreign authority, shall cease," he declared. Five months later he announced that he was "reestablishing a normal situation of sovereignty, in which that which is French, as regards land, sky, sea and [armed] forces, will in the future be under French command alone." He was kicking SHAPE, and the American army, in the pants and out of France.

Some thought that de Gaulle's assertion of national independence meant the end of the Alliance. France was its geographical center. How could it exist outside? De Gaulle gave NATO a year to find new headquarters—until March 31, 1967—and after shopping around at various sites, Belgium, for many of the same reasons that the Common Market had selected it, became the host country. SHAPE moved from Rocquencourt to Casteau, in the Belgian coal-mining region near the French border where the British Expeditionary Force fought its first battle in World War I. The NATO Council, representing the political leadership, transferred from Porte Dauphine, on the edge of the Bois de Boulogne in Paris, to a site between the center of Brussels and Zavantem International Airport. De Gaulle, refusing to make an absolutely clean break, retained France's seat on the Council. But France was completely detached from military planning activities.

Institutions have a way of surviving, and NATO was no exception. The move, under the overall charge of General Lyman T. Lemnitzer, the NATO commander at the time, was a masterpiece of accurate planning, and, if anything, the NATO machinery and bureaucracy was probably strengthened by it. Changing headquarters required an exhaustive analysis of just what functions were performed, how they were performed, and why. This had an efficiency effect that probably could have been achieved by no other means.

If a conclusion was to be drawn, it was that France needed NATO more than NATO needed France. One effect of the de Gaulle edict was suddenly to deprive a number of French communities of the profitable presence of the American military establishment. But even more important than the economic dislocation was the anxiety of French military men over the enforced isolation from their allies. As the years passed, especially after de Gaulle's departure from power in April, 1969, the French high command showed increasing eagerness to resume cooperation with the Allies. During the Soviet-led invasion of Czechoslovakia in August, 1968, the French were already exchanging intelligence information with NATO. In 1971, the French navy was participating in NATO Mediterranean exercises, while French aircraft were taking part in NATO reconnaissance of Soviet fleet movements in the Mediterranean

De Gaulle had set himself up as the champion of an independent Europe, and in many ways his ideas touched a common chord among the European peoples. But as the de Gaulle era drew to a close, the American military-industrial-monetary presence was still deeply rooted in the continent. The American presence was there because nothing, as yet, had developed that could replace it. The continent could not depend on the deterrent capabilities of the *force de frappe,* the leadership of French industry, or the appeal of the French franc to compete in the coming decades in a world of superpowers. The only answer was to try to "relaunch Europe" by striving again for that evanescent union.

In December, 1969, the Six met at a summit conference at the Hague, in an effort to gather a new momentum toward union after the divisiveness of the de Gaulle years. The results of that conference, in the turreted Hall of Knights, across a cobblestoned courtyard from the Dutch Parliament, were to shape European events well into the 1970s. The six chiefs of state decided to intensify their economic union, form a monetary and political union, and negotiate once again with Britain.

7

Knock Three Times: End of an Era

Dean Acheson once validly summed up most of British postwar history by observing that Britain had lost her empire and had not yet found a role. One by one the colonies of Asia, Africa, and the West Indies had won their independence. Only the ties of an amorphous Commonwealth joined the new nations to Britain.

Many Britons thought the Commonwealth an adequate substitute for a role in Europe. It provided the nationalistic attachment to the fixtures of former power, the sentimental association with "kith and kin" (in the ever smaller white Commonwealth), the idealistic notion of a union of all races and therefore an elevated world order, the practical consideration of trading benefits, including those politically invaluable cheap food supplies for the British housewife.

If being at the center of all this was not sufficiently reassuring, the British always had their "special relationship" with the United States to augment their influence in the world.

Yet, new political, social, and economic forces were undermining these comfortable attitudes of the British public. As the Commonwealth grew larger and more racially diverse, it became less of a political or even a moral force in the world and more a simple band of nations without any real concerted purpose. By contrast, a formidable economic and political power center seemed on the verge of creation in continental Europe. Unless Britain acted, she would have no voice in this development.

While controlling her vast empire, Britain, in her role of the continentals' "perfidious Albion," had always worked toward maintaining a power balance across the channel, playing one power off against the other. The new voluntarily formed power structure cast doubts over the continued effectiveness of such policies. Britain risked becoming a passive spectator on the world scene.

British attitudes toward the Commonwealth were also changing. Britain was the mother country, but racist feelings inside Britain were pushing both Labor and Conservative governments into enforcing ever tighter bans to keep the black Commonwealth immigrants outside. Britain found herself repeatedly arraigned at Commonwealth conferences, accused of racism because of her immigration controls and of softness toward the white-dominated governments of Rhodesia and South Africa. Pshychologically, it was becoming ever more difficult for even the most idealistic supporters of the Commonwealth to accept the anti-British assaults. "Those bloody black dictators have some cheek lecturing us," was the way one company executive put it during the fracas over Rhodesia's declaration of independence in the mid-1960s.

While the free movement of citizens to the mother country had been halted by the British, changes in trade patterns were calling into question the value of the Commonwealth preference system. British trade with the continent of Europe, even when it was forced to jump over the tariff walls, was growing. The Commonwealth countries themselves were developing new trading allegiances within their own regional groupings. Australia, for instance, was looking far more to Japan as a trading partner than to Britain. In 1970, more than 25 percent of Australia's exports, primarily raw materials and food, were being bought by Japan, compared with only 12 percent by Britain. In the same year Britain's exports to the EEC for the first time were larger than they were to all the Commonwealth countries.

Similar patterns affected investment. British corporations were putting most of their money into the Lowlands and into France and Germany. Relatively little was going to places like Malawi or Kenya.

As trade and investment grew with the continent, so did the

awareness that Britain was being discriminated aginst in the continental markets because of the progressively duty-free access that Common Market states were enjoying in each others' markets. Furthermore, Britain was being excluded from the potential benefits of an enlarged home market. The continental companies were growing in size and power because of these advantages and were already challenging British exporters in their traditional markets of the Commonwealth.

The British prided themselves on their special relationship with the United States, but this too was coming under something of a cloud. The elements of the relationship were the sentimental attachments between the two English-speaking peoples, the friendships that developed between leaders of the two governments in the Eisenhower and Kennedy years, and, in more practical terms, the nuclear knowhow that the United States transferred exclusively to Britain. But the effects of all this were not entirely salutary. The British were lulled into a deceptive sense of confidence, encouraged to think that they really didn't need the continent, and that if they ever got into trouble the United States would always be at their side. The special relationship worked at counterpurpose to the American goal of a politically united Western Europe. It was a relationship, Harvard Professor Richard Neustadt observed in his book *Alliance Politics,* woven out of "muddled perceptions, stifled communications, disappointed expectations, and paranoid reactions."

In the early months of 1961, there were signs that the British Tory government under Harold Macmillan was becoming increasingly aware of Britain's exposed position on the fringes of the changing continent and was preparing to do something about it. The early British attitude that the Common Market would never work was proving delusive as successive tariff cuts intensified the discrimination against British industry. Britain, furthermore, had been excluded from those Fouchet Plan talks over a political structure (see chapter 6), and this deeply worried the British Foreign Office.

Finally, George Ball and others in the Kennedy Administration were repeatedly urging the British to find their place in Europe. "So long as Britain remains outside the European Community, she is a force for division rather than cohesion, since she is like a giant lodestone drawing with unequal degrees of force on each member state,"* Ball told Edward Heath, number-two man in the Foreign Office, in March, 1961. The American Trade Expansion Act, the legislation that was to lay the foundation for the Kennedy Round, included a provision that would have widened the president's tariff-cutting power if the British were inside the Community. This was a calculated effort by the Kennedy men to nudge the British into action. All the European exporting states, not least Britain, wanted to expand their markets in the United States.

The mounting pressures began having results. On July 31, 1961 (a little over four years after the Treaty of Rome was signed) Prime Minister Macmillan announced to the House of Commons that the government was prepared to see if mutually acceptable conditions for membership in the Community could be worked out. Negotiations finally opened on November 8 in Brussels.

From the outset the British insisted that the problems raised by membership—for the Commonwealth, for EFTA, for the British farming community—had to be resolved in all their detail before a treaty of accession was drawn up. This approach barely concealed what was still only a lukewarm commitment to the whole venture. A surer course would have been to negotiate on general principles and work out the details of adjustment from the inside as a member, as Jean Monnet counseled. But the simple fact was that the British were far from certain, even at this juncture, that they wanted to join. This was understandable in view of the radical and uncomfortable changes (higher food prices, for one) that were involved in membership. Under such conditions the negotiations were already under a severe handicap.

Predictably, the negotiations got bogged down in a series of endless debates over protecting Commonwealth trade interests (weeks were spent simply on what duties to levy on Australian kangaroo meat) and over adapting British agriculture to the Community. "The British were prepared not so much to join the Community as to 'embrace it,' " wrote Richard Mayne, a former

* *The Discipline of Power*, Boston, Little, Brown and Company, 1968, p. 79.

Commission spokesman in Brussels, in his book *The Recovery of Europe.** Britain was still driven by the desire to dissolve the EEC into that giant free trade area, perhaps including the Commonwealth and the United States as well as Western Europe.

In the critical debates over agriculture, the British were reluctant to convert from their program of direct subsidy payments to farmers and low prices to the diametrically opposed methods of support through protection barriers and high prices being evolved by the Community under the whiplash of France.

The farm question was a fundamental stumbling block because of the domestic political considerations in both camps. The basic fact was that there were many more farmers in France than in Britain. France needed to placate her farmers because their large numbers represented a point of potential social unrest. The British were chiefly concerned with maintaining cheap food prices.

With less than 5 percent of the working population on the land, the British Treasury paid farmers "deficiency" payments, so called because they were designed to bring incomes to levels on a par with other sectors of the population. The British farmer was therefore not wholly dependent for his livelihood on the prices he charged for his product in the market. As the world's biggest food importer, Britain could continue her decades-old policy of buying at the cheapest world market prices without damaging the living standards of her farmers.

The Community as a whole, and France in particular, had well over 20 percent of the working population on the land in the late 1950s (a figure that was to drop substantially as industrialization and urbanization intensified). Because the numbers were so much higher, the Community worked the problem of farmer support from a different angle. Internal food prices were set at relatively high levels. A protectionist frontier barrier, the variable levy, was put into effect to bring the cost of imported food to the Community's internal levels. Proceeds from these levies were then used to subsidize agricultural exports. Traditional food-exporting countries such as the United States, Canada, and Australia saw their

*Weidenfeld and Nicolson, London, 1970, p. 269.

markets displaced in the late 1960s and early 1970s by the Community system of farm support and complained vociferously. In effect, the EEC was making these countries share the cost of European farm support.

In the Community the consumer paid to support the farmers; in Britain, the taxpayer. While it seemed to amount to the same thing, there were important differences. As already noted, the British system kept food prices low. But in the continental bloc, where many more farmers were involved, direct treasury subsidies would have meant the disbursement of vast sums. Almost inevitably strong parliamentary pressures would have arisen in the more industrialized states of the bloc such as Germany and Holland, where there were fewer farmers, to reduce the payments. By discouraging food imports from outside the Community and forcing the consumer—and indirectly the foreign farmers who were losing markets—to foot the bill, the system was less vulnerable to political pressures. Yet, under the Community system farm support became such an expensive proposition (the high food prices produced enormous surpluses) that the member states had to chip in anyway with treasury payments to the Community farm fund to meet the full costs. As predictable, pressures arose to trim the costs.

There was naturally a good deal of resistance in Britain to acceptance of the continental system. Not only would it mean higher food prices; it also would aggravate social injustice. Food represents a larger portion of a poor man's budget than a rich man's.

But the British hadn't the slightest chance of changing the Community system. France counted far too much on the rewards the Community's support mechanisms and protected farm market would bring to her unruly peasants. De Gaulle intended to exact to the fullest measure the farm concessions he had won from the Germans in return for acceptance of industrial free trade.

As the negotiations dragged on, the British finally decided in 1962 that they had to accept, at least in principle, the Community system. But again the negotiations bogged down, this time over the special transitional arrangements London was seeking to adjust to the radically new policies on agriculture. The French quite simply mistrusted the British, suspecting that Whitehall wanted to maintain special privileges that would be difficult to take away once Britain was a voting Community member. There was a further complication. The Community had not yet fixed the common price levels for the bulk of its farm products. France felt with good reasons that Britain would work from the inside to keep prices low and weaken, if not destroy, the common farm system that was evolving. In any such endeavor, Britain would certainly have found allies. France, alone among the Six, produced enough food to feed herself and still have a substantial surplus for export.

As French suspicions mounted during the farm debate, a crisis was developing over Britain's Big Power posture in the nuclear field. This was to have a decisive bearing on the way things turned in Brussels. Rising costs and sticky technical problems forced the British in 1960 to scrap their intermediate-range ballistic missile known as Blue Streak. This was to be the delivery vehicle for the British nuclear deterrent. Britain at the time had only a fleet of 180 long-range V-bombers to perform this function. New defense systems were coming along that would prevent the bombers from ever getting over their targets. To stay in the deterrent business, Macmillan turned to the United States, which was then building the Skybolt missile. After visiting President Eisenhower at Camp David, the prime minister was able to persuade the United States to provide Skybolt, a 1,000-mile-range air-to-ground missile which could be mounted on the V-bombers, as a substitute for Blue Streak, under favorable financial terms.

But the American Skybolt program began running into the same kind of difficulties that had plagued Blue Streak. In an economy move in 1962, Defense Secretary Robert S. McNamara decided Skybolt was no longer needed. The United States was already deploying Minuteman intercontinental ballistic missiles and was building new Polaris submarines that could launch an atomic warhead from the depths of the sea. Macmillan, seeking to capitalize on the "special relationship," flew to Nassau in the Bahamas on December 18, 1962, to try to get President Kennedy to reverse McNamara's decision. Macmillan returned not with Skybolt but with Polaris. Britain salvaged token superpower status.

The Nassau agreement, as George Ball observed in *The Disci-*

pline of Power, showed in "especially vivid light" the unhappy effects of the special relationship. Nassau perpetuated the discriminatory nuclear relations between the United States and Britain; it falsely encouraged the British to continue thinking they could play an independent great-power role; it deflected Britain from coming to terms with her European destiny; it provided the occasion, if not the cause, for General de Gaulle four weeks later to veto British entry into the Common Market. Harold Wilson, who became British Prime Minister less than two years after Nassau, put it more bluntly: "Nassau," he said in a speech at Bristol in 1966, "slammed the door of the Common Market in Britain's face."

De Gaulle said three years later at a press conference:

> Not that we despaired of ever seeing that great island people truly wed its destiny to that of the continent, but the fact is that [Britain] was not then in a position to apply the common rules, and that it had just, in Nassau, sworn an allegiance outside of a Europe that would be a real Europe.

Britain, to de Gaulle, was the Trojan horse for American domination of Europe.

The veto came at a press conference on January 14, 1963. Reporters, summoned to the gilded, tapestry-hung hall of the Élysée Palace in Paris, were told by the towering, bulbous-bellied man in a blue suit that Britain was "insular, maritime, bound by her trade, her markets, her supplies to countries that are very diverse and often far away." De Gaulle went on to say: "How can Britain, as she lives, as she produces, as she trades, be incorporated into the Common Market as it was conceived and as it works?"

The veto exploded like a bomb on the sceptered isle. The public humiliation over exclusion from the continental club, which de Gaulle may have wanted to heap on the British to settle scores after France's exclusion from the British-American nuclear partnership, drew out fierce British indignation and the feeling of betrayal by an ally. It also shocked France's partners. When the veto was announced at the new foreign ministry building in Brussels, opposite the hulk of the nineteenth-century Palais de Justice (largest construction in the world of its day), newsmen saw tears in the eyes of Paul-Henri Spaak.

There was anger as well as shock among the Five. Britain had been denied a hearing by the action of one government. The communitarian ideal of mutual agreement by consensus was dead. De Gaulle was, in fact, challenging the others to accept his concept of the Community—a Europe of nation-states instead of a United States of Europe—or to go on without France and almost certainly destroy the Community. He was confident the partners would not press for dissolution, and his instinct proved correct. The German-French partnership was the key to the Community's survival, and within a week de Gaulle had outflanked his critics by getting "that good German," Adenauer, to sign a treaty of reconciliation with France.

Some of the anger against the veto, it turned out later, may have been emblazoned a little too brilliantly on the sleeve. Despite their protests, none of France's partners probably was really prepared in 1963 to see the British join. While they might not have staged the coup de grâce so brutally as the General, they could well have set the membership price so high that Britain could never have paid. De Gaulle's intervention permitted them to profess loyalty to the cause of British membership without having to prove it.

All were in favor of getting Britain to help shape the Community in the 1950s, but the passage of years had altered the configuration. As the 1960s rolled on, the Community began the process of developing and refining its internal structure. Each member was fighting battles as part of the constant trade-off of interests that had to go on for this internal development to proceed. Had Britain somehow managed to join in 1963, her entry would have hopelessly confused matters because of what would undoubtedly have been the weakest of commitments, reflecting the deep divisions within the country over the advisability of a permanent link with the continent.

While there had been hints that a veto was coming, the timing was a total surprise, even to the French foreign minister, Maurice Couve de Murville, the rarely ruffled aristocrat from a wealthy French Protestant family, who had to maneuver in the backwash at Brussels. De Gaulle had made his government into a constitutional monarchy in all but name. Elected as president of France, he had framed the constitution of the Fifth Republic to give the presidential office more power than any other democratic leader in Europe. In his own eyes, he was the embodiment of France, declaiming policy often without deigning to inform those who had the more lowly task of carrying it out.

The British may not have been so ill-informed about de Gaulle's intentions as the public was led to believe.* Some historical accounts suggest that de Gaulle had warned Macmillan at a private meeting between the two leaders on December 15–16 at the hunting lodge of Rambouillet, in a forested park between Paris and Chartres, that the negotiations would probably have to be suspended. Macmillan, trying to save the talks, made a vague offer of nuclear cooperation between the two countries—an offer described later by Denis Healey, who became defense minister in Harold Wilson's Labor government, as a "humiliating fiasco." Writing of the meeting at Rambouillet, de Gaulle—who left an abundant record of his career—spoke of Macmillan in these pungent terms: "This poor man, to whom I had nothing to give, seemed so sad, so beaten, that I wanted to put my hand on his shoulder and say to him as in the Edith Piaf song, *'Ne pleurez pas, milord.'* "

The divisions within Britain had made Heath's job as chief negotiator almost impossible. The bulk of British public opinion still believed that the "wogs" started at Calais. The opposition Labor party had been demanding terms impossible for the continentals to meet. While most Tory MPs supported the government's initiative, many were against any form of association that didn't put Britain first in Europe and the world. In trying to convince continentals of Britain's sincerity, Heath—who was firmly committed himself—caused resentments at home. In trying to soothe domestic opinion, he raised fresh doubts on the continent.

With the veto there was a remarkable change in public opinion.

---

*Geoffrey de Courcel, Ambassador to London, did know, however. He was one of de Gaulle's few confidants, having been an aide to the General during the World War II years.

There was now a villain in the piece ("How could de Gaulle treat us like that after all we did for him during the war?"), and the reappearance of a common enemy did much to restore unity. Almost all Britons wanted what they knew they could not get so long as de Gaulle was in power. The grass now looked much greener on the continent. This rather superficial change of heart led to a somewhat disingenuous conversion within the Labor party.

Labor leader Harold Wilson, a rotund, pipe-smoking Yorkshireman, characterized by British cartoonists as a teddy bear, moved into Downing Street after the general elections of October, 1964. The first socialist prime minister in thirteen years, he pressed ahead, despite a mere three-seat majority in the House of Commons, with a program to renationalize the steel industry, raise taxes for middle- and upper-salaried classes and for business enterprises, increase some social welfare benefits, and defend the parity of the pound sterling at $2.80. After the general election of March, 1966—in which Wilson, battling for the first time against the new Tory party leader Edward Heath, liberally increased Labor's majority—he actively began looking at Common Market possibilities again.

Although Wilson had won the endorsement of the electorate, his program had done little to restore the health of the British economy. Britain was plagued by the lowest growth rate of any major country (mainly because excessively high taxes choked off incentive), and the pound was under almost steady attack by speculators who thought it would have to be devalued. To hold the pound's rate, Wilson was forced to move Britain ever deeper into debt with the United States and the International Monetary Fund. Against this cheerless economic setting the Common Market issue was a godsend. There were apparent political gains to be made in grappling with de Gaulle and in trying to undercut Tory leader Heath, who had remained, despite the veto, a strong champion of Common Market membership. Wilson could furthermore portray himself as actually trying to improve the economic fortunes of the nation by establishing links with a wider European market. It was a policy that would cost nothing more than the rhetoric involved in promoting it, since the chances were minuscule that de Gaulle could be budged from his opposition to British membership. In fact, many skeptics argued that Wilson was indeed counting on de Gaulle's hostility and would not have known how to react were the doors to Europe suddenly opened.

In those years of economic weakness and Gaullist banishment of the mid-1960s, London became the "swinging" city of Europe, a development that at least on the psychological plane helped prevent the continent from forgetting about Britain. Apart from the tales of woe being told daily in the foreign exchange departments of the financial district, no one was taking things very seriously, and this airy, spicy insouciance brought forth an odd outpouring of talent that served as a pole of attraction for the continent. Shunned by the Common Market, unenthusiastically embraced by the United States, increasingly criticized by the Commonwealth, Britain seemed to have nowhere to go, a point brought home by one London satirist, Peter Cook, who quipped that the British Isles were destined to sink giggling into the Atlantic. Nothing was sacred. Malcolm Muggeridge took off against what he considered to be the needless luxury of maintaining a royal family; David Frost and Bernard Levin lampooned the government, trade unions, and even the British worker on the liveliest television program of the decade, "That Was the Week That Was." The Establishment nightclub in Soho, birthplace of the satirical movement, poked fun at the same targets. Even the staid *Times* of London, once the chief organ of government, was caught up in the irreverent current. To its anonymous Parliamentary Correspondent, Sir Alec Douglas-Home, who succeeded Macmillan as prime minister, presented the "gawping visage of a bifurcated owl" one day in the House of Commons. These were the years when the mop-haired Beatles, who had created a sensation in the hypersonant Liverpool rock club known as The Cavern, had just moved down to London, when the gambling clubs and the discothèques were multiplying like the miniskirts on Kings Road, when Mary Quant and a host of others finally prised the well-bred English girl out of her classic twin-set and pearls. Talent was bursting forth in the theater, in furniture design, in the oases of continental chefs suddenly springing forth in the desert of London gastronomy.

On November 10, 1966, Wilson announced to the House of Commons that in light of a "deep and searching" review the government had made of the problems of Britain's relations with the Community, "a new, high-level approach must now be made." He assured the House that he "meant business."*

Between January 15 and March 19, 1967, Wilson and his foreign secretary, George Brown, made an official tour of the Common Market capitals to gauge the chances for a new entry bid. Newsmen promptly and irreverently dubbed the entourage the "flying circus." It is doubtful that Wilson learned anything he didn't know before. The line-up was more or less unchanged. The French were still hostile, even to opening negotiations; the Five, in varying degrees, wanted Britain in. The trip, however, did give Wilson the international attention he coveted. There had been a good deal of curiosity about the man; now he was on center stage. Wilson used his international forum to try to turn around one of de Gaulle's main arguments for refusing the British—that Britain was a Trojan horse for American domination of Europe.

This was a period when all of Europe was worried about the technological superiority the United States had acquired in key modern industries—electronics, data processing, atomic power, commercial aircraft—a superiority promoted in large measure by the existence of a large single market, vast sums of government money spent on defense and the Apollo moon project, and a generally liberal educational process, as opposed to the elitist system of education in Europe. The technological gap, combined with the increasingly large European base that American industry was building and the ability of the American military, scientific, and industrial establishment to buy out the best brains of Europe, had left Europeans feeling both inferior and insecure. "Fifteen years

---

*Lord Wigg, a close friend and confidant of the prime minister in those days, had this to say about Wilson's conversion in memoirs published in early 1972: "Wilson's swing from being a strong antagonist of the Common Market to becoming a protagonist ready to run risks to secure Britain's entry, took its place among other historic phenomena exemplified by Paul's conversion on the road to Damascus. The one difference was that, judged by his subsequent actions, Paul's conversion was sincere." (*George Wigg,* by Lord Wigg, Michael Joseph, London, 1972, p. 339).

from now," Jean-Jacques Servan-Schreiber, the French journalist-politician, wrote in *The American Challenge,* "it is quite possible that in 15 years the world's third greatest industrial power, just after the United States and Russia, will not be Europe, but American industry in Europe."* De Gaulle had tried to weaken the American grip by pulling the French military units out of NATO and striking at the privileged role of the dollar in the international monetary system. But his divisive nationalism, especially in his adamant refusal to consider a wider European grouping that might somehow be mobilized against the American challenge, was keeping Europe in second-class status.

Wilson, in his speeches in the six capitals, in his press conferences and numerous private meetings with journalists, held out the prospects of a European technological community competing with the United States as an equal. Britain was prepared, he said, to merge her not inconsiderable scientific and technological prowess in key sectors to achieve this goal. Britain was prepared, he also said, to work with the Six toward forging closer political and economic unity. He warned that if Europeans did not get together the continent was destined to play the role of "industrial helot" to the United States. Much of this was rhetoric. Wilson's record as an opponent of Market entry during the debates in Britain during the 1961–63 negotiations was well known, and many continentals doubted the sincerity of so rapid a conversion. But the words, nevertheless, struck a responsive chord. Wilson was cleverly using one of de Gaulle's own arguments about the evils of American industrial domination to knock at the Common Market door a second time.

Most evidence pointed to Wilson's use of the Common Market issue as an instrument to keep his own cabinet together and take the British public's mind off the economic decay of the nation. But his decision to reapply for membership in an announcement to the House of Commons on May 2, 1967, was still a highly significant act. Regardless of his motives, both major parties were now for the first time behind the European venture.

Le Défi Américain, Editions Denoël, Paris, 1967, p. 17 (translated from the French).

The House of Commons overwhelmingly approved the decision to apply, and on May 11, Britain's ambassador to the European Communities formally deposited the application at EEC Council headquarters in the Brussels Palais des Congrès. Denmark, Norway, and Ireland had let it be known that they too would apply for membership once Britain did, and within hours of Britain's action in Brussels ambassadors of those important British trading partners filed into the cavernous Palais, on a hill overlooking the Renaissance Grand Place of Brussels, and also deposited their formal applications before the Council.

Only slightly more than four years had elapsed since de Gaulle's veto. For Britain they were years of economic crisis, humiliation before international bankers, receding military power, and growing political isolation. They were years in which the Common Market, all the more because of the rejection by de Gaulle, seemed to offer the only hope. Later, when it was within reach, the Market was seen in a much colder light.

It is almost certain that the Labor party would have fought membership, had the opportunity to join arisen in 1963. By 1967 Wilson, for his own special reasons, brought the Labor party round. It was inevitable, with the combined pressure of the two parties inside Britain, with the increasingly active support Britain was getting from the friendly Five inside the Community, with the weakening of de Gaulle's grip on France, and with the deteriorating relationship between France and Germany, that something would have to give.

But while many saw the inevitable attachment of Britain to the continent (including de Gaulle himself, who once was reported to have said in a private conversation that Britain would eventually join the Community, not under Wilson but under Tory leader Edward Heath), the move was to come only after painful setbacks as well as progress.

Only sixteen days after the four ambassadors had trooped into the Palais des Congrès, with all the rhetoric about a new united Europe hardly yet muted, de Gaulle struck back. Britain was still not "mature" enough for membership, he announced, frigidly and loftily dismissing all Wilson's talk about meeting the "American challenge." Almost as an afterthought, de Gaulle offered Britain the second-class status of association with the Community, in effect putting Britain in the same rank as Greece and Turkey (which already had formal association agreeements with the EEC).

An immediate confrontation with the Five was avoided when the EEC Council of Ministers delicately put the dossier aside for a few months by asking the Commission to draw up a report on the advisability of opening negotiations. The report was completed in September. It came out unequivocally in favor of negotiations but also contained ammunition for de Gaulle in its analysis of the British economic situation.

The pound had been under almost continual pressure in the foreign exchange markets since the fall of 1963. Its weakness was a sign of Britain's lack of competitiveness in world markets. Morris cars from Birmingham, steel knives from Sheffield, the merchant and passenger vessels from the shipyards on the river Clyde were not selling as well in world markets as competing products from Germany, Japan, Belgium, and Italy. Prices were not low enough. There were too many strikes and tea breaks. Salemanship lagged. Quality fell behind because of insufficient investment. Management by and large was hardly aggressive and badly needed to be upgraded. Taxes were punitively high, discouraging incentive. The Common Market's external tariff kept British sales on the continent from expanding as fast as they might have. Finally there was the problem of the sterling debts that Britain had run up in World War II and had never been able to repay. Most of Britain's former colonies, which made up the sterling area, decided after the war to keep their money in Britain because it was earning high rates of interest. Yet, there was always the danger that they might withdraw it en masse, cashing in their pounds for the gold and dollars the Bank of England had in such limited supplies, and tossing Britain into bankruptcy. The threat of withdrawals, a nightmare for all British prime ministers and chancellors of the Exchequer, forced them always to watch the balance of payments and therefore to keep a tight rein on the economy, which in turn checked growth.

One of Wilson's biggest mistakes was not to devalue the pound when he came into office in the fall of 1963. This would have lowered the price of British products in foreign markets and given exports and the reserves a big boost. Had there been any domestic criticism, he could simply have shoved the blame onto the Tories, who had run up big balance-of-payments deficits in the months before losing the 1963 elections. Wilson didn't act then for two reasons. He was afraid that Labor, which had devalued the pound in 1949, would be branded the party of devaluations. Far more important in Wilson's considerations, however, was the relentless pressure from the United States against any precipitate currency action.

The American Treasury was worried about an attack against the dollar if the pound were devalued. Although few Americans realized it at the time, there were portents of trouble of even greater magnitude than Britain's after years of excess dollar spending abroad. The United States was still running large trade surpluses, but tougher competition from Japan and Western Europe, inflation in the United States and the massive overseas investment, military and aid spending were already tending to make the dollar an overvalued currency. Devaluation of the pound, the second most important trading currency, would inevitably expose the dollar even more to the forces of speculation. The American troubles were temporarily masked by the size of the United States economy. But officials in Washington, worried by the trends, promised Wilson enormous quantities of financial assistance to help him defend the pound at the unrealistic rate of $2.80.

By the time the EEC Commission's study was published in 1967, Wilson was deeply committed to holding the rate. Although it was written in the obfuscatory language of bureaucrats, the Commission's report said in unmistakable terms that the pound must be devalued. Once again, as they had periodically since 1963, the speculative forces began to attack, but this time the United States and the other nations that had organized a consortium to support the pound threw in the towel. Within two months the British had devalued by 14.3 percent, dropping the parity of the pound to $2.40.

French ministers seized on the section of the Commission's report on Britain's finances to argue that since the British position was so weak there was no point in even considering the opening of negotiations. When Britain was in healthier condition, smooth, icy French Foreign Minister Couve de Murville said disdainfully, perhaps the dossier might be reopened. At a Council of Ministers meeting in Luxembourg on December 19, five of the six foreign ministers said they were in favor of opening negotiations. Couve said no. France had delivered her second veto. De Gaulle commented later that the reopening of negotiations would have been a "step toward surrender" by the Six to *"les Anglo-Saxons,"* the pejorative term he used to describe the bogeymen of the English-speaking world.

Wilson came out of that initial encounter badly scarred, but Britain's allies on the continent were determined to continue exerting pressure on the French. Although there was no question of overriding France's veto (and probably destroying the Community in the process), the Five and particularly the Dutch, who were the most friendly to Britain, found it intolerable that the clear wishes of the majority were being consistently blocked. They refused to let the matter drop and began a series of moves to outflank the General. The main activity centered on bringing Britain into the continental councils in fields where the veto would not apply, such as technology, defense, and foreign policy. There was a feverish swirl of diplomacy, but in the end nothing came of it all except that Britain's case stayed at the top of the European file. Yet, even this was not insignificant. It was in sharp contrast to the way Britain's case was forgotten or at least shelved after the first veto.

Initially, the major initiatives came from the Benelux countries and Italy. Finally Germany stepped in with a plan of its own. This was important because it again underscored (in contrast to 1963, when Bonn docilely accepted the French veto) France's isolation. The German plan, presented to an EEC Council meeting in March, 1968, provided for progressive mutual lowering of tariff barriers in a commercial agreement to be formally considered as the first step toward full membership. While not opposed to a commercial accord, France rejected any declaration of future intentions and countered with her own idea—a commercial agreement that would be open not just to Britain but to all interested European states.

After countless hours of theological debate in heated Council of Ministers meetings, the then German Foreign Minister Willy

Brandt returned to the attack in October, 1968, presenting detailed proposals not only for the German type of commercial agreement (leading to full membership) but also for meaningful technological cooperation and permanent contacts between the Community and the four applicant countries.

The French found reasons for rejecting the German formula, but the relentless pressure on de Gaulle was at last having some effect. At a council meeting in November, 1968, the French said for the first time that they were willing to permit discussions between the Community and other countries, including Britain, on technological cooperation and the harmonizing of industrial patents. Once again the French said they were willing to make limited trading arrangements but without guarantees of ultimate membership.

Against this background, de Gaulle's political position inside France was continuing to weaken. The worker-student riots in the streets of Paris the previous May and June raised questions about the effectiveness of his internal policies. He had earlier tried to win over workers by promoting a liberal program for worker "participation" in industrial decision making. This won him little worker support, but it gained him enemies in the community of big business. In the end "participation" was never implemented. Other segments of French public opinion were alienated by his refusal to permit Israel to take delivery of advanced Mirage fighter aircraft (which had already been paid for) and by his generally pro-Arab stand in the Middle East. The pro-Arab policies combined with strong anti-American positions in other areas of foreign policy led many Americans to cross France off their European vacation itineraries and to stop buying French wines. Apart from his denunciation of the war in Vietnam, his foreign policy was considered at the time by many to be petulant, invidious, and extreme. With his withdrawal from the NATO military command and his struggle to undermine the dollar's hegemony, he seemed intent on destroying the entire Atlantic structure without being able to provide a meaningful alternative. Nowhere was gratuitous arrogance in foreign policy more in evidence than in his calculated interference in the linguistic, ethnic, and economic quarrel in Canada. On a trip to French Canada he dangerously agitated the already combustible separatist feelings with his 1967 declaration, from the steps of the Montreal City Hall, *"Vive le Quèbec libre."* Not even the French Canadians appreciated his interference.

An unrepentent, mischievous de Gaulle, even while he was being increasingly characterized inside France and outside, perhaps unfairly, as a dotty old man out of touch with the world, made one more flamboyant gesture of defiance in his European policy before stepping down as president of France. This became known as the Soames Affair of February, 1969.

The portly, genial Francophile Christopher Soames, epicurean British ambassador to France and son-in-law of Winston Churchill, received an invitation on February 11 to come over to the Élysée Palace (a couple of doors down from the British embassy on the rue du Faubourg St. Honoré) for a private chat. Soames wanted to sound out the General on the development of Europe and the role Britain should play. It turned out to be an extraordinary conversation. De Gaulle, Soames later reported to the Foreign Office, had said he had played no part in the creation of the Common Market and had no particular faith in it. If Britain and the other applicants joined, the EEC would no longer be the same, which would not necessarily be a bad thing, in de Gaulle's view. Soames said that de Gaulle wanted to see it change into a loose form of free trade area, which is what Britain had always wanted anyway, with supplementary arrangements to exchange farm products. De Gaulle then proposed in the dialogue with Soames that Britain should join France in secret discussions to create this enlarged European Economic Association. Reviving the old directorate idea with a twist, de Gaulle said the new association would be controlled by France, Britain, and Germany.

Wilson and the Foreign Office smelled a trap. Refusing to enter into any secret deal with the General, they promptly leaked Soames's account of the conversation, first to the German chancellor, silver-maned Kurt-Georg Kiesinger, and then to the other Common Market governments. Soames, feeling betrayed, was enraged, and so were the French. "The French fury," as Wilson was to observe later in his memoirs, "knew no limit." Then followed the battle of the leaks. The French leaked a special version of the affair to the French press; the British responded with their own version to the British press. The French then served notice that they would take no further part in the only political organization that linked Britain to the Common Market countries, the Western European Union, which was being used up to that point as the instrument to keep Britain's Common Market application alive. As the recriminations flew back and forth across the Channel, British-French relations, as Wilson commented, sank to the low level at which they had been after de Gaulle's first veto in 1963.

Wilson maintained, a little weakly, that the decision to inform the Five of the Soames-de Gaulle conversation was largely the doing of the Foreign Office. Regardless of the apportionment of blame—or credit—disclosure proved to be the only action Britain could take to get out of the trap.

To accept the offer of a three-power directorate and negotiate secretly with the General would have put Britain in the class of conspirator and revived all the old charges about perfidious Albion. For if the British didn't inform the Five, the French probably would have, and could have used the revelation as an argument to support France's contention that Britain wasn't really serious about joining the Common Market. Britain would then have been seen as double-crossing her stanchest supporters within the Community, the Benelux countries, which had long feared a situation in which the big powers would gang up against them. And yet, to reject the General's offer was tantamount to writing off a future European role. The British, fully aware of de Gaulle's eroding power base, probably felt they had nothing to lose by their unconventional riposte. They had more or less concluded that they could never get into the Common Market while de Gaulle was in power.

De Gaulle resigned two months later, in April, 1969, after a referendum for constitutional changes was rejected by French voters. De Gaulle chose to interpret the defeat as a loss of confidence in him. But his only son, Philippe, said in a television interview in June, 1971, that his father had planned to resign anyway before reaching the age of eighty—that is, sometime before November 22, 1970. He intended this, said Philippe, in a reference to Marshal

Pétain, because "there have been sad and unfortunate examples, in France at least, of octogenarian chiefs of state."*

De Gaulle resigned in April, and in the following months Georges Pompidou, a wily Auvergnat, a former Rothschild banker steeped in history and the classics, a self-made man, a politician to his fingertips, was elected president of France. Pompidou had earlier served as de Gaulle's premier, but was dropped after the uprising of May-June, 1968, in an effort to meet the public's demand for change in France. Some French commentators speculated that he was sacrificed because he was rising too fast as the General's rival. He had negotiated the labor agreements that got the workers back to the factories and had become by far the most impressive political figure in the Gaullist entourage.

As president, Pompidou sought to give France a new image. The months in purdah had embittered him against the old-line Gaullists, but while be branched out on his own, he could not afford to break completely with the past. He carefully shaped his policies, downgrading, while still heeding, the doctrinaire elements of Gaullism—particularly de Gaulle's semi-mystical concern about *"la grandeur"*—and upgrading practical economic considerations. The first sign that there was a new, cool-eyed man at the Élysée was the decision in August to devalue the franc, a move that the General had refused to take, even though it became necessary with the outpouring of reserves after the worker-student uprising of May-June, 1968, because of the damage it might have done to French prestige. The devaluation, reducing the price and thus increasing the demand for French exports, was part of a long-range Pompidou plan to improve French competitiveness and stimulate industrial growth. Pompidou was convinced that this was the only

* *International Herald Tribune,* June 19, 1971, p. 1. Pétain was eighty-four in June, 1940, when he signed an armistice with Hitler and organized the Vichy government that collaborated with the Nazis during the war. De Gaulle, even while naming his only son after Pétain, never forgave his old commander for working with the Germans and had him condemned to military degradation and death in August, 1945. Later on the sentence was commuted to life imprisonment. Pétain died on July 23, 1951, at the age of ninety-five. While many regarded him as a traitor others revered him as a hero who had stood by a stricken France.

way to prevent future social uprisings and to get France in a stronger position in relation to West Germany. Germany's industrial output was still 50 percent greater than France's, but France's faster growth rate, in the 1960s and at best through the early 1970s, was expected by the futurologists, such as Herman Kahn's Hudson Institute, to make her the number-one industrial power in Europe in the 1980s.

Pompidou also looked at the British case with a more practical eye. He had none of de Gaulle's complexes about *"les Anglo-Saxons."* If the British still wanted to join, and were willing to pay the price, and the Five still wanted them in, then France might make a bargain. Pompidou sensed that it was in France's long-term interest anyway to have the British in. Germany's power was growing so much inside the bloc that Britain was needed to redress the balance.

Conditions improved for the trade-off when, in September, Willy Brandt, the German Socialist leader, became chancellor and immediately proceeded to revalue the German mark upward, a move that the earlier government under CDU (Conservative) leader Kiesinger had rejected, even though the case for revaluation was compelling. Kiesinger was motivated by some of the same considerations as de Gaulle. German prestige seemed to be at stake in making an unwanted currency change. The French devaluation followed by the German revaluation restored a balance between the French and German economies, and this had the immediate effect of improving the state of political relations between the two countries. Pompidou then called for a summit conference of leaders of the Six to examine the question of Community development and enlargement. The prospects were that it would produce results.

The leaders of the Six met in the medieval Hall of Knights at the Hague on December 1 and 2, 1969, and agreed on three cardinal points: to open British membership negotiations (wanted by the Five), to establish permanent farm financing regulations (wanted by France), and to try to create a monetary union over the next decade (wanted by all Six).

The state was thus set for the third and decisive round in the struggle over British membership. Only two weeks before the formal opening of the talks in Luxembourg's modern Kirchberg Center, British voters, in the biggest election upset in a quarter century, dismissed Harold Wilson and brought Tory leader Edward Heath to Downing Street with a mandate to lead the country for five years. There was now a completely new set of main characters: Pompidou, the chain-smoking, practical politician who would strike a bargain if the terms were right; Brandt, the hard-drinking European federalist and socialist who had fought Nazi persecution as a youth and who had always believed that Britain must join; and Edward Heath.

Heath, who was determined to bring Britain into the Common Market, had impeccable "European" credentials.

"And so I would say to my colleagues," the new prime minister had said in Brussels just after the first veto, winding up his job as negotiator, "they should have no fear. We in Britain are not going to turn our backs on the mainland of Europe or on the countries of the Community. We are a part of Europe: by geography, tradition, history, culture, and civilization. We shall continue to work with our friends in Europe for the true unity and strength of this Continent." If anything, his conviction was even stronger in 1970 than when de Gaulle's veto was slammed on the table in 1963.

Like Pompidou, Heath was a practical man. He saw his country floundering in a welter of confusion and contradictions and was determined early that Britain could thrive only as part of a wider European grouping.

The son of a shopkeeper in the resort town of Broadstairs on England's southeast coast, Heath was taught early to believe in the virtues of self-reliance and hard work. On scholarship, he went to Balliol College, Oxford, got himself elected to the House of Commons, and by indefatigable efforts and some luck rose swiftly in Conservative governments from whip to Lord Privy Seal (the post he held as Common Market negotiator) to president of the Board of Trade.* He had achieved a reputation for being uncompromis-

---

*This was the biggest and probably most inefficient government department in Britain at the time. Awed by Heath's capacity for work, one high Board of Trade offical commented at lunch in 1963: "Heath has shaken up this ministry as no one has before."

ing, tireless, and efficient, and when Sir Alec Douglas-Home lost to Wilson in 1963, the Tory party chose Heath to give it a new image. Heath lost badly to Wilson in 1964 but managed to hang on to the Conservative leadership long enough to ride to unexpected victory in 1970.

Both Pompidou and Heath wanted the negotiations to succeed. Heath saw membership as the only way to foster the economic revolution necessary to get the growth rate and efficiency quota up in Britain. He believed in the "cold bath" effect of foreign competition and in the stimulus of an enlarged market area. He furthermore saw that in a world of two or three superpowers Britain would have no influence except as part of a broader European grouping. Membership was thus a way to rebuild national self-confidence and self-respect, after years on the dole. "I have always had in my mind's eye a vision about the people of this country," Heath once said. "I have wanted to see them look up instead of seeing them always looking down,"

Pompidou saw Britain, the largest food importer in the world, as a major market for French farmers and as a counterweight to the power of West Germany. So long as the British question remained dangling, the situation in Western Europe would remain unstable, Pompidou told visitors in 1970. Pompidou badly wanted stability, both internal and external, to concentrate on his highest-priority objective, the doubling of French industrial output in the decade of the 1970s to try to catch up with Germany.

Pompidou and Heath saw each other as allies in the Community debates over supranationalism. Representing two of the oldest nation-states in Europe, they were in no hurry (and knew it would be politically impossible anyway) to cede, at least in the short term, any significant degree of national sovereignty to central institutions. While they recognized that this might come about eventually, they believed that if it did it would have to be a natural process resulting from the convergence of national aims by the great European states.

"There is not one European nation," Pompidou said on British television on May 17, 1971. "There is the British nation, the French, the German, the Italian, and so forth. Therefore, I do not believe in a purely technocratic or administrative power that could impose itself upon the several nations and states. After all, the existing Council of Ministers is already an embryo of a confederal government."

At a summit conference in Paris on May 20 and 21, 1971, Heath told Pompidou that there was "an identity of views" on this point. The two men also found it was both "desirable and possible" to reach a rapid agreement on the principal issues before the negotiators in Brussels who were trying to agree on the terms for membership.

A few feet from where de Gaulle issued his 1963 veto, Pompidou, with Heath at his side, spoke these words to newsmen in the early evening of May 21: "Many people believed that Britain was not and did not wish to become European and that she wished to enter the Community only to destroy it or to divert it from its goals. Many also thought that France was ready to use all pretexts to put up a new veto to the entry of Britain. Well, mesdames et messieurs, you see before you this evening two men who are convinced of the contrary."

That statement duly signaled the end of a chapter. The following month in Luxembourg, Britain's chief negotiatior, Geoffrey Rippon, and the foreign ministers of the Six, came to a final agreement on the terms, meeting in the same building, the Kirchberg skyscraper, where the negotiations had begun twelve months earlier. Rippon and France's foreign minister, Maurice Schumann, broke out the champagne as Schumann told a 5:30 AM press conference ending the final negotiating session: "This is the end of the beginning; it opens the way to great achievements for Europe."

Despite the convergence of views of Pompidou and Heath, sealing an agreement had not been easy, as the duration of the final negotiating session readily showed. The British had to get terms that would be acceptable to the House of Commons and the public. The continentals had to strike a bargain that would satisfy the British and yet maintain the integrity of the Community institutions, principles, and laws as they had evolved over fifteen years.

The critical issues were the amounts that Britain would pay into the EEC budget over a transition period and guarantees for New Zealand's British-descended dairy farmers, who depended heavily on British markets. The British ceded on another important issue before it became divisive by agreeing to a gradual phasing out of the reserve role of sterling. A compromise on the budget kept Britain's net cost to what was probably the minimum acceptable to the Six. Rippon won guarantees enabling New Zealand to keep 71 percent of its British market over five years, New Zealand's welfare being important because of the influence it would have on Tory MPs voting on crucial Market legislation in the House of Commons.

At the time the agreement was initialed, 60 percent of the British public was recorded in public opinion polls as being against joining. But 70 percent believed that membership would come anyway. The most vocal opposition came from Labor supporters, and Wilson sought to gain cheap political advantage by turning the party against its previous endorsement. He was castigated by the press and some of his own supporters for his tergiversations. Bitter strife broke out within the parliamentary party, leading to the resignation of deputy leader Roy Jenkins, the most ardent "European" on the front bench and a rival to Wilson as the leader of the party.

Wilson vacillated again, denying that he opposed membership outright, saying that he was opposed only to the terms, which he asserted were not good enough for Britain and would be renegotiated by a future administration.* George Thomson, who had been Rippon's predecessor in the earlier Labor government and who had opened the membership negotiations in Luxembourg, flatly contradicted his party leader, declaring that the Rippon-Heath terms were the best possible. In Brussels it was often commented that since Heath's personal commitment to the Community was never in doubt, the Tories probably were able to extract even more concessions from the Community than a Labor government could have obtained.

A hard core of Tories, led by Enoch Powell, the cantankerous,

---

*In the early 1960s, Wilson also pledged a future Labor government to renegotiate the Polaris missile agreement Macmillan brought back from Nassau. This was to appease left-wingers who wanted Britain to give up a deterrent. Wilson conveniently forgot about this pledge during his seven years as prime minister.

brilliant Greek scholar, fanatic individualist, and racist, was also against membership and was determined to bolt party ranks when the crucial votes came, but the split in the Labor party assured passage of the European Communities Bill in the House of Commons. Under the British parliamentary system this was all the ratification that was needed. The anti-marketeers said Heath should have taken the issue to the people in a referendum, but this simply was not the British way of doing things (even Wilson could agree with Heath on this point), and that was that.

By the end of 1972, Heath, as the *New Statesman* observed, was like Henry V about to launch his forces against Agincourt, saying, "I can see them stand like greyhounds in the slips, straining upon the start. The game's afoot: Follow your spirit and upon this charge cry, 'God for Teddy, England, and the Common Market.' "

8

From Sovereignty
to Supranationality?

Into the early 1970s the Common Market remained a grouping of sovereign states which had obtained, through a series of compromises, a balance of mutual advantages. Never was there a question of forcing a member government to act against its will on an issue of overriding national interest. Pressures could be brought to bear against one government that seemed to be blocking the will of the majority. But, in the end, progress depended on that government's freely-made decision. Usually, it would not bow until it saw the chance of gaining concessions in another field. It could take months, and in some cases, years—as in the episode over British membership—before the right conditions were present to strike the bargain. Even when the conditions seemed to be met and the ministers had gathered to act (generally with a self-imposed deadline hanging over them), it would frequently be many hours into the night, with dramatic midnight calls to capitals, before the big decisions were taken. Much of this was simply playing to the gallery. It was easier for ministers to explain their actions to home constituents if they could show that the big decision was a hard one taken after a long, grueling bargaining effort.

These procedures were far from what the founders of the Common Market had in mind. They felt that there had to be supranational decision-making authority if their Community was to amount to anything more than a regrouping of the alliances that had failed so dismally throughout past centuries in keeping peace in Europe. They had given strong powers to the Executive Commission. They wanted the European Parliament to play a vital role in Community affairs. They wrote into the charter a provision for majority voting in the Council and supplied the date—January 1, 1966—when this should take effect.

As the community developed in the early 1960s, establishing its common farm policy, reducing internal tariffs, and building up a common external tariff wall, the forces were gathering for a conflict between the initial concept of a federal Europe with central institutions and the Gaullist concept of a confederation of sovereign states banded together because of a concordance of mutual interests. With the date for majority voting written into the treaty, there was little way of avoiding an open clash. On one side was de Gaulle, the proud, self-willed, self-styled embodiment of the French nation. On the other side was Walter Hallstein, the shy, solitary, autocratic German law professor who had become the Commission's first president.

Hallstein was determined to get majority voting introduced. This would mean an end to the veto power that permitted a single state to impose its will on the others. Only de Gaulle had used it. Hallstein knew that de Gaulle would fight its termination, but he also felt that de Gaulle might be swayed if the terms were right and if sufficient pressure could be exerted on France by the others.

As president of the Commission, it was Hallstein's job to frame proposals for the Council of Ministers. In March, 1965, he announced at a Brussels press conference a complex plan for financing the Community budget, which was to become the first shot in the battle. In effect, the plan was designed to give France something that she wanted while exacting a supranational price for the concession.

Most of what the Community spent each year went into a farm fund that was used to prop up the prices that farmers in the six countries obtained for their products. France was the principal agricultural supplier in the Community; therefore France was the country to benefit most from Community farm spending. The farm program was financed by payments into the farm fund from the national treasuries, payments that were related under a formula to each nation's economic strength. So while Germany and France put the most in, France, because of her large farm economy, took the most out.

Neither France nor Germany was entirely satisfied with this system. Bonn was beginning to complain that payments were getting too large. The Community's relatively high price levels were causing surpluses, and the surpluses were costly. France was worried lest Bonn or another capital decide to put ceilings on payments because of the rising costs. France wanted an arrangement under which there would never be any question about each nation's contribution: in other words, she wanted a permanently enshrined system for feeding Community money to French farmers.

This is where Hallstein saw his opening. The Community had a huge foreign trade turnover. The common tariffs on industrial imports and the common levies on farm imports were pocketed by national treasuries. Hallstein proposed that these receipts be turned over automatically to the Community institutions, that the powers of the European Parliament be strengthened to watch over the other institutions, and that the Council shift over to majority voting.

It was an imaginative and audacious plan. In one fell swoop a supranational community would be created, a new Europe would be born. The founding fathers would smile down on Professor Hallstein and say "well done."

The Dutch, German, and Italian delegations supported Hallstein, but de Gaulle reacted as if stung by a Rhenish wasp. His representatives in Brussels said there was no question of even compromising along lines of the Commission's ideas and warned that France would feel obliged to withdraw if the others tried to gang up against her. In June, 1965, at a critical council meeting in Brussels, Foreign Minister Couve de Murville received instructions from the Élysée to pull the French delegation from Brussels. The Community, instead of being reincarnated, experienced perhaps its gravest crisis. For seven months it was a paralyzed Community of five. Midway through the crisis de Gaulle denounced the Hallstein Commission as a "bogus" executive body and a "technocratic, irresponsible, stateless apparatus." The Commission published an article shortly afterward personally attacking de Gaulle.

So frayed were tempers that suggestions began circulating that the Five should simply let France stew and invite Britain in her place. Britain wisely offered no encouragement, preferring to sit out the crisis in a neutral corner. Cooler heads in the capitals of the Five prevailed. The Community had begun as a French idea. France was its geographical center. Without France there was grave doubt whether it could survive. Inevitably, signs began appearing in the fall that the Six were going to patch up their differences.

On January 17, 1966, the six foreign ministers met again for the first time since June at a suspenseful council in Luxembourg. The result was to shelve all elements of the Hallstein plan, including majority voting. The decision taken in the Grand Duchy, a return to the status quo ante bellum, kept the Community intact, but only by halting the process of federalism. Future decisions would be taken, as in the past, only when there was a consensus of all the member states. There was no question of enlarging the power of central institutions.

Yet, while the Luxembourg agreement could be characterized as a complete victory for de Gaulle, the text left the door open for some type of majority voting principle to evolve in the future. The Six agreed that when very important interests of one or more member states were in question, they would *try* to reach, within a reasonable period, solutions that could be adopted unanimously. They could not agree on what might happen if they did not reach unanimity. The communiqué noted that France considered that when very important interests were at issue, discussion should continue until unanimous agreement had been reached. The difference of opinion was noted.

All this was important in terms of the Community's future development. The Five left unsaid what might happen if unanimous agreement could not be reached, but they were obviously leaving the door ajar for some type of future agreement on majority voting, after the de Gaulle era when French resistance might have softened. The de Gaulle-Hallstein confrontation dramatically demonstrated that the Six had yet to—and might never—reach that point of political, economic, and social integration where they could act with a common purpose as a United States of Europe.

Hallstein was trying to push the states too fast and de Gaulle simply blew the whistle. The acrimony was to be regretted but the incident itself was probably salutary. Hallstein's federalist vision was too much that of the Procrustean bed, and the states weren't prepared to have their limbs cut off to fit into it. If de Gaulle hadn't been there to say *"non,"* someone else undoubtedly would have. One of the inconsistencies in the positon of the Five and of Hallstein revolved around the question of British membership. They were in favor of it, de Gaulle was against it. Yet, de Gaulle's victory in the end made it possible for the British to join. Britain was as much intent on preserving sovereignty as France was. The British were to have a hard enough time swinging into step with the continental bloc without also having to accept a tight set of federalist rules that they had no hand in writing.

There were forces for integration and disintegration within the bloc, but the forces for integration were stronger. In the late 1960s and early 1970s the community, responding to internal pressures and external challenges, especially from the United States, was developing in inchoate form a common identity and personality. Again it was the French, representing the lowest common denominator* who set the pattern for this development. At a press conference in Paris on January 21, 1971, President Pompidou went well beyond de Gaulle's rabid nationalism in sketching a view of the future.

> The idea of achieving confederation on the basis of technical organizations, of commissions, is an illusion that has already been swept away by the facts. The government of Europe can only arise out of the gathering of national governments, joining together to take decisions that are valid for all. Today it is the Council of Ministers, which brings together the foreign ministers and, when necessary, the technical ministers who, in fact, also hold specialized meetings. In a final phase, these ministers might have nothing

---

*The French obtained maximum bargaining power through a policy of calculated obstinacy that drove their partners up the wall. But there was a certain logic and consistency to the French position. They never make promises they couldn't keep, unlike some other members, particularly Italy.

but strictly European duties and will no longer be part of the national governments.

Here, for the first time, the French conceded the need for some kind of "European" authority that went beyond the nation-state. Pompidou blithely skipped over the stages of development and ignored the key role that would have to be played by a European Parliament once the "European" ministers were installed. And the ministers, of course, would have to be answerable to something beyond national parliaments if they were to be an effective force in shaping European policies. But all this was very much in the future. Pompidou's point was that once a European identity was established, the rest would fall into place.

Later Pompidou spoke of a "separation of powers" within the Community. He said that the principal countries should each have a "vocation." France, which was "friends with everybody" east and west, naturally had the political vocation. (Pompidou wanted a political secretariat based in Paris.) Benelux, with its great ports of Antwerp and Rotterdam, would be the center for international trade. Germany would be the center for industry, and Britain, with the resources of the City of London, the financial center.

It was all very neat and logical. But would it work, and if so, how? One would have to come back in the mid or late 1970s to find those answers.

As Western Europe searched for an identity, a personality, varying national priorities and preoccupations slowed and at times halted the process of integration much as the sectional rivalries did the federal union of the United States. The American example was forever cited by the Europeans who wanted to construct a unified continent; yet, even if a parallel could be drawn between the Europe of multicultured, industrialized sovereign states of the twentieth century and the thirteen agrarian colonies of the eighteenth century, the length of time and problems in bringing the United States together were often overlooked. Even into the Great Depression of the 1930s the regional differences in the United States were so wide as to prevent Washington from having full control over money and credit policies. Federal Reserve Banks from the urban regions strongly resisted giving credits to the depressed farm belt. The structure of the Federal Reserve System with its quasi-autonomous regional banks gave play to varied and often contradictory monetary philosophies. Monetary policy in the United States was a policy of consensus, but sometimes it was difficult to know what that consensus was.

Since regional and national differences ran far deeper in Europe, it was only realistic to measure the process of integration against a long time chart. The only sector apart from the common tariffs where the EEC, by the early 1970s, had achieved any degree of integration was agriculture. Early in the new decade the first tentative steps were taken to try to achieve a monetary union. Later in the decade, once the British were fully paid up members and the American military presence in Germany was withdrawn or sharply reduced, there would be renewed talk, and possibly some action, to create a defense union. Coordination of foreign policy, which began in a loose, informal way in 1969, looked forward to the establishment of a political secretariat. All of this would mean the gradual transfer of political authority from national to central bodies. It wouldn't happen overnight. There would be fantastic brawls before the consensus was established. There might even be some pulling apart before things were put together again, perhaps in a different form. But the forces pushing the continent together were still greater than those pulling it apart.

Again it was more the external threat than internal compulsion. Earlier the threat had come of the paranoid aggressiveness of the Soviet Union. Later it came from the insouciant aggressiveness of the United States as it promoted a new world monetary and trading order to increase jobs in the United States and add to the power of American companies overseas. There was a new game in world politics: getting the other fellow to pay to solve your social problems. In devising their common farm program the Europeans showed a certain expertise in the game.

What was happening down on the farm?

Although there had already been a massive flight from the land by 1970—at the rate of 500,000 farmers a year—there were still too many farmers in the six countries, too many small landholders who, despite the high price supports, found that their income was falling far behind the earnings of industrial workers. In 1970, agricultural workers amounted to 13 percent of the total EEC work force: they had made up 16 percent in 1965, 24 percent in 1955. While Germany, Holland, and Belgium had under 10 percent of their workers on the land in 1970, France still had about 15 percent and Italy 22 percent. In both the United States and Britain, farmers made up much less than 5 percent of the working population.

Social problems arose in absorbing farmers into the labor force. Jobs were not that plentiful, particularly for men whose training did not go much beyond tractor repair or handling a team of oxen. The farmers were unhappy about moving and resisted in a number of ways. Farm organizations brought heavy political pressure on governments to raise price levels. They were backed up by action on the local level. Hardly a week went by when farmers in some part of the Community didn't show their anger. They dumped manure on country roads, rolled out tractors to tie up traffic on holiday weekends. They marched on towns occasionally, attacking local police stations. And sometimes they marched on the cities.

On March 23, 1971, some 80,000 farmers from all six countries converged on Brussels for what became a violent demonstration aimed at influencing decisions of the Community farm ministers, who were debating price levels for the coming season. Carrying heavy wooden pitchforks, the farmers tangled with the Brussels riot cops, probably the toughest in Western Europe, and by the end of the day one farmer demonstrator lay dead and 140 persons were injured. Two weeks earlier a smaller group of farmers, herding their cows ahead of them, had forced their way into the chamber at the Palais des Congrès, where ministers were carrying on another farm debate. One burly farmer slopped a glass of milk on the green felt table after having drawn the liquid warm from the swaying spiggots of his beast. Several ministers, more accustomed to agriculture in the abstract, nearly fell over in their chairs. When the farmers were finally expelled, custodians of the Palais scurried about the halls with mops and shovels.

In the earlier years of the Common Market, while a policy of high price supports was being shaped, farmers thought they were finally being assured a good living. Many who lived on marginal tracts borrowed extensively to buy modern equipment. Later they found that they had acquired nothing but debts.

One of the difficulties was the diversity of the Community. To placate the farmers, common price levels were set at relatively high levels. But, in an area that stretched from the cold, damp Baltic coast to the hot Mediterranean shores of Sicily, comprising exceptionally rich and exceptionally poor farmland, too much was given to some and not enough to others. With high prices for grains, for instance, the wheat growers of the Beauce (the extremely fertile region running southwest from Paris to the Loire) stashed away pieces of gold and took winter vacations in the Canary Islands. But the wheat growers of West Germany, with poorer soil and smaller tracts, proclaimed that they were hardly being helped at all and demanded still higher prices.

Farm authorities not only had their farmers to worry about; they had the outside world. Bowing to internal pressures to raise prices in a protected market, they ran into stiff complaints from traditional food-exporting countries such as the United States, Canada, and the developing countries, which saw in the common farm program one of the greatest trade-diverting instruments of the postwar period. President Nixon's economic offensive against Europe, Japan, and Canada, launched on August 15, 1971, when the dollar's convertibility into gold was suspended, had as one of its targets the weakening, if not the complete dismantlement, of the Common Agricultural Policy (CAP). Americans thought it unfair that they and the other traditional food-exporting countries were being called on to help subsidize the Community farmers when the European states were themselves rich enough to take on the job.

Early in 1972, President Nixon's adviser on international economic affairs, Peter G. Peterson, had this to say about the CAP in a special report:*

By any measure, the Community's policy has displaced imports, increased self-sufficiency, and forced exports onto world markets at distress prices. This system is the essence of mercantilism,

*A *Foreign Economic Perspective,* U.S. Government Printing office, December 27, 1971, p. 22.

forcing more efficient farmers in other countries to bear the costs
which the Community itself ought to pay for internally. As a
result, European consumers eat less well, and American and other
farmers live less well.

That was pretty tough talk for a public statement. Privately,
American officials were even abusive. "Those fat cats don't realize
the world's changed, and we're no longer paying their bills," was
the way one American representative put it to this correspondent
in 1971. But the Europeans, particularly the French, regarded the
CAP as the cornerstone of Common Market integration. President
Pompidou said, in a television interview on December 22, 1971:
"Everyone talks to us of integration and union; yet, in the only
domain in which we have realized this union for the moment
[agriculture], they want to weaken it. Well, let me tell you that if
the Common Market for agriculture is weakened, at that moment,
there will be no hope for economic and monetary union."

The first regulations of the CAP went into effect in 1962, and by
1972 the following commodities were covered: cereals (wheat, bar-
ley, rye, maize, and rice); pork, beef, and veal; eggs and poultry;
milk and milk products; sugar; fruit and vegetable; wine. To maintain high farm incomes, support prices for these commodities were
fixed at well above the world market price. (The support price is
what the EEC authorities promise to pay the farmer if he can't get
a better price in the market.) Imports of these commodities were
subjected to a variable border levy that automatically lifted their
price to the level of the highest price in the Community. This
assured domestic producers a preference in the home market. Receipts from the variable levy were then used to finance export
subsidies for the surplus foods the Community wanted to sell
abroad. Dairy products overflowed in the late 1960s. Karl Schiller,
Germany's economics minister at the time, calculated in 1969 that
the amount of unsold butter in the Community was equivalent to
the weight of the entire population of Austria. (With all that Sa-
chertorte and Schlag consumed daily that must have been quite a
load.) The high price levels certainly contributed to overproduc-
tion.

So the CAP hit the traditional food suppliers two ways: by reducing market growth for them inside Western Europe, a traditional importing area that was becoming increasingly self-sufficient in foods that were produced more efficiently elsewhere; by intensifying the competition in third markets. The United States and Australia were particularly upset in the late 1960s when EEC grains were dumped in Japan.

The United States served notice as far back as 1962 that it would demand compensation for trade losses as a result of the CAP. Other food exporters had the same rights under the GATT rules. The claims could have involved enormous sums. But President Kennedy held back. Captivated by the idea of constructing a "twin-pillar" (some called it the dumbbell) Atlantic partnership, the president wanted no economic confrontation with Europe at this time. Kennedy instead got a commitment from the Europeans that they would at some appropriate time "reconsider with the United States government . . . the overall commercial relations between the two parties." That time came in 1973 when negotiations began over the broad sweep of commercial relations in the industrialized world. This extensive review entailed a fresh look not only at the CAP but at the preferential agreements the EEC was signing with countries of Africa and the Mediterranean littoral. The preferences, in effect, made Europe and Africa into a north-south trading bloc that discriminated against North and South America and the countries of Asia. What particularly angered American officials was the EEC's demand for concessions from the developed countries as the price of granting them concessions or preferences in the European market.

But in the 1960s such issues, always simmering a little below the surface, never attracted much attention. One reason was the American preoccupation with Southeast Asia and China. Then, the EEC itself was not fully developed because of the French vetoes of British membership. Furthermore, there was an agreement in 1967 on the Kennedy Round, reducing tariff barriers around the world. But with the EEC enlarged in the 1970s and the United States increasingly concerned about its commercial posture in the world, the new trade negotiations began taking place in an atmosphere of bitterness and tension. While the United States could point to the inequities of the CAP, particularly the variable levy, the Community could show that the United States hadn't done at all badly when the export figures were toted up. Between 1958 and 1970 American food sales to the Community more than doubled, from $900 million dollars to $2 billion.

So, while the EEC farmers complained that they weren't being protected enough, the outside world, and particularly the United States, was getting after the Community for too much protection of its farmers. Yet, time was working in favor of resolving this problem. Inevitably, as Europe's industrialization continued apace, the farm population was dropping. Dr. Sicco Mansholt, the glossy-domed, droopy-jowled Dutch agronomist who was vice president and later president of the EEC Commission and its chief farm strategist through the 1960s and early 1970s, tried to help the process along by proposing, in 1968, a program of financial incentives to induce inefficient farmers to leave the land. Under the Mansholt Plan there would have been a 12 percent reduction in agricultural acreage by 1980, a decrease of 3.6 million people in the farming population, consolidation of the smaller and most inefficient farms into larger units, and increased mechanization. The far-reaching proposals were not accepted by the individual member governments because they would have cost too much. But a watered-down version of the plan was finally adopted in March, 1971. The EEC Council agreed to provide pensions of $600 a year for farmers between fifty-five and sixty-five who were willing to give up farming, and to offer low-interest loans for modernization and enlargement of their spreads to farmers who could show that their farms were capable of being efficient units.

Following the defeat of Hallstein's proposals for a self-financed Community, treasuries of the member states continued to hand over funds for the budget under a formula relating payments to economic strength. In the late 1960s, the budget was running at more than $3 billion a year, 95 percent of which went into farm support. With costs continually rising, the French, who got most of the benefits, wanted to build the common-financing principle into a more permanent structure. Otherwise, one of the member states might be tempted to decide unilaterally that the cost of farm support was too great and stop or reduce its payments. Following the compromise reached at the Hague summit in December, 1969, an intensive series of negotiations got under way to meet the French demands.

Hallstein, in 1965, had tried to extract immediate supranational concessions for permanent budget arrangements. What was worked out in a marathon Council meeting, which ended finally at 2 AM on Demcember 22, 1969, was much softer. But there was a supranational kicker all the same, which after long arguments the French finally accepted.

A progressive scale was worked out so that agricultural import levies and industrial tariffs collected by member states, together with up to 1 percent of the receipts of the value-added tax, the complex type of national sales tax introduced in the 1960s, would flow automatically into the EEC budget by 1978.

Of potentially greater significance was the decision to give the European Parliament in Strasbourg, which never had any real power, final authority over the disposition of some of the resources. The Parliament would be able to determine how funds were spent for the everyday administration of the Community. Heretofore the Council of Ministers, representing the national governments, had final authority over everything. It was tempting to recall the shift of power from the Stuarts and later monarchs to the Parliament at Westminster once it got the power of the purse.

Another reason for envisaging a more centralized and integrated Europe was the move beginning in the early 1970s to establish a single currency for the Common Market. The dismantling of trade barriers provided a balance of mutual advantage that made it almost unthinkable to go back to the old days of protectionism. A common currency, by stimulating trade and increasing the mobility of capital and labor, could provide a similar dynamic for prosperity and growth.

In the United States no one has to change money when he crosses state lines. An Albany manufacturer selling to a Chicago wholesaler doesn't worry about the devaluation of money in Illinois. Oil-rich Arab sheiks and treasurers of multinational corporations don't accumulate the money of Montana because they think it is destined to appreciate in value. Yet, the Common Market nations, except for Belgium and Luxembourg, which had their own private monetary union, all had separate currencies. Despite the integration of tariff and farm policies, there were still formidable monetary barriers between the states and wide differences in economic performance that kept the currencies separate. In a monetary union these barriers and differences would have to disappear.

When one talks of putting francs, marks, guilders, lire, pounds, and crowns into a single pot, the real issue is the merger of national personalities. Could nations with separate traditions, cultures, and languages, could regions as poor as Italy's Mezzogiorno or as rich as Germany's Ruhr, achieve the required harmony of interests or agree to sufficient redistribution of resources to make centralized decision making and a common currency possible? The answer seemed to be "yes, but it will take many years and many disappointments."

The aim of ultimate monetary unification was historically unprecedented. In the past monetary unification came after not before political unification, as was the case with both Switzerland and Italy in the nineteenth century. Or it involved the acceptance by a small country of the medium of exchange of a bigger neighbor, as was the case with Luxembourg's monetary union with Belgium. From 1873 to 1915 there was a Scandinavian monetary union in which banknotes of each country circulated freely in the other member states. But this was the era of the gold standard. Each currency was fully backed by gold in a simpler, less socially conscious era, before governments began managing currencies to pursue the objective of full employment.

Before a single currency could be created in Europe, coordinated economic, monetary, and fiscal policies were needed to provide balanced rates of growth, inflation, and employment. In effect, a Community-wide regional policy had to be set up so that poor areas—Sicily, southwestern France, parts of Scotland and Wales— would get new purchasing power. This would require investments on a massive scale, and some authority to decide the priorities.

Submerging nationalities was, of course, a highly delicate operation. What would happen, for instance, if a German chief of something equivalent to a Federal Reserve System for Europe decided that interest rates were too low in France or that there was too much money chasing too few goods in Italy? Serious, perhaps fatal conflicts would arise if the actions prescribed to correct these imbalances led to excessive unemployment and severe social disturbances. France or Italy might simply decide that the game was not worth the candle and quit the monetary union. In such a case, what would happen to their membership in the Common Market or to the Common Market itself?

These were grave questions which no one really had the answers to in the early 1970s. The magnitude of the adventure and the possible dangers weighed heavily in favor of caution as the Community charted a master plan for monetary union. The summit conference at The Hague at the end of 1969 started things off. Luxembourg's Premier Pierre Werner, a brimmingly effusive politician and financial expert in his own right (he was also the Grand Duchy's finance minister), was given the important task of sketching the first outlines of a monetary union plan. Working with a body of specialists from the member states, he faced those same issues that had dogged the Community for so long in the debate over supranationality. But there was one key difference. He had a mandate from all six governments to produce something.

France was no longer the odd man out. Georges Pompidou, the former Rothschild banker who had become France's new president, became, in fact, the adopted father of the idea. Pompidou had quickly grasped the importance of monetary cement to hold the customs and (even more important to France) the farm union together. Furthermore, monetary union was another way of reinforcing Germany's ties to the Common Market at a time when Germany's attentions were being drawn eastward by Willy Brandt's policies of seeking better relations with the Communist countries. Despite reassurances that Germany was still wedded to the Community and the Western alliances, France was more than a little worried over any moves the no longer slumbering giant made that might alter the power position in central Europe.

The debates within the Werner Committee and later in the Council of Ministers as the Six prepared to adopt a working plan for monetary union by 1980 showed that while France was for the plan in principle, the old Gaullist objections about giving up sovereignty were still a force to be reckoned with. The Germans were afraid that monetary union would mean they would have to pay the bills for their less disciplined neighbors. Therefore, Bonn was insisting on strong controls to keep spendthrifts in check. France, naturally, fought hard against any loss of monetary independence, and finally, after months of haggling, a compromise was struck. In the first stage, the Six were to coordinate their economic policies more closely, comparing notes on budget and fiscal policies but still reserving the right to pursue independent policies. They recognized, however, that later supranational institutions might be necessary. President Pompidou, for instance, conceded that a central nerve center was needed to manage a common pool of reserves and handle other jobs. Another provision provided Germany (or any other country) with the right to withdraw from the plan between the third and fifth year if it did not like the way it was going. It could bow out, in other words, if things got too costly and the others didn't want to change their ways. Hans de Koster, the Dutch secretary of state in the foreign ministry, put it this way: "We are like the couple who have an engagement party. If, over the next five years we don't get married, we return the gifts."

Progress in the phased plan for union was to be marked by a narrowing of margins of fluctuation of the EEC currencies to the point where they would be locked immutably and move up or down in value as a single unit. In early 1971, central bankers in the EEC installed hot-line circuits for instantaneous communication with their colleagues in the other centers and took other action to prepare for the progressive slimming of the margins. "There is a strong incentive built into the plan to move forward," said France's Foreign Minister Maurice Schumann, presumably because the economics of the Six would be so interdependent that it would be unthinkable to break up. He called the process that had begun "irreversible." Subsequent events showed his assessment perhaps a bit too optimistic.

The six EEC countries on April 23, 1972, began the formal

coordinated efforts to limit the maximum spread of their currencies to 2 1/4 percent, supporting the plan with mutual lines of short-term credit. The 2 1/4 percent was half the margin theoretically allowable under the Smithsonian Agreement of December 18, 1971, under which the dollar was devalued and the monetary system was made more flexible. It was a plan to create a "snake" in a tunnel, the snake being the EEC currencies fluctuating narrowly together and the tunnel representing the extent to which the snake could swing up or down against the dollar. Britain and Denmark, in anticipation of their membership, became additional coils of the snake on May 1, and Norway on May 23. In ten years, if things went according to plan, all variations in exchange rates of the EEC currencies would be completely eliminated. The snake would get thinner and thinner. In effect, there would be a single currency.

But within a few weeks of Norway's linkage the exchange markets began showing signs of entering one of their then increasingly frequent rounds of agitation—this time over what nearly every specialist agreed was an overvalued pound. Soon waves of money from the multinational companies, the central banks of Middle Eastern kingdoms, Communist countries and such other countries as Israel and Spain, from big and little commercial and private banks, and from opulent investors such as Greek shipping magnates and American millionaires living in Paris engulfed the market and pressed the pound hard against its lower fixed limit. Because the pound was part of the snake there was less room for the British authorities to maneuver. It looked like it would be 1964–67 all over again with Britain accepting huge quantities of short-term credits, this time from her continental partners, to defend an unrealistic rate for the pound. But Heath had learned Wilson's lessons and did what was becoming the fashionable thing; he floated the pound. He detached it from all commitments to maintain fixed margins and let it adrift in the markets to find its own level. In January, 1973, Italy followed Britain's example. These were the two countries in the Common Market with the most serious economic and social problems. They quickly showed that they could not stick out a monetary union, even in the most embryonic form, for very long. They had to master their internal problems first.

Yet, a few years earlier the EEC was in some danger, not because of experiments to create a monetary union but because of experience that showed the divisions that could result if monetary harmonization did not take place. Spurred by freer internal trade, the economies of the EEC states had been drawing together, but not close enough to prevent imbalances. These were chiefly noticeable between France and Germany.

The rate of inflation in France was twice that of Germany, which meant that over the years German goods became increasingly competitive. It wasn't only France that felt the effects of German strength in world markets; it was practically every other country in the world, except Japan, which was doing the Germans one better. Germany had an undervalued currency. France, unable to keep up, had an overvalued currency. But for reasons of national prestige neither country wanted to alter the value of its money. In 1968 de Gaulle characterized devaluation as "the worst possible absurdity." German Chancellor Kiesinger said at the same time that the mark's parity would stand "for eternity."

Maurice Couve de Murville, French premier at the time, publicly accused the Germans in a French television broadcast of deliberately weakening the French economy. The point was that with an undervalued currency the Germans were exporting more goods and taking jobs away from France and other countries. Wars had been fought over far less in earlier years. For their part, the Germans could not understand why they should be forced to accept the consequences of an upward revaluation that would make exports more expensive and probably less competitive. Germans thought they were being punished by other nations, especially France, for working harder. It was a delicate, dangerous situation between countries that were not too long ago at war.

In 1961 the Germans had upvalued the mark by 4.75 percent. That was the result of pressure by President Kennedy. Pressure by the Americans, and particularly Kennedy—that was different from pressure by de Gaulle. In 1961 Germans were especially dependent on United States military support. That was the year the Russians built the Berlin wall to stop the movement of East Germans to the West. It was a year of high Cold War tensions. Yet even with all these reasons for bowing to American pressure, Chancellor Ludwig Erhard and other Bonn politicians were criticized for their action in the ensuing German recession. Kennedy was the first American president to worry about the balance of payments. He felt that a German upvaluation would help relieve some of the pressure on the dollar that was being reflected at the time in the gold market. "There are two things that keep me awake at night," Kennedy said once, "Berlin and the balance of payments."

France was spending more than she was earning overseas. Germany's position was just the reverse: it was earning more. Both governments adopted a series of economic measures to try to restore equilibrium, but, as was the case with Britain in the period prior to November, 1967, when the pound was devalued, the measures were insufficient. The power of international speculators and those who were simply trying to preserve their financial assets was too great—and getting greater. Billions of dollars moved into the German central bank, while billions of dollars were squeezed out of both the Bank of France and the Bank of England, all in defending unrealistic rates. The Bretton Woods system (see chapter 2) had set up procedures under which currency adjustments would be infrequent, a last resort when all other measures had been exhausted. The experts came to realize in the 1967–69 crises that something else was needed to encourage countries to make currency changes before a full-scale crisis was upon them.

In the early 1970s the monetary authorities of the United States, Western Europe, and Japan were trying to work out a new system that would encourage smaller and more frequent parity changes. An adjustment would then become simply another tool in monetary management.

De Gaulle's resignation in April, 1969, finally paved the way for the adjustment in France. His successor, Georges Pompidou, measured France's interests with a cooler eye. A decision to devalue the franc by 12.5 percent was taken on July 16 and announced to the world on August 8, when most of Europe was on vacation. France's reserves only a few years earlier, when General de Gaulle was challenging the preeminence of the dollar and trying to restore the world to a gold standard, had been among the highest for any industrial country. But now, without devaluation, they would have been completely eroded by the end of 1969. A decision by France's financial experts had actually been taken to devalue the franc the previous November, but this had been vetoed by the General.

The change in Germany came in October, 1969, when the mark's value was increased by 9.2896 percent. Here, too, a change of government was necessary. After general elections in September, Socialist Willy Brandt became chancellor, leading a coalition that excluded the Christian Democrats under Kurt Georg Kiesinger but included Walter Scheel's Free Democrats. On September 29, one day after the federal elections, the caretaker cabinet detached the mark from its internationally agreed peg and let the rate float. This was in anticipation of a formal revaluation by the Social Democrats. As the minority partners in the former coalition, the Socialists had been in favor of revaluation since the previous March.

With the mark-franc adjustments and an end to speculation against the pound, relative peace came to the European monetary scene for the first time in five years. It was during this period that the Common Market leaders decided that somehow future crises of this sort, which had spurred nationalistic feelings to an extent not seen since the war, had to be avoided at all costs.

Yet peace proved to be short-lived. Next time it was the crisis of the overvalued dollar, and, basically, of the monetary system itself. This too was to affect French-German relations and put another obstacle in the path of monetary union.

Economic and monetary integration was essential if the EEC was to amount to anything more than a customs union with pretensions. But there was still another driving force behind the adoption of monetary union as a long-range goal. This was the desire to be liberated from the influence of the dollar.

The dollar was battering the Europeans right and left. Surplus greenbacks had been generated by two decades of excessive spending by the United States culminating in the spectacular dollar's 30 billion deficit in 1971. The quantities were just too much for any government to control. So governments had little choice but to swallow dollars and accept the inflationary consequences of a ballooning of their money supply or regurgitate them and accept the deflationary consequences of an upvaluation of their money. For a couple of years the Europeans did both, while trying to put pressure on the United States to ease up on the outflows. Preoccupied with Southeast Asia, the United States didn't listen, or didn't want to listen, and followed what has come to be known as the policy of benign neglect. It was not an American problem, but a European problem, American officials said. Meanwhile, American companies, armed with bundles of depreciating dollars, continued to buy up companies in Europe in a demonstration of naked financial power. Germany, which was fast accumulating most of the American paper, had no overseas investments to speak of. Germany was a creditor without assets.

The background to all this was the change in the constellation of power in the world, a change that had not yet been taken into account in the structure of international payments. While the United States monopolized the world's wealth, the dollar had been installed as the sun of the Bretton Woods solar system. By 1971 it was still the sun, but there were other strongly competing sources of energy.

Germany and Japan, thanks to new industrial plant after the war, financed in large measure by the United States, and thanks, of course, to their own not inconsiderable industriousness, had emerged as giant exporters. Embracing Germany, the Common Market exported more than the United States.

Then there was a certain inequality in monetary and trading rules, built into the system after the war to help the recovery effort of other nations but operating to American disadvantage twenty-five years later. Trading blocs were tolerated by the rules but they inevitably discriminated against those who weren't members. Exchange rate adjustments were permitted to other nations, but since the dollar was at the center of the system, a reference point for all other currencies, it could not change. Its value was determined by what other countries decided as the dollar relationship of their currencies. Most other countries had devalued against the dollar, leaving it exposed. So, until December 18, 1971, with the first dollar devaluation of the postwar era, the dollar had become an overvalued currency with no real powers of correction. The United

States may have been buying up other countries' companies, but the actual work to fill the export orders was being done by foreign, not American, labor at a time when the high unemployment and social disorder showed that the United States badly needed to put men to work.

The Vietnam War was another element in the picture. While the American buildup in Southeast Asia began in 1965, President Johnson was unable to get the war adequately financed by the American taxpayer until 1968. The war was being fought on credit, other people's credit, the credit of those dollar holders abroad. The American government was simply printing money with the result that the United States went through one of the severest rounds of inflation since the Republic was founded. Until 1970, when the inflation got out of hand, Paul A. Volcker, the deputy treasury secretary for monetary affairs, thought the dollar's adjustment could be handled by somewhat greater flexibility for other currencies in the exchange markets, that is, by allowing them wider bands of fluctuation against the dollar. "It was the inflation that murdered us," he told a small group of correspondents in Rome's Excelsior Hotel in November, 1971.

By the middle of 1971 the evidence of economic slippage of the United States could be read starkly in the figures for foreign trade, which showed a deficit for the first time in the twentieth century, and in the American reserve figures. Ten years earlier, when gold reserves were still over $15 billion, President Kennedy was already worried. In July, 1971, despite what had been for years a de facto ban on dollar conversions into gold, the stocks had dropped to the $10 billion level. Perhaps even more significantly, the American overseas indebtedness to foreign official institutions had ballooned to more than $40 billion. Officially, therefore, the United States owed four times more than it could pay under the Bretton Woods arrangements. Washington was inflating not only the United States but the world. And conditions were to get much worse. By 1973 official dollar indebtedness had doubled to $80 billion.

It had all come about because the changing forces in the world prevented the United States from earning enough to finance its commitments. "When the Nixon administration came into office

[January , 1969]," Secretary of State William P. Rogers said in later 1971, "the United States was over-extended and under-appreciated." Aside from military expenditures, much of the money that was leaving the United States—capital outflows, the trade deficit, tourist spending, foreign aid—was being put to productive uses abroad. This was good for the foreign countries, because it helped create jobs. Dividend income returned to the United States, which helped big American corporations and gave the United States its biggest plus in the payments ledger. But it didn't create jobs in the United States at a time when jobs were needed. (Repatriated earnings of American subsidiaries abroad in the 1970s were running about \$2 billion a year higher than corporate capital outflows.)

Companies expanded overseas because production costs were lower in foreign countries and productivity rates higher, signs that the dollar was overvalued. Confirmation that the dollar's exchange rate was all wrong finally came with deterioration in the overseas commercial accounts. Those great surpluses of the early postwar years of the "dollar gap" had completely disappeared.

On August 15, 1971, following a period of heavy speculation against the dollar, mainly by international companies and banks moving funds out of the United States, President Nixon announced formal suspension of the dollar's convertibility into gold, a 15 percent tariff surcharge, and a series of measures to try to curb domestic inflation. He then invited other countries into currency negotiations to try to work out a new exchange rate for the dollar. At first the United States insisted that other countries had to upvalue, make trade concessions, and contribute more toward defense costs before the surcharge would be lifted. Finally, after a depression in the stock market and mounting anxiety over the possible outbreak of a trade war and worldwide recession, a compromise was struck in which the United States devalued against gold, other major countries either held their old parities or upvalued, and trade and defense negotiations were put off for later settlement. The agreement of December 18, 1971, the so-called Smithsonian Agreement because it was signed at the Smithsonian Institution in Washington, was the first multilateral currency realignment in history.

For a while the exchange markets settled down. After the disturbances connected with the float of the pound at mid-1972, there was actually a reflow of dollars back to the United States. But again peace was to be short-lived.

In the first three months of 1973, the monetary system itself was under attack and from the crisis that broke out over that period a new monetary system began to take shape. It came into being not by design but by the force of circumstances. Its main characteristics were floating rates with rules that would hopefully prevent exchange rate wars and foreign exchange controls to keep speculators at bay and maintain orderly market conditions.

What led to all this was the second devaluation of the dollar on February 12, 1973, fourteen months after the first, followed by a breakdown in confidence that forced closing of official trading in foreign exchange for more than two weeks in March while a series of crisis conferences were held in Paris and Brussels. It was essentially the story of the tailor with the prosperous mail-order business. Clients send in measurements and get splendid suits. One day the tailor wakes up to find the meter measures only 90 centimeters. He makes some changes and with some difficulties is able to continue the business. The next week the meter changes again and the tailor is barely able to keep up. A week later, the meter changes three times, and the poor tailor doesn't know what to do. Finally, he sends out word that clients must come to the shop if they want a suit. Business drops off and the tailor has to fire some of his personnel.

Luckily, up through 1973 the shrinking dollar did not cause any loss of jobs, but it did create a host of problems for the Europeans, and particularly France and Germany.

Because the Germans, for a variety of reasons including the need for a counterweight in the *Ostpolitik* negotiations with the Russians, wanted American troops to remain in Germany, Bonn showed more sympathy than France toward the United States. And with Congressional pressures rising to bring the troops home or at least reduce their numbers below the 300,000 level of the early 1970s, the Germans were even more receptive to American demands in hopes of checking neo-isolationist and protectionist forces in the United States. Of course, the troops would not remain in Europe forever. But they represented a major element in the status quo that all governments, even the administrations in Paris and Moscow, wanted to retain. For France they were assurance that German armies would not again cross the Rhine. But the French could never publicly admit this.

In addition to their different structural relationships with the United States, the French and Germans had different monetary philosophies. The French believed in dirigisme, which means a high degree of bureaucratic control over economic life. In Germany dirigisme smacked of the discredited National Socialist economic policies of Hjalmar Schacht, Hitler's financial wizard. The Germans said they believed in free market solutions to economic problems.

So when the excess dollars sloshed over Europe, France and Germany, though trying to reconcile their differences for the sake of an EEC monetary union, were again shoved into the ring for a fight that neither country wanted or was prepared for. Valery Giscard d'Estaing, the haughty French finance minister, and Karl Schiller, the German economics minister, not a little supercilious himself, were the two principals, and their personalities clashed as well as their views. As *Le Figaro* put it, both maintained a "cordial dislike" of each other. Rules of political economics went by the board. It was the right-of-center Giscard who was the dirigist and the socialist Schiller who plumped for the free market. So deep was the disagreement between the two men that the monetary union plans were shelved from the spring of 1971 to the spring of 1972. It took a Brandt-Pompidou summit meeting and the eventual resignation of Schiller to get things moving again.

When the second crisis erupted in 1973 France and Germany hit it off better. Along with four other countries in the enlarged Common Market of nine, France and Germany decided to link their currencies in a stable relationship—the old "snake" again—while the six as a unit floated against the dollar. As currencies no longer had to maintain fixed limits against the dollar, it became the same without a tunnel or, as wags quickly dubbed it, the snake in the grass. The other four were Belgium, Holland, Luxembourg, and

Denmark. Britain and Italy continued their independent floats.Ireland, dependent on Britain because of her close trading relationship, did what Britain did. These three promised that they would seek ways to participate in the joint float sometime later. So in the face of the forces of disintegration unleashed by the dollar glut, the EEC retained, at least through early 1973, most of its monetary initiative. The health and length of life of the snake would depend on the ability of the EEC nations to harmonize economic performance, to bring their rates of growth, unemployment, and inflation together and to transfer resources from rich to poor regions.

In Paris diplomatic circles in the early 1970s one often heard these words: *"Il faut piéger les Allemands en Europe."* ("We must trap the Germans in the construction of Europe.") In other words, the Common Market was a means of maintaining peace and stability in Western Europe, something of immeasurable benefit to the United States, which fought in two European civil wars this century, and to the rest of the world.

> In the process leading toward Western European integration we have always known that, as Western Europeans developed collective policies and a collective identity, their views and ours would not always coincide and transitory differences would develop. In the economic field this has happened from time to time over the years, but we have resolved our disputes without damage to the underlying strength of our relationship.

Those disputes referred to by Secretary of State William P. Rogers in a speech in December, 1971, were bound to get sharper as the decade proceeded, and it was almost certain that if Europe moved in the direction of political union (which was what monetary union was all about), the underlying strength of the relationship would change. The hope was that the deep respect for liberal democratic institutions in both the United States and an enlarged Common Market (with the leavening force of Britain and the liberal Scandinavian democracies) would help insure there would be no rupture.

9

Ostpolitik:
The Hazards and Hopes

A quarter-century after World War II, the legions of NATO and the Warsaw Pact were still facing each other across a divided continent. Borders were sealed by barbed wire, concertina rolls, machinegun towers, and malevolently roving searchlights—searchlights that skittered nightly across the Wall and empty rows of warehouses that separated the two Berlins.

Yet, in twenty-five years the relationships had altered substantially. A French word, *détente* (relaxation), had crept into the English language to express the new situation. While military units were still dug in, a military confrontation seemed far less likely. The fears for security were far less acute as the peoples of East and West Europe struggled for advancement, demanding higher standards of living, more consumer goods, and a measure of independence from their superpower patrons.

In the Soviet Union itself more reliance on profits and greater powers for managers were hailed as a cure for the nation's ills as far back as the Twenty-third Soviet Party Congress of 1966. Five years later, in April, 1971, at the Twenty-fourth Congress, party leader Leonid I. Brezhnev told the delegates in his opening address:

> We have had many years of heroic history behind us, comrades, when millions of Communists and non-party people conscientiously accepted privations and hardships, were content with the bare essentials and denied themselves the right to demand any special amenities. But that which was explicable and natural in the

past, when other tasks, other undertakings, stood in the forefront, is unacceptable in present conditions.

A resolution of the Communist Party Central Committee and the Council of Ministers, published in January, 1972,* called for more and better goods, packaged foods, self-service stores, polite clerks, and even the creation of a consumer research council.

The Soviet Union had already dramatically showed that it could not ignore consumer needs when, in 1968, it ordered construction by the Fiat Automobile Company of Turin, Italy, of a plant beside the Volga River to turn out 660,000 cars a year by the mid-1970s.† This and other undertakings would eventually have an impact on the allocation of resources, meaning less money for guns. "Once the Soviet people begin to move about on their own wheels, they will never be the same again," George Ball wrote in *The Discipline of Power.* "They will insist on paved roads and borscht bars and jukeboxes and filling stations and motels—and maybe, god knows, even clean rest rooms." But all this would probably take an awfully long time. The domestic price of a Zhiguli, what the Russians called their new Fiats, was equivalent to three or four years' wages for even the well-paid worker, and closer to ten years' for others. And demand for private cars so outweighed the supply that the average Russian considered himself lucky just to get on the waiting list, which was several years long. By 1972, total car ownership in a population of 240 million was only 1.5 million. Some 200 million Americans, by contrast, owned 100 million cars.

"It is only a step," the London *Economist* said in the spring of 1971, "from being an aggressive consumer who demands material

*By the end of 1975, the resolution called for 40 percent of total retail trade volume to be dispensed through self-service outlets. One reason for this push was the sheer inefficiency of traditional stores, where a customer had to stand in line to select what he wanted, stand in line to pay, then join a third line to collect what he bought.

†During the Stalin era, cars were considered a luxury and production was limited largely to vehicles for official use. Khrushchev (1953–64) considered car ownership by the public to represent a wasteful use of resources and began promoting instead the development of an extensive car rental network, which never materialized.

satisfaction after years of neglect to becoming a militant citizen demanding the return of his political rights." Brezhnev's problem in the early 1970s was finding ways to check the development of that militant citizenry without resorting to the discredited Stalinist modes of repression. One reason why the Russian leadership moved so slowly in supplying consumer needs was that it was both cautious and afraid.

Yugoslavia became the economic model for Eastern Europe. Breaking with Stalin in 1948, Marshal Tito embarked on a gigantic program to turn an agricultural society into a prosperous industrial state. Yugoslav reformers emphasized profits, self-management, and a free market. Some of the same ideas were being advanced in the Soviet Union by Professor Evsei Liberman of Kharkov University and applied initially to improve the efficiency of tractor production. The goal was to shift from the orthodox practices of centralized planning to a system in which business enterprises produce what they want, compete for domestic and foreign markets, and share their profits with their workers. One of the effects, however, was that the authority of the Communist party could be weakened. The key function of running the economy was taken from the party and given to the skilled technocrats, who might or might not be party members. There was not a wide gap between greater economic and greater political freedom.

With these implications for the Communist power structure, economic reform proceeded slowly and in a contradictory fashion throughout the bloc and even in Yugoslavia. The Soviet leaders were prepared to accept it so long as the primacy of the Communist party was not challenged.

On the night of August 20–21, 1968, General Ivan G. Pavlovsky, Soviet deputy defense minister, moved 250,000 Warsaw Pact troops into Czechoslovakia and ordered the arrest of the country's progressive leaders. That brutal intervention, in which more than two hundred Czechoslovaks were killed, was mounted because, in the view of the Kremlin, Czechoslovak party leader Alexander Dubcek seemed to be losing control. He had sown the seeds of democracy, perhaps unwittingly, by opening up Czechoslovakia's borders, giving the green light to economic reform, loosening censorship, permitting the recorded expression of minority opinions within the party, and even allowing non-Communist political "clubs" to take root. So severe was the Soviet repression that by 1972 the political, intellectual, cultural, social, and economic life of the tragic state was still undergoing a purge. Under the occupation, conservative forces moved back into positions of power, and Dubcek was banished to his native Slovakia, where he worked as a garage foreman for the Bratislava city parks department. As liberal students, journalists, intellectuals, and other "counter-revolutionaries" who had played a part in the Prague Spring of liberalization in 1968 were rounded up and put on trial, fears grew for the safety of Dubcek, who, in 1972, was still living quietly on the outskirts of the Slovak capital with his wife and three sons, leading a better life, up to that point at least, than most earlier fallen Communist leaders. Gustav Husak, the new party leader who had spent eight years in prison while Czechoslovakia had been in the Stalinist grip of former party leader Antonin Novotny, pledged that there would be no political trials. But presumably he had to give way under pressure from the hardliners in the party leadership who had shamelessly welcomed the Soviet intervention in August, 1968, as necessary to snuff out the counter-revolutionary fires.

The Soviets justified the intervention by inventing the Brezhnev Doctrine of limited sovereignty, under which Soviet armies had the right to intervene throughout Eastern Europe if the principles of Marxist-Leninism, as interpreted by the Kremlin, were in danger. There were repeated rumors in the postinvasion period that Moscow would also apply the doctrine against Yugoslavia and Rumania, which, like Czechoslovakia under Dubcek, were also following separate roads to socialism. Even while Yugoslavia had started going its separate way a generation earlier and Rumania was becoming more and more energetically independent (courting both China and the United States), the Kremlin leadership stopped short of intervening in these two countries for a number of reasons. For one, there was the uncertainty of the Western response. NATO was caught off guard by the Czechoslovak invasion, but leaving aside this technical failing (a result in large measure of superior radar-blocking equipment by the Soviet forces), the Western allies were hardly disposed to intervene in Czechoslovakia and risk a major war. American warnings against wider Soviet moves, together with what in both the Rumanian and Yugoslav cases almost certainly would have been far more active resistance by the local armies and civilian populations, made new invasions for the normally cautious Kremlin leadership a much riskier affair—especially since the long-range policy was still to achieve a relaxation of tensions with the West. "You cannot have detente in Europe and war in the Balkans," a Yugoslav official told *New York Times* correspondent Alfred Friendly, Jr., in 1971. Another major reason was that control of the Communist party in both Rumania and Yugoslavia was unchallenged. With the leadership strong in both countries there was stability, one of the major aims of Soviet policy within the bloc.

Czechoslovakia under Dubcek was not stable. Strategically situated in central Europe between West Germany and the Soviet border, Czechoslovakia was a country where, in the spring and summer of 1968, it looked like anything might happen. The winds of change were blowing in Prague as they never had in Belgrade and Bucharest. In fact, the model for Prague's liberal reformers was Willy Brandt. Perhaps Moscow might have applied other pressures against Dubcek, who as an unsophisticated party bureaucrat elevated suddenly to high office probably did not fully appreciate what was happening. But the Kremlin was obsessed at that time with China. And to deal with that problem it needed stability on the west. Said Zygmunt Broniarek, chief correspondent for the Warsaw party newspaper *Trybuna Ludu,* sipping twelve-year-old scotch one evening in August, 1968, in Prague's Alcron Hotel, "The Soviet Union had to secure its western frontier."

Michel Debré, the French foreign minister at the time, called the invasion of Czechoslovakia "an accident on the road" to detente, and while that comment may have been seen at the time as representing a cold, cynical disregard for the Prague tragedy, it was to prove a surprisingly accurate assessment of the situation. The invasion neither checked economic liberalization from spreading through the bloc nor did it sap the spirit of national independence.

Neither did it stop West Germany on one side and Russia and Poland on the other from drawing closer together to try to heal the still open wounds of World War II. As soon as Czechoslovakia was quiet again (with its frontiers sealed and its liberals incarcerated), Moscow and the Western nations renewed their efforts to relax tensions, but this time it was done in a more coordinated way, bloc to bloc. Neither side was much troubled by moral considerations.

Moscow's objectives were the confirmation of the postwar division of Europe, the weakening if not the destruction of the European Common Market, and finally the easing out of Europe of the American military and economic presence. Moscow sought Western recognition of the postwar boundaries between East and West to maintain its grip over the Eastern bloc and to insure stability in case hostilities arose on the China frontier. Wary of the increasing economic strength of the EEC and its potential political muscle if the states were ever united, Moscow offered both peace and pan-European cooperation to try to undermine the Western structure. With the United States out, Russia could become the dominant power. Western Europe would then become "Finlandized"—an infelicitous word invented to describe creation of a neutral region friendly to Moscow. Once its European hegemony was established Moscow could then more comfortably deal with rising consumer expectations both in the Soviet Union and Eastern Europe.

These were compelling motives for the Soviet Union. As for the Western Europeans, they badly wanted to reconcile East-West differences and to reduce the tensions on the continent. But they were determined also to move forward with their plans for economic union, forging, at perhaps some later date, a political union.

The Soviet Union had always considered the Common Market as a Cold War instrument. Neither Moscow nor the Eastern European capitals (until the 1970s) recognized it in any formal sense. Communist parties in the West reviled it as a tool of NATO and American neo-colonialism. But because the Community was such a large factor in world trade, because it lay right next door to Eastern Europe, and because trade policies for the Communist countries were about to be decided in Brussels at the Community level, the Common Market was difficult to ignore.

The Russians and especially the Eastern Europeans were feeling increasingly uncomfortbale over trade diversion. Integration in the West inevitably meant some discrimination against Eastern goods, especially farm products in competition with those produced inside the Community. To forestall what might have been a crisis-torn rupture, the Community postponed the effectiveness of its common commercial policy for Communist countries until 1975. Individual members could continue having bilateral trade relations with individual members of the Eastern bloc. But all the bilateral agreements had to expire by 1975. If the Eastern countries and Russia wanted to do more business with Western Europe, they would have to deal with the Community institutions. In April, 1972, the Moscow party leader Leonid I. Brezhnev announced that the Soviet Union recognized the reality of the Common Market, anticipating the moment when Moscow would have to deal in trade negotiations with Brussels, but at the same time he said that Westerners had to recognize the reality of Communist Eastern Europe.

The Communists had formed their own economic bloc, the Council of Mutual Economic Assistance (Comecon), to counteract the pressures in the West, but vastly different levels of economic development within the bloc, the absence of market-based pricing standards or effective competition, and the demands, not for Eastern goods but Western technology, combined to inhibit Comecon's development. So in the broad strategic design Moscow would have liked nothing better than to see the EEC disintegrate. But because of the trade pressures all the Communist countries had to come to some accommodation, especially after January 1, 1973, when Britain, Ireland, and Denmark joined the EEC. "It seems increasingly easy nowadays," wrote Michael Simmons, East European correspondent of the *Financial Times,* in 1971, "to meet an ambitious young Communist who is writing a heavily-documented doctoral thesis on 'The Effects on My Country of a Larger EEC.'"

Yugoslavia became the first Eastern European nation to deal with the Community's institutions by negotiating and signing a trade agreement in 1970 that chiefly guaranteed it greater markets for beef exports to Italy. Rumania in 1972 formally petitioned the EEC to give it the trade preferences on industrial and semi-industrial goods that the EEC was already providing for some ninety developing countries. Poland, Czechoslovakia, and Rumania were members of the GATT. Hungary had an application on the table in 1972, while Bulgaria had observer status. They were all hoping through their GATT associations for better relations with the Common Market, perhaps through improved facilities for selling farm products, which, with raw materials, made up the majority of their exports to the West.

For the Eastern Europeans it was a delicate balancing act to promote their own national interests with the Common Market while not going so far as to attract Soviet tanks to their cities.

Rumania asserted itself in the early 1960s, in response to former Soviet party leader Nikita S. Khrushchev's plans to keep it forever in inferior status within the Comecon bloc as an agricultural supplier. This was part of the Soviet proposal to promote a specialization of activities within Comecon that would insure Soviet economic as well as political hegemony. The Rumanian leadership reacted violently.

Party chief Nicolai Ceausescu not only stepped up the country's industrialization program but began shifting Rumania's trade so that by the late 1960s more than half of its business was with the West. In the political sector, he began flirting with Peking, absolutely refused to permit Warsaw Pact maneuvers on Rumanian soil, and, two years after the Warsaw Pact invasion of Czechoslovakia, defiantly invited President Nixon to Rumania.

While asserting his independence, Ceausescu retained perhaps the tightest party control of any Eastern European leader. There was never any toying with democracy the way there had been during the Prague Spring. Ceausescu thus maintained the Kremlin's principal objective in the bloc—stability.

After the 1956 revolution in Hungary, power in Budapest went to Janos Kadar, who was almost universally reviled as a brainwashed puppet of the Soviet secret police. After consolidating his power, Kadar opened up the pressure valves in 1968 with a major economic reform program aimed at giving consumers some of the products they had been deprived of since the war. Kadar was doing what Dubcek and his economic chief, Ota Sik, had tried in Czechoslovakia, but Kadar acted without doing anything that could be considered as undermining the authority of the party.

The Hungarians freed their market mechanisms, geared production to what they could sell, both domestically and in the West where they could earn hard currency, and emphasized the profit motive as an incentive for efficiency. Plant managers were no longer tied to rigid wage policies. They had to think in terms of profits. About forty of the largest enterprises were authorized in 1972 to deal directly with Western concerns and determine their own investment areas.

By 1972 there were the trappings of Western-style competition in the retail market, with price wars being fought by competing enterprises and increased use of advertising and promotional gimmicks. A consumer research magazine appeared in Budapest in 1970, the first in Eastern Europe. Called *Nagyiti* (Magnifying Glass), it sought, according to its editors, to "put pressure on industry and trade" by guiding consumers in their decisions. In an early issue nine brands of men's shirts were studied. All but a Yugoslav import were panned. Similarly, it surveyed seven makes of refrigerators. The only Soviet model, a Saratov, got a "so-so" rating because it was "out of date."

Economic reforms were signs of recognition by the leadership of the Eastern bloc of a tide of popular feeling that could not be easily suppressed.* Even in postinvasion Czechoslovakia, while liberals were being purged, a policy never acknowledged by the government was carried out to keep factory workers content by giving them relatively high pay. Gustav Husak was shrewder in this regard than Polish party leader Wladislaw Gomulka, who fell from power at the end of 1970 because of a worker revolt.

Just before Christmas that year the Warsaw apparatchiks an-

---

*Appeals to the consumer and understanding of market psychology were still at a primitive stage. A tale of some Rumanian businessmen with a toaster illustrates the point. The Rumanians, according to Dan Morgan, the Eastern European correspondent of the *Washington Post,* had devised an excellent toaster that could be sold in the United States market for one-tenth the price of an American-made toaster. But the toasted bread would not pop up. All the Americans had to do, the Rumanians said, was to give up their absurd preference for pop-up toasters.

nounced a dramatic rise in food prices along with a two-year wage freeze. Colossal economic mismanagement by the regime meant that workers would be forced to accept a sharp cut in their living standards. This was too much for the men who worked in the relatively prosperous Baltic port cities of Gdansk, Gdynia, Sopot, and Szczecin.

Workers from the Gdansk shipyards, wearing their hard hats and swinging their stevedore hooks, were the backbone of an angry crowd that marched into the center of Gdansk to protest the food price increases on Monday, December 14. Refusing to disperse, the marchers were struck by elements from the militia, and as the first casualties were taken the industrial workers in Gdansk and other port cities, rallying around the shipyard men, laid down their tools and began a general strike, an event that was nearly unprecedented in a Communist country.

As the strikes spread from the port cities to other areas of the country, the government was forced either to make concessions or gear itself for a full-scale worker revolution. The government opted for the former course and began negotiating with strike committees that had been formed in the factories, something it would never have done under normal circumstances. In these strike committees the workers had reinvented their own form of democracy. Each committee was composed of elected delegates. Party membership was not a bar to election, but neither was rank in the party regarded as a qualification.

Eyewitness reports brought out the extraordinary daring of the crowds. When soldiers were besieged in the Gdansk party building, they fired a warning burst through the windows, but their shots, according to the local paper *Glos Wybrzeza* (Voice of the Coast), were greeted by "a chorus of laughter." The paper said that the following day "a group of youths decided to run at the tanks to test the reaction of the soldiers. . . . it ends in tragedy. . . . there are two dead and 11 wounded."

Officially, the number of persons killed in Gdansk and Gdynia was placed at forty-five, but unofficial reports mentioned hundreds dead and said the number of wounded may have run into the thousands. Fighting had spread as far as two hundred miles westward to Szczecin, which for ten days was under administrative control of strike committees. A strike newspaper, *Glos Szczecina* (Voice of Szczecin), was published during this period.

The riots led to the ouster of Party leader Wladyslaw Gomulka and his replacement by Edward Gierek, a former coal miner who led the party organization in Katowice, Poland's leading industrial city, a smog-laden depression in the coal and steel region of Silesia. Under Gierek, Silesia came to be known as the Polish Katanga. As Moise Tshombe ran Katanga as his personal fief in the early days of Congolese independence, so Gierek was the undisputed boss in Silesia.

Gomulka had come to power in almost identical circumstances after the "bread and freedom" riots in Poznan in 1956. Because of the parallel some wondered whether conditions would really get any better under Gierek or whether he, too, would eventually make a mess of the economy. His record in Silesia provided some hope. The workers of the province were the best paid in Poland and, mainly because of Gierek's unchallenged power within his domain, they were not hit by the wage freeze. During the troubles in the north, they stayed on their jobs. It was often said that if there were shortages of sausages, ham, vodka, or television sets elsewhere in the country, the shops of Silesia would be well stocked for Gierek's miners.

Gierek did not announce any important changes in policy. But he did indicate that he would press for more consumer-oriented production and less centralization of industry. Anything more might well have provoked the Russians, who were strangely quiet during the port city outbreaks. His modest statements impressed many Poles, but others remembered Gomulka's promises in 1956 and his failure to deliver.

Both Gomulka and Gierek said they would try to improve relations with the Roman Catholic Church, which had remained a power the equal of a strong political party in opposition. Gomulka ended up in interminable arguments with the church and finally broke contact. By March, 1971, Gierek had arranged the first high-level meeting between church and state in eight years—between Stefan Cardinal Wyszynski, the Polish primate, and Piotr Jaroszewicz, the new premier. Three months later, the government gave the church full title to nearly seven thousand former German church buildings in the territories acquired from Germany after World War II. And in February, 1972, the church was freed from the obligation of reporting income and expenditure and of maintaining records of assets. In return for these long-sought concessions, Cardinal Wyszynski petitioned Pope Paul VI to redraw diocesan boundaries in what had been Germany to reflect the postwar territorial changes.

Declaring that the port cities' conflict reflected "honest attitudes and motives," Gierek acted without fanfare throughout 1971 and 1972 to improve the flow of information between rulers and the ruled, boost family allowances and pensions, and enlarge home market supplies of goods. This helped reinforce the truce between workers and the regime, but it didn't get rid of one of the biggest social problems, plant absenteeism. A couplet that went the rounds in the factories perhaps explained why:

> Whether you work or you shirk
> You're sure to be paid because the Party's afraid.

Worker uprisings, while infrequent, had taken place within the bloc as early as 1953. On June 17 of that year the workers of East Germany rose in revolt against the norms imposed on them by party leader Walter Ulbricht, and for twenty-four hours the future of Communism in what was to become Russia's strongest satellite seemed to hang in the balance. In a play called *The Plebeians Rehearse the Uprising,* Günter Grass recounts that all that revolution needed was a leader, but that the one man who could have provided a voice, playwright Bertolt Brecht, had spent his life telling Germans they should live without heroes. Brecht passed, and the revolution died as Soviet tanks rumbled into the streets of East Berlin.

In Berlin in 1953, in Poznan and Budapest in 1956, in Prague in 1968, and in Gdansk and the other port cities in 1970, the picture was much the same—women shaking their fists and taunting soldiers, youths tossing stones at tanks, screaming their defiance, and getting killed. This reporter, in Prague on August 21, 1968, saw part of the battle for the Prague Radio building on Vinohradska Street as Soviet troops tried to occupy it, forcing tanks through flaming barricades of overturned cars and derailed trolleys. Waving Czechoslovak flags, youths ran out into the street to try to set the Soviet tanks afire with flaming rags, newspapers, and branches from fallen trees. Others tossed mattresses, wooden crates, and garbage cans onto the tanks. One tank was left a flaming wreck and two retreated in flames a few hundred yards from the Radio building. Four young Czechoslovaks were slain, one with his head blown off, after a machine gun from a Soviet tank opened up on their truck. One youth with a slit abdomen was lifted into an ambulance, barely alive. Earlier in the day Soviet machine gunners had raked the façade of the National Museum, at the head of Vaclavske Namesti. A student, tears in her eyes, looked up at the damage and said, "Not even the Germans did that."

In 1955 the Soviet Union ended the occupation of Austria by agreeing with the United States, Britain, and France, the other occupying powers, to sign a State Treaty of peace. Austria's independence and territorial integrity were restored, but at a price set by the Russians of large reparations, strictly observed neutrality, and Austria's exclusion from any type of union with the renascent West Germany. Although the smaller country's efforts to accommodate itself to economic integration in the West were severely hampered, the conditions were readily accepted. It marked the Soviet Union's single backward step since the war in Central Europe, and while not fully understood was deeply appreciated by Austrians.

Against the stirrings in the East came the attempt by one of the Western leaders, Willy Brandt, who had become chancellor of West Germany in the fall of 1969—the first postwar Socialist chancellor—to bring about a completely fresh relationship between East and West. Brandt, who won the Nobel Peace Prize for his efforts, was the natural-born son of a salesgirl in the Baltic port city of Lübeck. He never knew his father and was raised by his mother's father, a gentle idealist who was also a Communist, from whom the young Willy drew much of his compassion for the sufferings of others.

In 1970 Brandt signed nonaggression treaties in Moscow and

Warsaw in which, for the first time in twenty-five years, Bonn recognized the status quo—the frontiers of Europe as they actually existed. Earlier governments had refused to acknowledge the loss of prewar Germany's eastern territories and had insisted that the Communist regime of East Germany be absorbed in an eventual reunification.

German security, Brandt believed, depended on clearing away the "myths" of the "temporary" division of Germany and the loss of the territories to Poland and Russia, and on beginning a reconciliation with Eastern Europe. To describe what was happening, German Foreign Minister Walter Scheel repeated a phrase of Bismarck's: "We have opened a door to the East."

The treaties effectively wrote off 39,000 square miles of territory of the former Reich, an area once occupied by some 6 million Germans. This was the land that Poland took in stretching its western frontier to the Oder and Neisse rivers. The river line separated Poland and East Germany. The East German Communist regime had already recognized the loss as one of its first acts as a new state. Many West Germans, except for unadaptable older refugees and some nationalists, accepted that the territories were irrecoverable, but earlier Bonn governments had taken the position that Germany's claim would be abandoned only as part of an overall peace settlement reuniting East and West Germany. Tentative Allied agreement at Potsdam had left the disputed territory merely under "Polish administration." The situation had produced only sterile dialogue at best, since Moscow was far from willing to accept German reunification.

The Polish-German treaty entailed "repatriation" of leftover Germans in the frontier regions and, when fulfilled, this provision was almost bound to aggravate a centuries-old homesickness among 400,000 other Germans living in Rumania. That ethnic minority had to be told by Ceausescu where its first loyalties lay. "The homeland of the population of German nationality . . . is Rumania, because here is where they have lived for hundreds of years. It is difficult for someone whose ancestors came to Rumania 800 years ago to say, 'I came from another place.' " In early 1970, Germans were being allowed to leave Poland by the hundreds in anticipation of treaty ratification.

Brandt went further than simply signing his name to the arid prose of two treaties. In an act of atonement that appeared to symbolize one of those turning points of history, Brandt, while still in Warsaw, knelt before the granite monument to the half-million Jews of the city killed by the Nazis. For millions of people in Europe, he seemed to be saying, "Now the war is really over."

Implicit in this Eastern policy (*Ostpolitik* in German) was the challenge to the Eastern bloc to expand its dealings with the West and perhaps allow greater freedom for the Eastern peoples. Brandt believed that Moscow wanted expanded trade with West Germany and Western Europe so much that it was ready for an easier political relationship. Fifty years earlier Lenin had remarked, "The steppe has to be turned into a bread factory and Krupp must help us with it." Time had, if anything, intensified the Eastern need for Western technology. The separate development of East and West under two different economic disciplines had left the East far behind.

Yet, despite the barbed wire and the machine gun towers, the East was never completely cut off. There had been increasing contacts, in which the Eastern European peoples saw for themselves that they were far behind.

Brandt's appeal was to the young in both camps, tired of the clichés of the Cold War. Almost half of West Germany's population in 1970 had been born after 1940. These people saw no reason why Germany should not resume its proper place in deciding the course of events in Europe. Orwell's 1984 vision of youths reduced to robots in a totalitarian system because they knew nothing better dominated early postwar thinking and generated deep pessimism about the future of the world. Communist totalitarianism seemed bound to become absolute and irreversible in Eastern Europe as a younger generation grew up knowing nothing of another world. But, in fact, it was the young who were leading the revolts against the Communist establishment. At the Charles University in Prague, Western journalists found sharp and accurate perceptions about life in the West by students who had never lived outside communism.

Even before Brandt's opening to the East, the West Germans were deeply involved in trade with the Eastern bloc. The volume of West German exports to the East in 1969 was at least three times that of any other Western country. Much trade was with East Germany, a rarely publicized factor in the spectacular industrial advances made by that country. (East Germany made some of the best computers in the Comecon bloc. Its television sets and home appliances were also of top quality.) But West German businessmen were also signing deals in Warsaw, Budapest, Bucharest, Sofia, and Prague. Of all foreign languages, it was German that was heard most often in Eastern European hotel lobbies and bars. The Warsaw or Budapest taxicab driver perhaps knew a few words of English, but he often fully understood German.

For many German industrialists Eastern Europe represented both a major growth market and a natural outlet for industrial and consumer products. The German government had also been generous with credits to enable the Eastern European purchasing agencies to buy German goods. *Ostpolitik* held out the promise of even larger credits and perhaps even the establishment of German-owned factories in the labor-surplus regions of the East, such as Poland. Faced with their constant shortage of workers, German industrialists often spoke of the natural labor market to the east.

Brandt aimed initially at a quid pro quo of modest concessions for West Berlin before turning the treaties over to the Bundestag for ratification. Throughout the postwar period, that city's legal status as part of the Federal Republic had never been clear.

West Berlin is not really tied constitutionally to West Germany. In 1949, when the West German constitution was promulgated, the Allied High Commission, then sovereign in the Western zones of occupation, had objected to a formulation of Article 23 of the constitution, which declared that Berlin was a state of the Federal Republic. Article 23 was retained anyway, but in practice the clause was honored mainly in ceremonial ways. West Berlin sent twenty-two representatives to the Bundestag, but they were delegated, not elected, and did not have the power to vote. Occasionally, West German party and government meetings were held in the city to emphasize its links with the West.

As an island of capitalist prosperity 110 miles inside East Germany, West Berlin was an embarrassment to the Soviet and East

German leaders, and, because of its never clearly defined attachment to West Germany, they periodically put pressure on the city's surface transportation links to the West, making life uncomfortable for the 2 million residents.

Khrushchev once remarked, "Berlin is the West's Achilles heel. Whenever I kick it, they say ouch." The Soviet leadership maintained that Berlin was a "separate political entity" and backed this up with a policy aimed at trying to squeeze out the Western military presence without triggering a war. The East German regime, while calling all Berlin its capital, had joined the Soviets in offering to make West Berlin autonomous—a free city—if the Allies would just get out.

As the quid pro quo for ratification of the Warsaw and Moscow treaties, Brandt won concessions from Moscow and its client state East Germany that would improve conditions for West Berliners and enable the city to remain a Western enclave.

Moscow, anxious to have the treaties ratified so as to consolidate its sphere of influence in Eastern Europe, signaled its willingness to make concessions by entering into a new round of "Big Four" talks on Berlin's future. On September 3, 1971, a Berlin treaty which, in Secretary of State William P. Rogers' words brought "practical improvements in and around the city without altering the status of Berlin or diminishing our rights and responsibilities there," was signed in a neoclassic building in West Berlin's Kleist Park by ambassadors from the United States, Britain, France, and the Soviet Union. For the United States, Ambassador Kenneth Rush said that the agreement was a sign of the Soviet Union's desire to move from confrontation to negotiation. Soviet Ambassador Pyotr A. Abrasimov said, in heavily-accented German: *"Ende gut, alles gut"* (All's well that ends well).

In the Berlin agreement, which was followed up by technical talks between the two Germanys on the concrete steps to be put into effect, Moscow undertook to assure that West German access to the city would be "unimpeded" and that communications between citizens of West Berlin and the surrounding regions of East Germany and East Berlin would be improved. The point was to remove the threat of East German harassment of rail, barge, and train traffic that had been a feature of life for the city since 1948 and to punch a few more holes in the Berlin Wall, allowing more West Berliners to cross over into East Berlin and East Germany. Officially they had been barred from East Berlin since 1966, and from East Germany proper since 1952. Thousands of West Berliners were able to take advantage of this provision as early as Easter, 1972, in tearful reunions with relatives and friends in both East Berlin and East Germany.

For their part the Western allies continued to accept that West Berlin was still not a part of West Germany and undertook to prevent the Bonn government from carrying out "constitutional or official acts" in West Berlin, as it had done as recently as 1969 by electing President Gustav Heinemann there. And since talks had to be carried on between East and West German authorities to implement the treaty, Bonn would be giving further recognition to the German Democratic Republic (East Germany's official name, cited seven times in the Big Four treaty).*

Moscow had long ago pulled East Berlin into the Soviet sector of Germany and then said, in effect, "What's ours is ours, what's yours is negotiable." It could do this because West Berlin was vulnerable. West Berlin was still vulnerable in 1972, but much less so.

When Konrad Adenauer was elected the first postwar chancellor of Germany in 1949, the country began a two-decade period of close

---

*The opposition Christian Democrats saw the Brandt moves as continuing the permanent division of Germany and therefore opposed ratification of the Moscow-Bonn goodwill treaty in the Bundestag. A "letter on German unity," stating the Brandt government's understanding that the treaty does not rule out the possibility of peaceful reunification was appended to the Bonn-Moscow treaty to try to overcome the CDU objection. When it looked as if it would be more difficult than anyone expected to ratify the treaty, Brandt announced that the "letter on German unity" would be brought to the "official attention" of the Supreme Soviet, thereby giving it a stamp of approval. The Kremlin was torn between the East German Communists, who considered division of the country irrevocable, and its own devoutly sought after aims in the West in which West German ratification figured as the kingpin. After extensive debate and intraparty wrangling the treaties with Poland and Russia were finally ratified in May, 1972, in the West German Bundestag.

cooperation with the West. But over the longer term of German history this postwar period represented a break from the pattern of policies that had brought Germany into closer contact with the East than the West. It was in the East that Germany's main expansion came as early as under the Teutonic knights and later under Bismarck and Hitler. Germans had settled thorughout the eastern lands, influencing the cultural and linguistic development as far east as Russia itself. The Russian Czars drew their wives from the German nobility, and under Peter the Great the Russian army was transformed to the Prussian model. It was the ideas of a German Jew, Karl Marx, that transformed the Russian social, economic, and political system. And it was Lenin who gave the Germans their biggest break in World War I. The German general staff used him as a time bomb, transporting him in a sealed railroad car across Eastern Europe to help take the Czarist armies out of the war after the Russian revolution in 1917. The treaty of Brest Litovsk, which finally ended the war for the Russians in 1918, gave the Germans for a brief period control of Europe east of the Rhine and enabled German divisions to be shifted from the eastern to the western front.

Between the two wars the two countries reached agreements with unhappy consequences, which were brought to mind again during the debate over *Ostpolitik*. At Rapallo in 1922 the Soviets secretly permitted Germany to develop new weapons in Russia in violation of the Treaty of Versailles. Publicly the two countries simply announced they had agreed to renounce all claims to war indemnities, to resume diplomatic relations, and to encourage commercial exchanges. Then, on August 24, 1939, Joachim von Ribbentrop, Hitler's foreign minister, met with Stalin and Molotov in Moscow to sign a nonaggression treaty. A secret agreement was tacked onto it, dividing the whole of Eastern Europe into Russian and German spheres of influence and partitioning Poland. Four days later Hitler invaded Poland to start World War II.

Even during the war, according to the British military historian Sir Basil Liddell Hart, the two countries' proclivity for making secret agreements came to the fore. Early in 1943, after Hitler had invaded Russia, Soviet Foreign Minister Molotov met von Ribbentrop behind the German lines to negotiate a separate peace. Liddell

Hart, in his *History of the Second World War*, quotes German military officers who attended as technical advisers as saying that von Ribbentrop put forward as a condition that Russia's postwar frontier should run along the Dnieper River, while Molotov said he wanted the original prewar frontier restored. They could come to no agreement, and the talks were broken off when it was reported that news of the meeting had leaked out to the Allies.

Brandt repeatedly told interviewers in 1970 and 1971 that he thought his *Ostpolitik* was safe because it was rooted in confidence in the American nuclear deterrent and in strong German participation in the creation of a united Western Europe. "West Germany is anchored to the West," Brandt declared in 1970. "We have not become friends of the Soviet Union or its system," Brandt told *New York Times* correspondent David Binder after a visit to the Kremlin's Black Sea holiday compound near Yalta to see Brezhnev in mid-September, 1971, "but rather we have become partners in a businesslike contract. . . ."

But there were others—within the political opposition in West Germany, in Washington, in Paris, and elsewhere in Western Europe—who voiced some misgivings over the whole Eastern adventure. Dean Acheson and George Ball, alumni of the State Department and ardent believers in a united Western Europe, were among the American skeptics. Acheson said that Brandt should be "slowed down in the mad race to Moscow." Ball said Brandt had legitimized the Soviets' Eastern European empire. "The treaty is useful to the Soviets, but what about the West?" Ball asked. "All that it offers West Germany," he continued, "is a promise of nonaggression, and one has only to recall Soviet tanks in Prague in 1968 to appreciate the total emptiness of such a pledge." Franz-Joseph Strauss, the conservative party leader in Bavaria, quoted Bismarck as saying "you don't make things move faster just by putting your watch ahead," in criticizing Brandt's policies while talking in 1971 to *New York Times* columnist C.L. Sulzberger.

Brandt was fully aware of his critics. But he thought he had the bulk of the German and the European people with him in his fresh approach to solve the musty problems of the Cold War.

10

The Quality of
Continental Life

The Paris of May, 1968, was something of a watershed in European social history. It had been possible until then to speak of "postwar Europe," after that it was not. As postwar Europe plunged into the past, the frustrations of a dynamically new society broke through the statistics. All the figures showed that housing was better, that social services were improving, that economic progress was being made, that cooperation on an international scale was possible. Europe was no longer in smoking ruins. Consumer needs were being met to some extent. But on a personal level this was no longer enough. Europe was still racked by inequalities.

In May, 1968, as the lilacs came into pale blossom in the Luxembourg Gardens, students at the Sorbonne demonstrated against the university's autocratic administration and anachronistic teaching methods and created a wave of protest that engulfed every major Western European country. The protests centered on far more than university reform. They were about the quality of life. The working man felt he wasn't getting a fair return on his labor. There were no longer the rubble heaps of war; nor were people still living in the bombed-out shells of buildings. But housing was still inadequate. Professor Jan Tinbergen, the Dutch Nobel Laureate in economics in 1969, talking with this reporter once, pronounced upon a failing of modern society—that no government had ever been able to build enough homes for its people.

There were the problems of overzealous police, women's rights, and immigration. There was the generation gap. "It was hard for him who had lived with one generation of men to plead now before another," Plutarch wrote, and these words could have applied to de Gaulle.

Students and workers felt left out of modern France, and just as the Common Market was linking the economies of Europe ever closer, so was it linking ideas. Never before did the Fiat worker in Turin, the Volkswagen worker in Wolfsburg, and the Renault worker at Boulogne-Billancourt have so much in common. It started in France because of forces at work that had much to do with the style and leadership of Genral de Gaulle. To some it was the Revolution of 1830 or of 1848 all over again.

Like John F. Kennedy, de Gaulle had little interest in domestic problems and preferred to focus on grandiose designs in foreign policy. He waved the tricolor, considering this adequate, forgetting that to his fellow Frenchmen a living wage, a TV, a place in a university, a car, a dishwasher, and a good August vacation were more important than *"Quebec Libre"* or the *"force de frappe."* Gaullist policy concentrated on a nuclear deterrent that was costing $2 billion a year and on building up vast hoards of gold to battle against American dollar hegemony. So intent was he on his foreign policy that he neglected the power base at home and ignored the signals that showed the stirrings of millions of Frenchmen. Prices were skyrocketing. Paris was becoming more expensive to live in than New York, supportable for Americans on American salaries but hardly comfortable for the Renault worker who was barely making a dollar an hour. Unemployment was mounting, especially among the youth. Job openings were few for the university graduates trained in the classics. Only a few could qualify for the *"Grandes Écoles,"* the French Ivy League, where the future was more assured. Peasants were blocking the roads with their surplus onions and potatoes, complaining that prices weren't good enough. Thousands of farmers were simply calling it quits and moving to the cities only to find it was tough to get a job. Regional differences were causing animosity. Administration was centralized in Paris, and money wasn't flowing fast enough to develop poorer districts in the southwest, in the coal-mining regions of Lorraine, in Brittany in the northwest.

There are 37,600 municipal councils in France, little ones for the villages and big ones for the cities, and then there is Paris. Paris had the balance of power, since it controlled the funds and appointed the prefect, or area governor. Projects which in a federalized country are handled locally, such as road and school building and public works, in France needed the stamp of Paris and the prefect. Sociologist Michael Crozier wrote in a book entitled *La Société Bloquée (The Blocked Society)* that France had "gone to the extreme of centralization, to the very point where we are blocked in a system that defies reform."*

The rigidity of society showed up also in the educational system. In France, and in fact all of Europe, higher education was available to relatively few students, a far lower proportion than in the United States. One reason was that there simply wasn't space enough. A low priority was given to university expansion programs. The selection process for a university, as a result, began at a far lower age than in the United States. A child's future was determined by his academic standing at the age of ten or eleven, making little allowance for late starters or those whose family backgrounds or cultural differences made it difficult to achieve high grades at an early age. Exams were designed to perpetuate a bourgeois elite. The selection process for the *Grandes Écoles* showed the same discrimination, in a more intense form. Legally these institutions, the real training ground for the government and business establishment, were open to all. And since it cost parents relatively little to maintain a student there, in sharp contrast to colleges in the United States, the poor were not excluded for being poor. But socially, the *Grandes Écoles* were something else again. The entrance requirements were slanted to favor those with a background and training available mainly to the privileged classes. The son of a graduate, as Sanche de Gramont observed in a portrait of France entitled *The French,* had a head start. Often he began preparing at the age of six. The percentage of peasant and working-class families in the *Grandes Écoles,* de Gramont wrote, was "almost nonexistent."

German, British, and Italian selection standards were similarly designed to keep privileges in the hands of the few and maintain

*Editions de Seuil, Paris, 1970, p. 210.

differences between the classes. The statistics showed a staggering underuse of brainpower in Europe. A study by the OECD showed that in the 1965–66 university year 22 percent of the youths in the United States in the relevant age group obtained a first university degree. The average in Europe was 5 percent. After the United States were: Canada (14 percent), the Soviet Union (14 percent), Japan (9.8 percent). In Britain, Belgium, and France it was between 4 and 5 percent. In Italy it was 3.5 percent, while Austria, West Germany, Switzerland, Denmark, and the Netherlands were all below 3 percent.

Even where attempts were made to increase the number of university places, these could hardly keep up with the demands of an increasing population. Starting early in the twentieth century universities were being built and expanded in the industrial cities of Britain to cater to local day students who couldn't make Oxford or Cambridge. These "redbrick" universities, named after the building material that was predominantly used, were never really sufficient in numbers or high enough in academic standing to shift the power away from the two medieval institutions.

A survey carried out by the European Graduate School of Business Administration in Fontainbleau found that European industry was run by a self-perpetuating upper-class elite. Three out of four top European executives were born into well-to-do families, while 16 percent came from middle-class background, and only 5 percent from low-income homes. A study by *Fortune* magazine in 1964 found that only 10.5 percent of American executives came from upper-class families.

With mounting frustrations, Frenchmen began questioning the wisdom of de Gaulle's policies. De Gaulle himself maintained an Olympian contempt for public opinion. The Fifth Republic's constitution gave the president enormous powers and a seven-year mandate. He was installed as a twentieth-century Bourbon sovereign and was not averse to consolidating his power by tightening up on state censorship, banning books, and firing critics of his administration in the state-owned television network.

What started as a student demonstration in the narrow, cobblestoned streets of the Left Bank was quickly picked up by the workers. Angered by authoritarianism in the universities, students wanted a measure of democratic control. Maoists and other radicals took over leadership and began engaging in pitched battles with the police, advocating the overthrow of society. Students joined the workers' strikes, but it proved to be an uneasy relationship. Far from wanting to overthrow society, the workers sought more of what society had to offer. They felt deprived of the material goods they weren't being paid enough to buy.

"From time to time," Professor Raymond Aron once observed during a Paris lecture, "France carries out a revolution, but never carries out reforms." De Gaulle, who attended the lecture, later told Aron, "France never carried out reforms except in the course of revolution."

Although the *"Événements de Mai"* took France by surprise, social unrest had been building up for years, as the simpler problems of physically rebuilding the continent gave way to more profound questions about where the new Europe was headed. On one hand there was a reaction to the growing materialism. On the other there was an intense desire for the better things of life.

A few years before the Paris riots broke out, the "Provos" (short for provocateurs) had started a not-so-quiet revolution in Holland. In 1966 they attracted widespread attention by winning a seat on the Amsterdam City Council. They read Peter Kropotkin, the Russian anarchist who said that revolutions are born out of hope rather than despair, and preached that all authority is fascist and that affluence creates the overacquisitive society. Their symbol was a white bicycle, which was also one of their more practical ideas for the city of Amsterdam. Cars would be banned from the inner city, and white bicycles would be left around for anyone to use, reducing pollution and solving—in a charming, if naïve, fashion—the urban traffic problem.* Another of their proposals submitted to the City Council was for minigardens to be planted on car roofs. "We wanted to provoke the entire system, which we felt was authoritariarn and unable to cope with the problems of war, pollution and race," said Roel van Duyn, a leader of the group who bore a striking resemblance to John Lennon.

---

*One damper to this idea was a city ordinance requiring parked bicycles to be locked.

The Provos eventually disintegrated into a rather dreary band of pot-smoking scruffy youth, but the idea of injecting a little life into one of the most rigid societies of Europe did not die. In 1970, there was a rejuvenation of the idea, a kind of Provo Reformation with the establishment of a new group called the Kabouter (Pixies). They also took to politics and won enough seats in the Amsterdam municipal elections to wind up as the third strongest party in the city government.

Anti-establishmentism, as seen in the radical and often whimsical social philosophy of the Provos and the Kabouter, had a profound effect on Dutch attitudes toward Roman Catholicism. Not content with the slow progress of reform in Rome, many Dutch clergy acted boldly to liberalize the religion in Holland. A revolutionary catechism, produced by Dutch theologians and endorsed by the Dutch hierarchy, limited doctrine to basic beliefs, but questioned others, such as the virginity of Mary and the belief that the Communion wafer is transformed into the body of Christ. The Dutch Catholics were far ahead of the Vatican in their liberal attitude toward clerical marriage and birth control, provoking the displeasure if not the outright wrath of the Curia and the Holy See.

But reforms did not proceed fast enough anywhere.

The ordinary working man in France felt that the much vaunted postwar economic progress was something that took place "up there" several strata up the social ladder. His housing was poor: while he saw magazine pictures of soaring new skyscrapers and new housing developments, he was far more likely to live in an old building and have to walk up six flights of stairs and have to use a communal toilet in the hall. Less than 20 percent of France's housing in 1970 had been built since 1960, and nearly half of it had been built before 1900. The rich could afford to maintain the old buildings; the poor could not. The worker perhaps had his inexpensive Renault and a telvision set, but the glitter of Paris was beyond him. Contributing to his restiveness at being excluded from the good life was the steady erosion of his standard of living. He never seemed to be able to catch up with price increases. A survey of Europe by the *Reader's Digest* in 1969 found 32 percent of the French population convinced that they were worse off than five years earlier; 11 percent said they were far worse off.

The problems were not confined to France. West Germany's Ministry of Labor and Social Welfare disclosed that in 1969 a quarter of the nation's working-class households had a net income of less than $200 a month, while 1.7 percent of the population owned 35 percent of the country's total wealth and 70 percent of the private industrial investment. The German news magazine *Der Spiegel* reported that at the end of 1967 independently employed persons had personal property and possessions—apart from their savings—of $13,000 each. The worker, on the other hand, had possessions worth less than $3,000. The magazine commented that even though four out of five working-class families had a TV set, and half of them owned a car, these were only superficial signs of prosperity. Solidly based wealth was the privilege of the very few.

E. A. Rauter, a Berlin author, estimated that in 1970 there were still 2 million West Germans living either in social welfare homes or in hovels such as dilapidated Nissen huts, cellars, and old railway cars. An official German report, published in November, 1969, estimated those living in inadequate dwellings at 500,000. Their quarters were termed "germ cells of dangerous illness, social decay and intellectual paralysis."

Southern Italy was always one of Europe's poorest regions, with an average income of less than $500 a year, but even in the prosperous north the inequality of living standards was in full view. According to an estimate made in 1970, there were 100,000 people living in shacks, cheap lodging houses, and old railway cars in Turin, a city dominated by the giant Fiat autoworks.

Housing was one major European problem. Immigration was another. In the nineteenth century there were massive waves of European immigrants to the United States. With two European wars in the first half of the twentieth century, the flight continued, but by the middle of the century the tightening of American immigration laws had slowed the flow to a trickle. Europeans then started moving about increasingly within Europe, political refugees moving from east to west, and those seeking jobs from south to north. At the same time there was the influx of people from former colonies—Indians, Pakistanis, and West Indians into Britain; Algerians and black Africans into France.

The industrialized countries, none with an adequate reserve of indigenous labor, depended on the immigrants to do the dirty, menial jobs that no one else would do. Pakistanis sweated out the night shift in a bellowing ironworks in Birmingham. Algerians swept the streets in Paris. Turks manned the jackhammers to construct the Munich subway and collected garbage from the streets of Stuttgart. Southern Italians assembled Volkswagens in Wolfsburg, Spanish maids waxed parquet floors in Paris and Brussels. Yugoslavs worked with Finns on the frigid catwalks of a Malmo shipyard.

A common labor market existed within the European Economic Community and also within the Nordic bloc. The Sicilian or Calabrian needed no special permits to work in Wolfsburg. The Finn could boost his earnings in Stockholm or Malmo, similarly without special permits. Each would gain social security benefits in his host country without losing accrued benefits in his native country. But coming into the bloc from outside meant a bewildering variety of forms to fill out before work permits could be obtained. The foreigners, or *"gastarbeiter"* (guest workers, as they were known in Germany), were second-class citizens whose work permits could be easily revoked if unemployment threatened the host country. Other treatment set them apart as inferior.

A Milan factory owner who employed Sicilians referred to them once in front of an American visitor as his "niggers." Words were scrawled on a poster in Lyon: *"Pas de travail pour les bicots"* (No work for the wogs). The foreigners were condemned to ghettoes around the railroad stations (the stations themselves becoming replacements for the piazzas of southern villages) or on the outskirts of the industrial cities and subjected to not so subtle forms of discrimination in bars, restaurants, and dance halls. Brawls broke out as local workers saw the foreigners competing with them for jobs and women. New rackets—such as trafficking in fake identity cards and work permits—were invented to exploit the foreigners. Around the factories arose another breed of sharks, the sleep merchants, who rented beds for three eight-hour shifts, reaching a twenty-four-hour-a-day occupancy. Many of the Algerians in France lived in colonies of fetid shacks known as bidonvilles. A *bidon* is a large can for carrying liquids. Once flattened, it is used as siding and roofing for these shacks. Although the French government has made attempts to close down these shanty towns, Paris was still ringed with them in the early 1970s. In the period between 1966 and 1970, the number of families living in bidonvilles around Paris jumped by 20 percent, to a total of about 25,000 people.

Resentments ran so deep in Switzerland, where one-fifth of the population and one-third of the work force was foreign in the late 1960s, that new work permits were almost impossible to get. In a 1970 referendum, the Swiss beat back, but only just, a proposal under which the foreign labor force would have been slashed by one-third.

In West Germany, with 2 million foreign workers in 1971, there was also a severe social problem, recognized implicitly by Chancellor Willy Brandt, who made an unusual radio appeal for "tolerance" in March, 1971. The "guest workers," said Brandt, were a "source of energy, which our country cannot do without."

Nowhere were the problems as keenly felt as in Britain, where by mid-1969 some 1.5 million "colored" people (a British term lumping together West Indians, Indians, and Pakistanis) lived with more than 50 million whites. One research organization, the Runnymede Trust, calculated that by 1985 the colored population would total 3 million, constituting 5 percent of the total population. At least two-fifths of the 3 million would have been born in Britain.

In the late 1960s the British, like the Swiss, acted to seal off their country from the flow of immigrants. Even with the relatively small numbers of colored people in Britain, race prejudice emerged at the grass-roots level and had a powerful influence on the policies of both major political parties. In opposition earlier in the 1960s, the Socialists had castigated the Tories as "racists," for restricting immigration from the Commonwealth. But later, when the Socialists came to power, they adopted even more restrictive policies.

Here were some views expressed to an American journalist in Britain in the mid-1960s. "I don't know what it is about the colored people, but I just don't like them," said an elderly woman—a long-time Socialist supporter. A Tory-supporting tin-mining executive in Cornwall said, "The trouble with you Americans is that you're giving too much away to your colored people. This is our country and we're not going to give it away." A housewife on the border of an airless black ghetto on the fringes of Birmingham said, "They smell different. They eat different food. They're not like us."

Men like Enoch Powell, a Conservative politician with a large "hard hat" following, played on the public fears. In a major speech on April 20, 1968, he said the colored people had already made the whites "strangers in their own country." He spoke of a white woman in his constituency of Wolverhampton (in the industrial midlands) followed down the street by taunting "pickaninnies," and quoted consituents as saying "in fifteen or twenty years' time the black man will have the whip hand over the white."

Powell drew a picture of a future Britain in which men "found their wives unable to obtain hospital beds in childbirth, their children unable to obtain school places, their homes and neighborhoods changed beyond recognition, their plans and prospects for the future defeated." Powell said that as he looked ahead he was "filled with foreboding. Like the Roman I seem to see the River Tiber foaming with much blood." The speech by the former Tory minister, the scholar puritan who "tells it like it is," caused a sensation.

Though the British were normally considered a tolerant people, these expressions of racist suspicions and resentments affected policy decisions. While shutting off the immigration flow, both the Tory and Labor governments sought to provide equal opportunities for the colored people already accepted in the country, but this was proving as difficult as it had been in the United States.

In the late 1960s and early 1970s, the troubles began to have a familiar ring. There were marches against the "pigs." The overwhelmingly white police force was accused of conducting "nigger hunts" as a form of amusement, of beating up blacks in the police stations around Islington and Notting Hill Gate in London, and in towns like Leicester in the midlands. Gangs of white youths wearing leather jackets and heavy boots were preying on "Pakis" and other colored people, and, inevitably, black power agitation began. A Race Relations Board was set up to hear complaints of racial intolerance, and in a high-minded but generally ineffective way, to do something about it. The "colored people" were still the first to be laid off; the rate of unemployment among colored men ran ten times as high as among the whites in the early 1970s.

The first-generation immigrant wasn't looking for trouble. He was willing to accept any kind of job and practically any form of discrimination, simply because conditions were better than at home. But his sons and daughters, born and bred in Britain, were not so docile. Britain was their home, and they were prepared to fight for their rights, as blacks were doing in the United States.

In November, 1861, the Goncourt brothers, who lived in Paris and kept voluminous journals on current affairs, wrote that "the day will come when all the modern nations will adore a sort of American god." Six years later, at the Universal Exposition in Paris, they were already speaking of the "Americanization of France." The Goncourts were referring, somewhat hyperbolically, to American freewheeling materialism and inventiveness and some of the new American products these had brought forth. A century later the process was continuing, and while it involved the deep penetration of American industry in Europe, it had an equally far-reaching impact on the social order.

Europeans were both fascinated with and repelled by the United States. They were attracted by some of the ideas and products, but were afraid of America's social problems which they saw being transferred to Europe by the industrial invasion. Inevitably, the United States was blamed for many things that went wrong in Europe. In fact, Europe's problems were not necessarily of American origin but were the mirror of any fast-growing, modern, greedy industrial society. The visible effects were often dismaying. *The New York Times* architecture critic Ada Louise Huxtable took a look at Italy and this is what she saw:

Historic hilltowns and mountain villages are being abandoned to decay. . . . Cities of baroque scale and splendor are inundated by jerry-built, unserviced, speculator highrises. Environmentally, the cure is often worse than the disease. Approximately 100,000 trees were felled along secondary roads from 1962 to 1964 to "promote" automobile safety. The automobile, in turn, has invaded plazas that are cultural treasures and gas stations elbow national monuments.*

Among the general European problems were the fairer distribution of wealth, the migration of farmers to the cities and the growth of large urban complexes, the problems of moving people, controlling pollution and crime, improving the quality and widening the accessibility of education, and treating the sick and aged.

British cities will be like New York in a few years, British liberal politician Emlyn Hooson predicted in 1970, and already in 1973 there were those "places where you just don't go at night" in London like streets in Soho and along the embankment at Charing Cross. Hooson cited the "electrifying" growth of cities, which were "drawing population from so many different backgrounds and were lacking any true community sense." He was describing the future of London or Manchester, but he could also have been looking at Paris, Frankfurt, and Düsseldorf, cities that were drawing workers from the Mediterranean littoral but also, and in increasing numbers, from black Africa.

British citizens had always taken a smug comfort in statistics showing more crimes in New York City than in all of Great Britain. However, with the spread of ghettoes in areas like Brixton, Peckham, Clapham, and Notting Hill, the rise of street gangs, the intensification of the drug problem, the distrust of the police by the minority groups, and the communitarian, some even said racist, strife in Northern Ireland, there seemed little chance that London and other cities could avoid catching the "American disease."

Drug addiction was becoming a serious problem in all major European cities by the early 1970s. In Stockholm, a park near the main public library was pointed out to a visitor as a place where hashish and heroin were openly sold. In dingy basement clubs along London's Bayswater Road couples sat staring blankly at the walls, smoking reefers and listening to the plaintive wail of a sitar recording. In Helsinki a youth leader told a reporter that drugs were being smuggled across the Soviet frontier for sale in Finland and Sweden. "We can't explain the drug traffic here any other

New York Times, May 14, 1971, section VII, p. 6.

way," he sighed. In Munich there were cases of teenagers dying from the after-effects of heroin. The tragedy of Harlem had fallen upon Bavaria.

The drug traffic was big and profitable. Investors were promised a 50 percent return on their money every month "without the slightest risk," according to one rich American woman living in Munich who had been approached.

Practically all cities were reporting an increase in the rate of crime. In Paris there were nightly shootings and knifings and muggings in the area between the Gare du Nord and Place Pigalle. Murray M. Weiss, the editor of the Paris *Herald Tribune,* was "rolled" one night in 1971 by teenage louts on the Left Bank. A muscular man on a motorbike in the French industrial city of Nantes patrolled dark streets looking for a lone victim to rob after midnight. Parts of Marseilles and Toulon, entrepôts in the French connection, were off limits for all but the most adventurous. This reporter himself was mugged one night in downtown Brussels.

Thefts were increasingly frequent. Some well-to-do Parisians complained that their Paris apartments were burgled on the weekends when they were away in their country cottages, and that their country cottages were burgled during the week when they were in Paris.

After attacks on subway personnel and the discovery of a ticket-selling racket, police patrols moved into the Paris Metro in 1971. Youths had been blocking the ticket-selling booths and forcing passengers to buy tickets from their friends. A profit was made on the difference in price between tickets purchased individually and those sold in booklets of ten. Unions threatened to strike if action was not taken "to assure the safety of riders and employees."

Kidnappings were also on the rise, and in a new twist the ransoms were set at a fairly modest level so that the average-income family could pay.

The French call their hoodlums *voyous,* and in 1970 two *voyous* were involved in a particularly shocking crime. Late at night, a driver had run out of gas and was walking toward a filling station on the outskirts of Paris. The two men, cruising around in a pick-up truck, stopped, offered to give him a lift, robbed him, and then, so that they could not be identified, gouged out his eyes. The victim was left writhing and screaming in the gutter.

As in the United States, there was a wide gap in outlook between different generations of Europeans. The youths of the early 1970s knew nothing of World War II except what they had read, and knew little of the war's aftermath of economic privation. Growing up in a period of increasing prosperity, they were less interested in money (perhaps because they had more of it) than their fathers had been, and more concerned with social injustice. Yet, they were not all as self-denying as St. Francis of Assisi. Industries prospered by catering to the young Europeans' keen appetites for snappy sports cars, cassettes, portable phonographs, nonconformist gear (costing as much if not more than the clothes their bourgeois parents wore), and a good hamburger at a yé-yé drugstore (in Europe an all-purpose boutique-cum-restaurant).

The young were, nevertheless, quicker to back the causes of social reform than their parents had been. In a long and bitter strike at the Batignolles metalworking plant in Nantes, lycée and university students left their classrooms to join the worker demonstrations for higher pay in early 1971. In 1969, London youths occupied a mansion in Piccadilly to protest against "slumlordism." In the Christmas season of 1970 youths demonstrated all over Europe against the cruel sentences given to Basque nationalists at Burgos, Spain, and to Jews in Leningrad who had tried to hijack a plane to flee to Israel. In September, 1970, left-wing students in Copenhagen disrupted the annual meeting of the World Bank and International Monetary Fund to protest against the "capitalist establishment" and the Vietnam War.

Even among youths who were destined for high posts in business there was a need to find a social justification in their work. In July, 1970, five students from the European Graduate School of Business Administration at Fontainebleau were discussing what they hoped to get out of the modern corporation. They wanted "meaningful" employment, they said, adding that they believed it was wrong for companies to try to squeeze the last drop of profits out of society. They were strongly critical, for instance, of the role of oil companies in the Nigerian civil war, which had just ended at a terrible cost in human life. They saw the war as essentially caused by a power struggle between competing corporations—imperialism in its crudest form.

Gerland Occhiminutti, a scholarly-looking young Frenchman, said: "There is no problem of eating today. That is the difference between us and the last generation. What we want out of a job is more than just money to buy bread. We feel we must accept a social responsibility."

As long-haired youths marched in the cities of Europe, they came into inevitable conflict with the forces of law and order. There were hundreds of occasions when phalanxes of helmeted, club-wielding police stared across no-man's-land at phalanxes of helmeted students. The riot squads, protected by shields, supported by water cannon and tear gas bombs, would often rush the students, who were armed with cobblestones, staves, and gasoline bombs. After breaking through the student lines the police struck at anything that moved. As these confrontations continued into the early 1970s the police, especially in Paris, because suspect of anyone with long hair, and made indiscriminate arrests which drove practically all youths and much of the general public against them. After one incident in the spring of 1971, in which a nineteen-year-old lycéen, Gilles Guiot, was unjustly accused of striking a policeman and was locked up for a week without bail and without even the chance to talk to his parents, practically all the younger students of Paris walked out of their classes to stage a massive demonstration against police brutality in the streets of the Latin Quarter. Guiot was finally released after an appeals court ruled that there had been a miscarriage of justice. In the aftermath of this case, the Paris police, their public image badly scarred, launched a public relations campaign to try to show that they were human beings like anyone else. Policeman led street-corner teach-ins to explain the pressures of their job.

Yet, there were positive results, too, from the "Americanization," or more accurately, the modernization, of Europe. Tourism, new roads, Eurovision, business contacts, and an increasing knowledge of English as the lingua franca combined not only to make a more mobile society in Europe but also to whittle away at the old frontiers. Amsterdamers who once motored no farther than Noordwijk on the North Sea for their summer vacations were packing kids into a Peugeot station wagon and driving down to the Costa Brava, perhaps picking up a couple of young German hitchhikers on the way. Parts of Italy that had been remote since Roman times were being discovered because the autostrada led there. Using the toll-free German autobahn, it was possible to breakfast in the shadow of Cologne's 700-year-old cathedral on the Rhine and dine by the 1,000-year-old fortifications of Bratislava on the Danube. Swedes took a car ferry to spend a weekend in the Baltic ports of Poland.

American products and commercial ideas were popular all over Europe. Women who once had their clothes made by seamstresses like Mimi in *La Bohème* were buying everything off the rack the way American women did. Everybody wanted a car, and by 1970, one out of every two families in Western Europe already had one. The cities were overwhelmed by them. In Paris, cars were slung over the sidewalks and traffic jams were monumental. In Rome it was worse. With their cars, Europeans discovered the long weekend, and demands were rising for a shorter work week.

Though Europeans had not yet adopted the American habit of shopping in quantity once a week, they were making increasing use of convenience foods. A supermarket was built in Brussels in 1967 with a 20-foot-long frozen foods case. By 1969 the store manager had rearranged the interior to accommodate cases measuring 60 feet. An increasing number of women were joining the work force and were spending less time in the kitchen, so there were plenty of customers for such frozen delights as Alaska king crab, braised endive and ham in cheese sauce, and black currant sherbet, which could be prepared in time to catch a Western on television.

Europeans were fascinated by the myth of the American West, perhaps because the cinema frontier culture was so remote from their own traditions. The "spaghetti western" came out of Italy, reshuffling the components of the American western into an intense, drooling saga of emotions. Replacing jodphurs with Levis, Parisians weekended on "ranches," galloping along on western saddles beneath the Big Skies of the Île-de-France. In West Germany a club was founded in which members dressed as Indians and weekended on the reservation in their own wigwams. One of the most popular comic books in Europe recounted the adventures of Lucky Luke, a cowboy.

In 2,500 years of civilization the Europeans have been almost continuously at war with each other or fighting invaders such as the Vandals and Huns, the Visigoths, Ostrogoths, Franks, Angles, Saxons, and Jutes. The postwar period saw an invasion by American business and American tourists. It was a peaceful invasion but perhaps more pervasive and more powerful in its impact than anything since Roman times. Not only did it bring American technology and American ideas, but also it grafted a single, common language on to the continent. The European shopkeeper had to speak a little English, as did the stewardess in the Lufthansa DC-9, or the chairman of a Belgian steel company. Business, technical, and trendy words and expressions were anglicized in French and German. A Frenchwoman welcomed you into *le living* instead of *le salon*. A French businessman explained that things weren't going too well in *le marketing* or *le planning*, while his banker friend discussed the flow of *le hot money*. The words are not only practical. As French linguist Robert le Bidois observed, "There is a certain snobbism in using American terms. It has become fashionable."

Europeans became anxious about the large-scale presence of American industry in Europe, but they also saw the benefits—increasing technological and management knowhow, the inflow of new capital, greater employment. American investments at times became highly political. In 1970, after the Ford Motor Company had been looking for a site in France to manufacture automatic transmission units, it decided to set up in Bordeaux instead of an alternative place near the Belgian border. The Ford move helped Premier Jacques Chaban-Delmas keep a National Assembly seat from Bordeaux.

American companies dominated many European industries. General Motors and Chrysler, for example, produced nearly one-third of Western Europe's cars in 1970. The International Business Machines Corporation controlled 70 percent of the European computer market. Coca-Cola dominated in soft drinks, which wouldn't be the case of course if Europeans didn't like to drink the stuff. The youth of France, which never took too kindly to milk, was switching from wine to Coke in the early 1970s.

A study by the Commission of the Common Market showed in 1970 that in France, West Germany, Italy, Belgium, the Netherlands, and Luxembourg, American subsidiaries represented 29 percent of the electrical industry, 60 percent of the production of carbon black, 15 percent of synthetic rubber, 80 percent of computers, and 95 percent of the production of integrated electronic circuits. The Commission found that American companies were able to use their enormous size as leverage to gain privileges that were not available to the smaller European enterprises. The Americans played European governments off against each other in the competition for the investment dollar. "It is undeniable," said the Commission, "that American investments [in Europe] generate progress, but the Europeans are not the main beneficiaries of this progress." The EEC executive cited the tax advantages that American behemoths were able to wangle out of host countries and the financial advantages they had in the capital markets.

"In addition to their market, their workers and their administrators, the European countries are at the same time bringing their savings to the American investor," the Commission said,* warning that the European governments had to adopt common standards in dealing with American corporations or face the prospects of almost total industrial domination.

Another thing that grated on European sensibilities was that major decisions affecting the economies of the individual host nations were taken not from the point of view of their national interest. The multinational company was motivated instead by what was good for it, or, in some cases when pressure was brought to bear, by what was good for its government. If things didn't suit the company in one country or region, it could simply pack up and

---

*For inexplicable reasons, presumably rooted in reluctance to exacerbate already strained relations between the United States and the Common Market, this report was never published. Extracts were made available to *The New York Times* (June 24, 1970, p. 65).

move without having to worry excessively about the social difficulties its exodus would cause.

The important EEC study cited some of the misgivings of Europeans, but, in fact, it was to the credit of American companies that they discovered the growing European market and capitalized on it well before the European companies knew what hit them. The Americans were better organized, more aggressive, more disposed to work with different nationalities (the Europeans were still hindered by national rivalries), and more willing to spend money to make money.

European executives, especially those of the older generation, tended to be more conservative and more set in their ways than Americans. As de Tocqueville said well over a century ago: "An American would be utterly wretched if condemned to minding his own business." A French banker told a reporter in the fall of 1970, "Mark you, the change won't really come until the old guard is gone. They were trained here in France; they speak French, think French. The younger people have worked overseas, speak English, German, Spanish, and Italian. They think internationally. There will be some sweeping changes when they get up to the level of being directors."

While Europeans were complaining about the penetration of American business on their continent, they were investing in the late 1960s at a faster rate in the United States than Americans were investing in Europe. West European countries poured $550 million into the United States in 1969, twice the amount they had spent two years earlier. The total foreign investment in the United States in 1969—in factories as well as stocks and bonds—was more than $90 billion, compared with the total foreign investment by Americans of $143 billion. Of the five hundred largest companies in the United States, about a dozen were owned or controlled by foreigners. Shell Oil and Unilever (so big and powerful was this company—Lux soap, Lipton tea—that it was sometimes known as the tenth member of the Common Market) were run by combined British and Dutch interests. Opening a can of Libby's tomato juice meant money in the coffers of Nestlé of Vevey, Switzerland, owner of 56 percent of Libby, McNeill and Libby.

It was the age of the multinational company on both sides of the

Atlantic, and as the powers of these companies grew, so unions began realizing that they too must act multinationally to meet the challenge. The late 1960s saw the first international union action in Europe. Ford workers went on strike in Genk, Belgium, in late 1968. Less than 100 miles to the east, at another Ford plant in Cologne, German workers said they would not accept any transferred work from the Belgian plant, in an unusual act of international solidarity. In the spring of 1970, Air Liquide, a French company controlled by the International Telephone and Telegraph Company, was struck. Workers at other Air Liquide plants in Europe offered to prevent delivery to France of the industrial gases the company makes. Perhaps the most significant action involved Philips Lamp, the big Dutch electrical company. Unions representing its 280,000 workers throughout Europe received assurances from management in 1970 that they would be given advance warning in case plant shutdowns were being considered. The unions also sat down with management to discuss, on a European scale, technological change as it affected employment, job training, and the harmonization of working conditions in the European plants. They hoped later to begin multinational bargaining over wages for all of Philips' employees.

But there were some major obstacles to multinational collective bargaining. Would national unions ever give up their power to an international bargaining unit? While workers were willing to refuse extra work diverted from struck plants in another country, would they be ready to lay down their tools in sympathy with striking workers in another country with whom they had little in common? In any case sympathy strikes were still forbidden by law in Germany and Holland in the early 1970s. Another obstacle was the spread of plant-level rather than industry-wide bargaining in Europe. It looked as if Europe would have to become an integrated economic unit like the United States before multinational bargaining became a reality.

Although economic and political forces seemed to be making European society more mobile, more compact, more homogeneous, only the most naïve would underestimate the diversity that remained as frontiers were crossed and regions folded into regions within nations.

Europe is made up basically of three different types of people—Teutonic, Alpine, and Mediterranean—with countless mixtures as evolved through centuries of interbreeding. The European speaks a score of languages and hundreds of dialects, and, despite the development of more mobile society since the war, he tenaciously hangs on to his regional roots. The Paris concierge who was raised in Castelnaudary in southwestern France still has goose fat shipped up by relatives so that she can cook in the traditional style of that region. You can go to Toone, a puppet show in Brussels, and in the unlikely event that you understand both French and Flemish you still won't catch the nuances. These come only if you know the dialect of Brussels. Luxembourgers, Liechtensteiners, Zurichers, Bretons, Toulousains, Bavarians, Welsh, and scores of other peoples all have their own separate dialect or language, often incomprehensible to outsiders, in addition to their national language. The regional as well as linguistic differences were for economic as well as cultural reasons a source of friction into the early 1970s.

In January, 1968, only four months before the riots erupted in Paris, Flemish students at Louvain University clashed with the French minority and the tough Belgian police, because the Flemings wanted to expel the French students. These were linguistic riots that led to the fall of the Belgian government. Belgium's difficulties illustrated the deeper European problem of regional separatism.

Belgium, spun off from Holland after the 1830 Revolution, is only a little larger than Maryland and has a population of 10 million. Three out of five Belgians are Flemings, who speak seventeenth-century Dutch. The others are Walloons, who speak heavily accented French. Until the postwar industrial boom in Flemish centers such as Antwerp and Ghent, Flanders was the poorer part of the country, its inhabitants dominated culturally and economically by the Walloons, who lived in the coal-mining regions to the south. The decline of the coal-based economy gave the Flemings a new awareness of their rights.

Belgium had already been divided linguistically, with Louvain (Leuven in Flemish) in the Flemish sector. But the 650-year-old university, through the long process of social and cultural elitism, was a stronghold of the French language. When French and Flemish competed on equal terms, variation of Gresham's law applied: French, being more universally accepted, drove out Flemish. The Flemish agitators saw the town of Louvain falling to the French-speakers unless the "francophones," as they are known, were driven out of the university. After weeks of riots, the crisis was finally settled when a newly formed Belgian government decided to construct, at great costs, a completely new university for French-speaking students at Ottignies, just over the line into Wallonia.

In July, 1971, a constitutional reform package giving added recognition to the country's division into Flemish- and French-speaking areas was approved by the Belgian senate. The country's four main regions—Flanders, Wallonia, Brussels, and the German border zone—were given more control over their own cultural and economic affairs. But the reform stopped short of complete federalism.

On both walls of the western Pyrenees are the Basques, who have preserved their language, Eskuara, which is totally isolated from other European linguistic families. With their distinct culture they are almost a separate nation. During the Spanish civil war, a Basque nation was, in fact, created,* and became a center for the Republican activities. After Franco's victory, the government went into exile and the Basques became victims of severe repression as the new *caudillo* (leader) sought to stamp out the culture of the rebellious people to the north. The French were far more tolerant of the Basques, permitting them to use the Basque language in school instruction and even to fly the Basque flag. Probably for these reasons there was never a strong Basque separatist movement in France.

Wales, Scotland, and Northern Ireland's six counties (Ulster) always merited special treatment in the so-called United Kingdom.

---

*The statute of autonomy was enacted on October 5, 1936, and two days later, in Guernica, José Antonio de Aguirre was elected president. Before the civil war ended, Guernica was practically bombed out of existence by German aircraft, marking the first of what were to be many massacres of civilians from the air in the twentieth century. Picasso, in his famous mural "Guernica," represented the scene as a nightmare.

The British cabinet held men specially responsible for these regions, who had to report to the prime minister and to Parliament. Until March, 1972, the Protestant majority of 1 million (mostly decendants of sixteenth- to eighteenth-century colonists) controlled a local assembly known as the Stormont, which operated shamelessly to prevent the 600,000 Roman Catholics of Ulster from obtaining equal rights. Agitation by the Catholics, followed by acts of violence by the Irish Republican Army, forced the British government to send troops to Ulster to suppress terrorism and keep the two warring communities apart. Finally, in March, 1972, Prime Minister Heath agreed to meet one of the main demands of the Catholics by suspending the Stormont and imposing direct rule from London. A secretary of state for Northern Ireland was named to join the secretary of state for Wales and the secretary of state for Scotland.

In the southeast of Europe, Trieste, on the Adriatic, was controlled in a fragile truce by Italians and Yugoslavs. Parts of the old kingdom of Macedonia, in the central part of the Balkan peninsula, were under the rule of Greece, Bulgaria, and Yugoslavia, and the issue of Macedonian nationalism was never far below the surface.

President Tito had declared to an interviewer in 1971 that the major achievement of his life was the creation of the unified state of Yugoslavia, but later in the same year demonstrations in Croatia, the most prosperous of the six constituent republics of the federation, showed that the structure Tito had built was in danger of cracking. Croatia, covering the bulk of the popular Adriatic coast, earned most of the country's foreign exchange. It wanted more control over its resources and destiny—more than could reasonably be granted by Belgrade without endangering national unity. Following weeks of student demonstrations in Zagreb, the capital of Croatia, the Croat Communist leaders, in a showdown with Tito, who is himself a Croat, resigned. The authority of the president had won. But what would happen when he was gone?

General de Gaulle once said of France that a nation that produced 365 different cheeses was ungovernable. There are also many different types of cheese in England, Holland, Norway, Denmark,

Germany, Switzerland, Italy. The Europe of regions had become a Europe of nations almost despite itself. Could the Europe of nations, with its fantastic diversity, ever become a continental confederation? This was the question men were asking in the early 1970s, and there was no easy answer. It was still difficult to imagine that a Hamburg longshoreman would accept a lower standard of living to help a peasant in the Dordogne or that a Calais shopkeeper would take up arms because Sicily was invaded. Strong forces, the forces of progress and the forces of tradition, were pulling both ways. So long as Europeans found a balance of mutual advantage in working together, they appeared ready to bury the differences and play the game of cooperation. But the game was played with great caution and reserve. Twenty-five years was not long enough to build a continent. In those twenty-five years no one nation had yet given up a significant amount of national sovereignty. Europeans still retained their regional and national perspectives, and while they talked a lot about a united Europe, they were not ready to rush into it, even though the forces of progress and the challenge of the United States were giving them a strong push.

Yet, there was still a feeling of inevitability about the whole movement, that what had been set in motion wouldn't stop until something had been achieved. Jean Rey, the dry, bespectacled Belgian lawyer who became chief executive of the Common Market in the late 1960s, was fond of saying that Europe was like one of those great Gothic cathedrals constructed slowly over the centuries, on which one generation of artisans took over the work of another.

Denis de Rougemont, the Swiss philosopher, asked in 1971 what he thought about the future of European unity, replied: "I think we shall progress toward federalist and regional solutions because there are no alternatives."

Index

Abrasimov, Pyotr A., 173
Acheson, Dean, 31, 59, 103
Action Committee for a United States of Europe, 64
Adenauer, Konrad, 5, 48–49, 53, 97, 111, 174
Adenauer Christian Democrats, 49
Africa, 141
Age of Austerity (Sissons/French), 17 n.
Agfa-Gevaert, 80
Agriculture, European, and Common Market, 106 ff., 132–43
Ailleret, Charles, 96
Air Liquide, 196
Albania, 40–41
Algeria, 9, 90–91
Alliance Politics (Neustadt), 105
Allied Control Council, 36, 47
Allied High Commission, 172
Amalrik, Andrei, 43
American Challenge, The (Servan-Schreiber), 116
American Trade Expansion Act, 106
Armand, Louis, 66
Aron, Raymond, 61, 92, 181
Asia, 141
Atlantic Charter, 27
Atomic power *See* North Atlantic Treaty Organization, Nuclear disarmament
Attlee, Clement, 29, 35, 36
Australia, 104, 141
Austria, 5
   educational elitism in, 180
   and European Free Trade Association, 87
   Soviet occupation of (1955), 169

Ball, George, 12, 98, 105–6, 109–10, 158
Bancor, 22
Bangui, Central African Republic, 10 n.
Bank of England, 118, 149
Bank of France, 149
Basques, regional separatism and, 198–99
Beatles, the, 114
Belgium, 39, 50, 53, 57, 59, 63, 74, 118, 144
   and Common Market, 83, 138
   Communist party in, 29
   currency float (1973), 155
   educational elitism in, 180
   and regional separatism, 197–98
   and Supreme Headquarters Allied Powers Europe (SHAPE), 101
Belle Epoque, La, 21
Benelux Convention, 53–54, 58
Benes, Eduard, 45, 46
Berlin, 12, 13, 36, 37, 47–48, 95, 168 *See also* West Berlin
Bevin, Ernest, 29–30, 34
Bidault, Georges, 60
Bidonvilles, 184–85
Binder, David, 176
Bismarck, Otto von, 175
Blue Streak missile program, 109
Bonn-Moscow treaty (1970), 169 ff.

Bosnia-Herzegovina, 41
Brandt, Willy, 5, 34, 48, 95, 120–21, 125,
    126, 145, 150, 161, 169–73, 174 n.,
    176, 185
Braun, Eva, 12
Brecht, Bertolt, 168
Brest Litovsk, treaty of, 175
Bretton Woods, and postwar economy,
    21, 24 ff., 149, 152
Brezhnev, Leonid, 157, 163, 176
Brezhnev Doctrine of limited sover-
    eignty, 160
Britain, 50, 147, 169
    and Common Market, 75, 78, 99, 110–
        14, 134–35, 147, 163
    and Commonwealth preference sys-
        tem, 103–4
    and crime, rising, 188
    educational elitism in, 179–80
    and European Free Trade Associa-
        tion (EFTA), 87
    and European Payments Union, 35
    foreign labor and racism, 104, 185–87
    France, and Common Market bid,
        82–102, 107 ff., 120
    Greece, intervention in, 29–30
    and International Monetary Fund, 23
    and Marshall Plan, 34–35
    Nassau agreement, 109–10
    postwar, 6–7, 15–17
    regional separatism, 199
    Suez Canal, nationalization of, 65–66
    and Western Europe unification
        efforts, 54, 55, 57, 59–61, 62
British-American Bizone, 38
British-American Loan Agreement, 27
Broniarek, Zygmunt, 161
Brown, George, 116
Brussels Defense Treaty, 50
Brussels World Fair (1958), 70 n.
Budapest, 168
Bulgaria, 40–41, 164
Burgos, Spain, 190

Canada, 50, 139
Castro, Fidel, 25
Ceausescu, Nicolai, 164, 170
Chaban-Delmas, Jacques, 193

Chiang Kai-shek, 58
China, 7, 58, 160, 161, 164
Christian Democratic Union (CDU),
    38, 150, 174
Chrysler Corp., 194
Churchill, Winston, 5, 15, 30, 35, 52, 54,
    57, 89, 90
Clayton, Will, 31, 32
Coca-Cola Co., 194
Colbert, Jean-Baptiste, 85
Cologne, Ger., 196
Committee of European Economic Co-
    operation, 33, 54
Common Agricultural Policy (CAP),
    139–42
Common Market, 71 ff.
    agriculture and, 106 ff., 132–43
    France, Britain and, 82–102, 107 ff.,
        120
    majority voting, 132–35
    sovereignty and supranationality,
        131–56
    See also European Economic Com-
        munity (EEC)
Commonwealth preference system, 84
    ff., 103 ff.
Communist Information Bureau
    (Cominform), 41
Communist party, 157 ff.
    in East Germany, 168–69
    in postwar Europe, 28–30, 39 ff.
    in Rumania, 161
    in Yugoslavia, 159, 161
Communist Party Central Committe,
    158
Community Food Aid Program, 78
Continental Can Co., 76–77
Cook, Peter, 114
Cooper, Richard N., 61–62
Cooper, Susan, 17
Copenhagen, student demonstrations
    in, 190
Coty, René, 90
Council of Europe, 54–55
Council of Mutual Economic Assist-
    ance (Comecon), 163
Couve de Murville, Maurice, 111, 120,
    133, 148
Croatia, 41, 199–200

Crozier, Michael, 179
Cuba, 25
Cyprus, 24
Czechoslovakia
  Communist coup in (1948), 40–41,
    44–47
  and General Agreements on Tariffs
    and Trade, 164
  and International Monetary Fund, 25
  and Marshall Plan, 34
  Soviet invasion of (1968), 101, 159–62

Daily Telegraph, 16, 17
De Aguirre, José Antonio, 198 n.
Debré, Michel, 161
De Courcel, Geoffrey, 112 n.
De Gasperi, Alcide, 5, 39–40
De Gaulle, Charles, 5, 11, 48, 54, 58, 69,
    73, 83, 87, 132–35, 148, 149, 178,
    180, 181, 200
  Britain and Common Market, 89–94,
    108, 110–14, 116 ff.
  and North Atlantic Treaty Organiza-
    tion, 100–102, 116, 121
  nuclear armaments, 96–97
  resignation, 121–24
  Soames affair, 122–23
De Gaulle, Phillipe, 123
De Gramont, Sanche, 179
De Koster, Hans, 146
De Lesseps, Ferdinand, 65
Denmark, 50
  and Common Market, 117, 147, 163
  currency float (1973), 156
  educational elitism in, 180
  and European Free Trade Associa-
    tion, 87
  and Nordic Council, 88–89
Der Spiegel, 183
D'Estaing, Valery Giscard, 155
De Tocqueville, Alexis, 195
Dillon Round, tariff talks, 100
Discipline of Power (Ball), 12, 106 n.,
    109–10, 158
Doorn's Automobil Fabrieken, 80
Douglas-Home, Sir Alec, 114, 127
Dresden, 37
Dubcek, Alexander, 46–47, 159–60, 164

Dulles, John Foster, 65, 94–95
Duyn, Roel van, 181

Eastern Europe
  Communism and postwar, 40 ff.,
    67–69
  and Marshall Plan, 34
  Soviet Union and, 157–76
  See also Europe
East Germany, 170, 172, 173–74
  and Berlin Wall, 94–95
  worker uprisings in (1953), 168
  See also Germany, West Germany
Eastman Kodak, 80
Eden, Anthony, 82–83
Eisenhower, Dwight D., 44–45, 94, 109
Erhard, Ludwig, 38–39, 148–49
Etzel, Franz, 66
Europe
  modern, 177–200
  postwar, 5–18, 19–20, 20–35
  See also Eastern Europe, Western
    Europe
European Atomic Energy Community
  (Euratom), 64, 69, 78
European Coal and Steel Community,
  53, 56–57, 59, 62 n.
European Communities Bill, 130
European Convention on Human
  Rights, 54
European Court of Human Rights, 54
European Defense Community (EDC),
  59–61, 62–63, 93
European Economic Community
  (EEC), 8 n., 53, 56, 64–69, 70 ff.,
  194–95
  agriculture and, 106 ff., 132–42
  Britain, France and, 99, 103–30
  and common labor market, 184
  Eastern Europe and Soviet Union,
    162–64
  and monetary unification, 143–56
  structure and organization, 70–81
  See also Common Market
European Free Trade Association
  (EFTA), 87–88
European Graduate School of Business
  Administration, 180, 190

European Investment Bank, 71
European Parliament, 77, 78–79, 132, 133, 136, 143
European Payments Union, 35
European Recovery Program, 34
European Social Fund, 78
Evens, Richard, 79

Fellows, Lawrence, 13
Fiat Automobile Co., 158
Figaro, Le, 155
Fil de l'Epee, le (de Gaulle), 89 n.
Financial Times, 79, 163
Finland, 43–44, 87, 88–89
Flemings, 197–98
Ford Motor Co., 193
Foreign Economic Perspective, 139 n.
Foreign labor and racism, 9–10, 183–87
Fortune, 180
Fouchet, Christian, 92–93
Fouchet Plan, 93, 105
France, 20, 35, 50, 57, 169
   in Algeria, 9, 90–91, 183–85
   and Common Market, 75
      agriculture and, 107 ff., 132–33
      Britain and, 82–102, 107 ff., 120
      currency reform and, 92, 124, 145 ff.
   Communist party in, 29
   and Euratom, 69–70
   and Germany, 37, 38, 53, 111
   in Indochina, 61
   and Marshall Plan, 34
   and NATO, 94, 99–102
   nuclear armaments, 96–99
   postwar, 6–7, 11, 15, 18
   social problems in modern, 182
   student-worker uprisings (1968), 124, 177–81
   and Suez Canal crisis, 65–66
   United States, postwar differences with, 90 ff.
France et Son Armeé, La (de Gaulle) 89 n.
Franco, Francisco, 33
Franklin, Benjamin, 31
Free Democrats (FDP), 49, 150
French, Philip, 17 n.
French, The (de Gramont), 179

French National Assembly, 60–61, 62–63
Friendly, Alfred, Jr., 161
Frost, David, 114

Gallois, Pierre, 99
Gdansk, Pol., 166, 168
Gdynia, Pol., 166
General Agreements on Tariff and Trade (GATT), 28, 141, 164
General Motors Corp., 194
Geneva accords, 61, 62
Genk, Bel., 196
George II, king of Greece, 29
George Wigg (Wigg), 115 n.
German Democratic Republic *See* East Germany
German Economic Council, 38–39
German Marshall Plan Fund, 34
Germany, 20, 36–51
   and Common Market, 120–21, 138
   currency reform, postwar, 38–39
   educational elitism in, 179, 180
   and France, 96–97
   history, 175
   Marshall Plan, 34
   postwar, 5–7, 12–15, 18
   See also East Germany, West Germany
Gerö, Ernö, 67
Gierek, Edward, 167–68
Giordani, Francesco, 66
Glos Szczecina (Voice of Szczecin), 167
Glos Wybrzeza (Voice of the Coast), 166
Gold standard, 21–23
Gomulka, Wladyslaw, 68–69, 165, 167
Goncourt brothers, 187
Gottwald, Klement, 34, 45–46
Grass, Günter, 168
Great Britain *See* Britain
Great Depression, 21
Greece, 24–25, 50
   and Common Market, 118
   Communist party in, 29–30
   U.S. postwar intervention, 29–30
Guernica, 198 n.
Guiot, Gilles, 191

Hadfield, E. M., 16
Hague summit conference (1969), 102, 125 ff., 143, 145
Hallstein, Walter, 79, 132–35, 142–43
Harris, André, 15
Hart, Sir Basil Liddell, 175
Healey, Denis, 112
Heath, Edward, 5, 106, 112–13, 117, 126–30, 147, 199
Heinemann, Gustav, 174
Hirohito, 19
History of the Second World War (Hart), 176
Hitler, Adolf, 5, 6, 12–13, 19, 20, 40, 43, 48, 52, 53, 89, 175
Ho Chi Minh, 61
Holland
   and Common Market, 108, 138
   currency float (1973), 155
   "Provos" revolution (1966), 181–82
Hooson, Emlyn, 188
Hudson Institute, 125
Hungary, 40–41, 42, 67–69, 164–65
Husak, Gustav, 160, 165
Huxtable, Ada Louise, 187–88

Iceland, 50, 87
Immigration, European, and racism, 183–87
Imperial Economic Conference, 85
Indochina, 61
International Bank for Reconstruction and Development *See* World Bank
International Business Machines Corp., 194
International Herald Tribune, 124 n.
International Monetary Fund (IMF), 21–25, 113, 190
International Telephone and Telegraph, 196
International Trade Organization, 28
Ireland, 117, 163
Irish Republican Army, 199
Israel, 65–66, 121
Italian National Assembly, 39–40
Italy, 39–40, 50, 59, 63, 118, 135 n., 144, 192

Italy
   and Common Market, 80, 83, 86, 120, 147
   Communist party in, 29
   currency float (1973), 156
   educational elitism in, 179, 180
   foreign labor supply, 72 n.
   living standards, 183
   and Marshall Plan, 34
   postwar, 7, 9, 11, 15

Japan, 7, 104, 118, 139, 141, 148, 149, 151, 180
Jaroszewicz, Piotr, 167–68
Jenkins, Roy, 24, 129
Joan of Arc, 82
Johnson, Lyndon B., 95, 152

Kabouter (Pixies), 182
Kadar, Janos, 68, 164–65
Kahn, Herman, 125
Kamm, Henry, 68
Karelin, 43
Kekkonen, Urho, 44
Kennedy, John F., 94–95, 98–99, 109, 141, 148–49, 152, 178
Kennedy Round, tariff talks, 88, 98–101, 106, 141
Keynes, John Maynard, 22, 23, 24
Khrushchev, Nikita, 69, 158 n., 164, 173
Kiesinger, Kurt-Georg, 122, 125, 148, 150
Kim Il Sung, 58–59
Korean War, 50, 51, 56, 58–59, 60
Kreisky, Bruno, 5
Kropotkin, Peter, 181
Krupp, Alfred, 14

League of Nations, 21
Le Bidois, Robert, 193
Lemnitzer, Lyman T., 50, 101
Lend-Lease Agreements, 27
Lenin, Vladimir, 171, 175
Leningrad, 190
Leopold I, king of Belgium, 74
Levin, Bernard, 114

Libby, McNeill and Libby, 196
Liberman, Evsei, 159
London, 114, 190
London *Economist,* 76, 158
London *Times,* 114
Louis XIV, 85
Louvain University, student riots at (1967), 11, 197–98
Luns, Joseph, 75
Luxembourg, 50, 53, 59, 63, 74, 84, 144, 155
Luxembourg agreement, 134

Macedonia, 41, 199
Macmillan, Harold, 82, 87, 94, 105, 106, 109, 112, 129 n.
Macrae, Norman, 76
Maginot Line, 89 n.
Mansholt, Dr. Sicco, 8 n., 142
Mansholt Plan, 142
Mao Tse-tung, 58
Marshall, George C., 31–34
Marshall Plan, 32–34, 46, 51, 53
Marx, Karl, 175
Masaryk, Jan, 34, 40, 46, 47
Masaryk, Thomas, 46
Massu, Jacques, 90
Maudling, Reginald, 87
Mayne, Richard, 106
McNamara, Robert S., 25, 109
Mein Kampf (Hitler), 13
Mendès-France, Pierre, 61
Messina conference, 63–64
Middle East, and Western Europe's energy supplies, 65–66
Mihailovich, Draja, 41
Mindszenty, Joseph Cardinal, 67–68
Minuteman missile program, 109
Mitford, Nancy, 35
Molotov, Vyacheslav, 61, 175–76
Monnet, Jean, 55–59, 63, 64, 90, 98, 106
Montenegro, 41
Morgan, Dan, 165 n.
Morgenthau, Henry, 18
Morocco, 9
Muggeridge, Malcolm, 114

Nagy, Imre, 67–69
Nagyiti (Magnifying Glass), 165
Nancy Mitford Omnibus (Hamilton), 35
Nantes, student-worker strikes in, 190
Nassau agreement, 109–10
Nasser, Gamal Abdel, 65
National Liberation Front (Algeria), 90
National Socialist party, 20
Nestlé Corp., 196
Netherlands, 50, 53, 59, 63, 84, 180
Neustadt, Richard, 105
New Statesman, 130
New York Times, 30, 62, 68, 161, 176, 187
New Zealand, 128–29
Nigerian civil war, 191
Nixon, Richard M., 27, 139, 152–53, 164
Nordic Council, 88–89, 184
North Atlantic Treaty Organization (NATO), 47, 50–51, 60, 62, 91, 94–95, 98–99, 100–102, 116, 121
Northern Ireland, 199
Norway, 50, 87, 88–89, 117
Nosek, Vaclav, 46
Novotny, Antonin, 160
Nuclear armaments/disarmament, 70–73, 96–99

Occhiminutti, Gerland, 191
Ophuls, Marcel, 15
Organization for Economic Cooperation and Development, 33 n., 84 n., 179–80
Organization for European Economic Cooperation, 84, 86–87
Ostpolitik, 171 ff.

Paish, Frank, 21
Pakistan, 9
Paris, 192
    bidonvilles in, 184–85
    cost of living in, 10
    crime, 189–90
    student-worker riots (1968), 121, 177–81
Paris *Herald Tribune,* 189
Paul VI, Pope, 168
Pavlovsky, Ivan G., 159

Pekkala, Mauro, 44
Pétain, Henri, 124
Peterson, Peter G., 139–40
Philips Lamp Corp, 196
Picasso, Pablo, 198 n.
Pieck, Wilhelm, 49
Plantagenets, 82
Plebeians Rehearse the Uprising (Grass), 168
Plutarch, 178
Poland, 36, 40–41, 165–66, 170–71, 172
  and General Agreements on Tariff and Trade, 164
  and International Monetary Fund, 25
  Poznan riots (1956), 68–69, 167, 168
  worker uprisings (1970), 165–68
Polaris missile program, 109
Pompidou, Georges, 5, 97, 124–28, 135–36, 140, 146, 149
Portugal, 9, 50, 87
Potsdam conference, 36, 90
Powell, Enoch, 129, 186
Poznan Poland, riots in (1956), 68–69, 167, 168
Prague, 44–45, 168–69
Prague Spring of Liberalization (1968), 160
Provos, 181–82
Pursuit of Love (Mitford), 35

Quant, Mary, 114

Rakosi, Matyas, 67
Ramadier, Paul, 39
Rapallo, 175
Rauter, E. A., 183
Reader's Digest, 182
Recovery of Europe (Mayne), 107
Reston, James, 30
Reuter, Ernst, 48
Rey, Jean, 200
Reynaud, Paul, 58
Rhosdesia, 104
Ribbentrop, Joachim von, 175–76
Rippon, Geoffrey, 128–29
Rockefeller, John D., Jr., 20
Rogers, William P., 153, 156, 173

Roman Catholic Church, 167–68, 182
Rome, 192
  Treaty of, 70, 72 ff., 86, 106
Roosevelt, Franklin, 15, 18, 28, 89, 90
Rougemont, Denis de, 200
Ruhr basin, 37
Rumania, 40–41, 160, 164
  and Common Market, 163–64
  and General Agreements on Tariff and Trade, 164
  and International Monetary Fund, 25
Runnymede Trust, 185
Rush, Kenneth, 173
Russia *See* Soviet Union
Russian-German nonaggression treaty (1939), 175

Saar industrial belt, 37
Santayana, George, 19
Schacht, Hjalmar, 155
Scheel, Walter, 150, 170
Schiller, Karl, 140, 155
Schlesinger, Arthur, Jr., 95
Schlieder, Willy, 77
Schuman, Robert, 53, 55–57, 66
Schumann, Maurice, 128, 146
Scotland, 144, 199
Serbia, 41
Servan-Schreiber, Jean-Jacques, 116
Shell Oil Co., 195
Sicily, 144
Sik, Ota, 164
Simmons, Michael, 163
Sissons, Michael, 17 n.
Skybolt missile program, 109
Slovenia, 41
Smithsonian Agreement, 147, 153
Soames, Christopher, 122–23
Soames Affair, 122–23
Social Democratic Party of Germany (SPD), 38, 39
Société Bloquée (The Blocked Society) (Crozier), 179
Sopot, Pol., 166
Sorrow and the Pity (film), 15 n.
Soustelle, Jacques, 87
South Africa, 104
South America, 141

208   *Index*

Soviet Union, 6–7, 18, 36, 52, 96, 137, 154–55, 157–76
  Austria, occupation of, 169
  and Berlin Wall, 95
  and Common Market, 162–63
  Communism and, 40 ff.
  Czechoslovakia, invasion of (1968), 101, 159–62, 168–69
  Eastern Europe, postwar policies in, 28–29, 37–50, 67–69
  educational elitism in, 180
  and Finland, 43–44
  and Hungarian uprising (1956), 67–69
  and International Monetary Fund, 25–26
  and Korean War, 59
  and Marshall Plan, 34
  in Middle East, 65
  and West Germany, 169–74
Spaak, Paul-Henri, 39, 54, 60, 64, 111
Spaak Committee, 87
"Spaghetti westerns," 192
Spain, 9
Stalin, Joseph, 36, 41, 42, 43–44, 46, 47, 50, 60, 67, 90, 159, 175
State Treaty of peace, 169
Stepinac, Aloysius, 41
Stockholm
  drug traffic in, 188–89
  Treaty of, 87
Strauss, Franz-Josef, 95, 176
Sudeten Germans, 37
Suez Canal, nationalization of, 65
Sulzberger, C. L., 176
Supreme Headquarters Allied Powers Europe (SHAPE), 100–101
Sweden, 10, 87, 88–89
Switzerland, 87, 144, 180, 185
Szczecin, Pol., 166, 167

Taylor, A. J. P., 89 n.
Thomas, Hugh, 84
Thomassen and Drijver-Verblifa, 77
Thomson, George, 129
Thousand Days, A (Schlesinger), 95
Tinbergen, Jan, 177
Tito, Josip, 41–42, 199–200
Toynbee, Arnold, 82

Trieste, 199
Truman, Harry, 30–31, 36, 50, 56, 58
Trybuna Ludu, 161
Tshombe, Moise, 167
Turkey, 9, 30, 50, 118
Twenty-fourth Soviet Party Congress (1971), 157
Twenty-third Soviet Party Congress (1966), 157

Ulbricht, Walter, 168
Unilever, 195–96
United Nations, 20
  Economic and Social Council, 27
United States, 135, 136–37, 160, 162, 169
  and Britain, 86, 103 ff.
  and Common Agricultural Policy, 139–41
  and Common Market, 99–100, 103 ff.
  dollar, devaluations of, 26–27, 119, 139, 150–56
  educational elitism in, 180
  and Europe, postwar, 6–7, 10, 13, 15 n., 18, 19–20, 23–29, 29–35, 52, 115, 154–55, 187 ff.
  foreign investment in, 195–96
  and France, 90 ff., 97–99
  and Germany, postwar management in, 38 ff.
  and Italy, 39
  and Korean War, 51, 56, 58–59
  in Southeast Asia, 141, 151
  and Soviet expansionism in Eastern Europe, 40–51
U.S. Department of Labor
Universal Exposition in Paris, 187

Valéry, Paul, 7
Valois, 82
Vandenberg, Arthur H., 30–31, 34, 50
Versailles, Treaty of, 18
Vers L'Armée de Métier (de Gaulle), 89 n.
Vichy government, 124 n.
Vietnam War, 27, 61, 152, 190
Volcker, Paul A., 152
Von Braun, Dr. Wernher, 16

Wales, 144, 199
Walloons, 197–98
Warsaw, 45
Warsaw Communist defense treaty, 67–68
Wartime United Nations, 21
Weiss, Murray M., 189
Werner, Pierre, 145
Werner Committee, 146
West Berlin, 48, 49, 172–74
Western Europe, postwar unification efforts, 52–64
  and atom bomb, 70–73
  and Common Market, 73–81
  and Eastern Europe, 67–69
  and Middle East, 65–66
Western European Union (WEU), 62
Western European Union Treaty, 96
West Germany, 50, 57, 90, 118, 162, 169–73, 174, 176
  and Common Market, 75 ff., 83–84,

    86, 88, 108, 120, 127
  agriculture and, 132–33
  currency reform and, 125, 145 ff., 150
  educational elitism in, 180
  foreign labor, and racism, 185
  and France, 53, 111, 125
  standard of living, 183
West Indies, 9
White, Harry Dexter, 24
Wigg, Lord, 115
Wilson, Harold, 110, 113–20, 122–23
Winter War of 1938–39, 43–44
World Bank, 24–25, 190
World War II, Europe's recovery from, 5–18
Wyszynski, Stefan Cardinal, 68, 167–68

Yalta Conference, 90
Yugoslavia, 9, 24, 25, 40–42, 159, 160–61, 163